Seven

THE ETHICS OF MANAGEMENT

A Multidisciplinary Approach

LaRue Tone Hosmer

Professor Emeritus of Corporate
Strategy and Managerial Ethics
Ross School of Business
University of Michigan

Special Edition for
University of Maryland University College

Boston Burr Ridge, IL Dubuque, IA New York San Francisco
St. Louis Bangkok Bogotá Caracas Lisbon London Madrid
Mexico City Milan New Delhi Seoul Singapore Sydney Taipei Toronto

The McGraw·Hill Companies

THE ETHICS OF MANAGEMENT
A MULTIDISCIPLINARY APPROACH, Seventh Edition
Special Edition for University of Maryland University College

This book is a McGraw-Hill Learning Solutions textbook and contains select material from *The Ethics of Management: A Multidisciplinary Approach,* Seventh Edition by LaRue Tone Hosmer. Copyright © 2011, 2008, 2006, 2003 by The McGraw-Hill Companies, Inc. Reprinted with permission of the publisher. Many custom published texts are modified versions or adaptations of our best-selling textbooks. Some adaptations are printed in black and white to keep prices at a minimum, while others are in color.

Printed in the United States of America.
4 5 6 7 8 9 0 QVS QVS 15 14 13

ISBN-13: 978-0-07-752235-3
ISBN-10: 0-07-752235-4

Learning Solutions Manager: Dave Fleming
Production Editor: Jessica Portz
Printer/Binder: Quad/Graphics

Contents

About the Author

LaRue Hosmer is a mechanical engineer who, in 1955, founded a company to build waste-reduction equipment for sawmills and paper mills. The company was sold in 1968, and Professor Hosmer returned to the academic community and received a PhD in Corporate Strategy and the Economics of Competition in 1971. He has taught at the University of Michigan ever since, with visiting appointments at Stanford, Yale, Virginia, the Naval Post Graduate School, and Alabama. His interest in ethics dates from experiences while running the machinery company, and he offered the first course in ethics of management at the Michigan Business School in 1984. He currently is emeritus.

Preface

The Growing Importance of Ethics in Management

The global economy is becoming far more complex and far more competitive. New technologies are being developed. New products and processes based upon those technologies are being designed. New markets are being opened, new sources of goods and services are being sought, and new types of investment are being used. The result is that employees at all levels within a business firm, not just those in the upper echelons and corner offices, are now being pressured to increase sales, reduce costs, and speed operations. Those pressures come in the form of performance rankings, monetary incentives, and employment threats. The problem is that the decisions and actions that are taken in reaction to those pressures may benefit the financial performance of the firm (measured by revenues, costs, and profits) but harm the social performance (difficult to measure, but represented by the overall well-being and satisfaction level of those associated with the firm as employees, customers, suppliers, distributors, creditors, stockholders, local residents, national citizens, and global inhabitants). These conflicts between the financial performance and the social performance of business firms are what this text terms the *moral problems of management.*

These pressures to act are immense, and students now within our classes are going to have to deal with the pressures, risks, and rewards of the exceedingly competitive global economy on their own, soon after graduation. They will encounter moral problems and will probably experience the temptation to "get along by going along." Yet, at the same time they should recognize the opportunity to "stand out by standing up." The most basic argument of this text is that all members of our ethics courses are going to have to learn how to *convincingly* present their proposed solutions to the moral problems they encounter in order to jointly serve their companies, protect their careers, and improve their societies. They have to convince the other managers within the company, both senior and junior, whose approval and cooperation they will need. There are, in my view, five steps in making such convincing presentations:

1. *Understand that moral standards of behavior differ among individuals.* Moral standards of behavior are the intuitive ways all of us just automatically feel about the decisions and actions that we believe to be right and fair and proper and those that we believe to be wrong, unfair, and improper. The difficulty is that moral standards of behavior differ among individuals, depending upon their personal goals, norms, beliefs, and values, which in turn are dependent upon their cultural and religious traditions and their economic and social situations. People within the global economy come from very different cultural and religious traditions and live in very different economic and social situations, and consequently their moral standards of behavior,

being subjective, are bound to differ substantially. Even people within the same company will differ on those four dimensions, particularly their economic and social situations where they hold different positions and have different relationships. The first step in seeking a resolution to a moral problem is to clearly understand the differing moral standards.

2. *Recognize that moral problems in business are complex and difficult to resolve.* Moral problems in business inherently involve some individuals, groups, or organizations associated with the firm who are going to be hurt or harmed in ways outside their own control, while others will be benefited or helped. Further, some of those individuals, groups, or organizations associated with the firm will have their rights ignored or denied, while others will have their rights recognized and extended. It is this contrast between benefits and harms, between rights and wrongs, all for different groups of people that make moral problems in business so complex and difficult to resolve. The second step in seeking this resolution is to clearly recognize the differing moral impacts.
3. *Define the moral problem in understandable terms.* Some managers within the organization may well benefit from a planned decision or action, and they may not have thought about any harm received by others. Other managers may well be pleased that their rights have been recognized, and again they may not have thought about any rights ignored for others. This is not a claim that most managers are so self-centered that they simply don't care about the harms and wrongs imposed by their firm upon other people; it is, instead, an observation that most people tend to focus firstly upon how a given decision or action affects them. The third step in seeking a resolution to a moral problem is to clearly identify the impacts, both positive and negative, to the various individuals, groups, and organizations associated with the firm. The final resolution will necessarily be a mixture of those impacts: the benefits received and rights recognized for some and the harms imposed and rights ignored for others. It is not possible to eliminate all of the harms and all of the wrongs, but it is possible to achieve a logical balance that can be viewed as the *most* right, fair, and proper of all of the alternatives.
4. *Apply objective, rather than subjective, methods of analysis to reach that logical balance.* It is almost never effective for a manager to recommend a resolution based upon his or her own moral standards of behavior. As explained previously, moral standards of behavior differ among people, and those differences obstruct agreement. It is necessary for managers to go further and *be able to convincingly explain why a given balance should be viewed as the most right, fair, and proper.* A convincing explanation requires objective methods of analysis rather than subjective standards of behavior. These objective methods of analysis include (a) economic outcomes based upon impersonal market forces (b) legal requirements based upon impartial social and political processes, and (c) ethical duties based upon universal moral principles. This entire process, which starts with understanding the differing moral standards and ends—hopefully—with a convincing balance of

economic outcomes, legal requirements, and ethical duties, is shown in graphic form here:

The Application of Objective Methods of Moral Analysis in Management

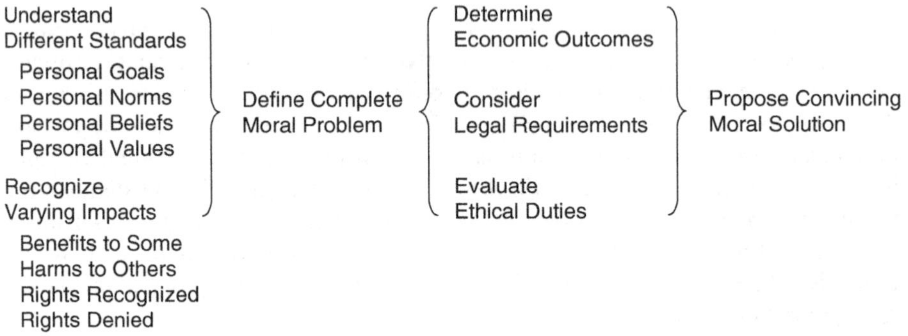

5. *Understand that the tripartite or multidisciplinary approach to a balance resolution is crucial.* People differ not only in their subjective standards of behavior and their personal evaluations of impacts; they also differ in their objective forms of analysis. Many people rely strictly on economic optimality. Others insist upon legal compliance. And a number go back to what they view as universal principles. The result can easily be confusion and misunderstanding. The managers in the room, the participants making the decision, are very likely to talk past each other, not with each other. What is needed to make progress is not a dominance of one discipline, but a logical balance among all three disciplines. That is the multidisciplinary approach recommended by this text.

The final argument of this text is that if this proposed decision process is followed on a consistent basis, with balanced multidisciplinary solutions that are either logically convincing to or fully understandable by all of the managers within the firm, eventually the result will be an increase in the trust, commitment, and effort evidenced by the individuals, groups, and organizations associated with the firm. Everyone wants to be treated justly in the workplace and in the marketplace, but the only way most people can ensure that just treatment in the future is to be associated with the managers of firms whom they trust because those managers treated them justly in the past. People tend to trust managers who have logically and understandably explained the economic, legal, and ethical foundations of their decisions and actions. The argument here is that trust leads to commitment; that commitment leads to effort; and that committed effort on the individual level is a basic requirement for corporate success in a competitively intense, technologically complex, and culturally diverse global economy.

It has often been said that ethics is essential for leadership. The argument of this text is that leadership is essential for ethics. Somebody has to be willing to stand up and say, "This is what we should do, this is why we should do it, and this is how we are going to do it." That is the combined character, skill, and ability that I think we should be teaching in our ethics classes. That, in my view, requires the unification of disciplines, not the separation of disciplines, and hopefully this text will forward that goal.

Health Care Insurance Companies and Payments to Customer Consultants

Almost all of the large and medium-sized companies within the United States feel obligated to offer health care insurance to their employees, either as a result of the terms of earlier labor contracts or as a consequence of their current need to attract and keep highly qualified workers. Many of the smaller, family-owned firms also offer this insurance; here the motivation is more often their personal relationships with employees whom they see every day, and want to help or reward, rather than the terms or conditions of union contracts and access to labor markets they want to maintain.

The problem is that health care insurance has become exceedingly complex. It is hard to select the right policies. Firstly, there is the issue of the medical conditions and diseases that are covered and the extent of that coverage. Health care insurers differ substantially in the conditions and diseases that are included within their policies, and in the nature and extent of the treatments that are provided. Secondly, there is the matter of the co-payments that are required. Health care insurers originally proposed co-payments as incentives to encourage patients to improve their lifestyles—to lose weight or stop smoking, for example—and thus reduce their demands on the health care system, but now it is alleged that co-payments have become more a means of blocking access to that system, and thus reducing the obligations of the insurers. Thirdly, there is the question of the overall cost. Health care insurers do not provide either diagnostic or treatment services; instead they pay others—hospitals, clinics, physicians, nursing homes, and pharmaceutical companies—for the needed services, and they negotiate the cost and quality of those services on a competitive or "preferred provider" basis, and then propose a level of annual charges that is hard to compare.

Most business firms (particularly those that are medium sized or small and family owned) and almost all public organizations (the school systems, police and fire departments, and city and state governments) don't understand this confusing mixture of coverages, co-payments, and costs; do worry about the continually rising level of annual charges; and frequently turn to health plan consultants for help. Some of these consultants are local 2- to 10-person organizations; others are much bigger regional or national corporations. All of them encourage a presumption that they act solely in the best interests of their clients. That presumption was called into question just recently through a series of revelations, many similar to the following account:

> When Kevin Grady took over as an employee-benefits consultant for the Columbus [Ohio] Public Schools District in 2001, he signed a contract promising to act "in the best interests" of the schools. The Ohio district agreed to pay him $35,000 a year to help it choose a health insurer. Officials thought that was all Mr. Grady was getting out of the deal.
>
> It wasn't. After the district switched its health insurance to UnitedHealth Group Inc. on what it says was Mr. Grady's recommendation, he started getting payments and other compensation from the big Minnetonka, Minn. insurer. "Thank you and United for the steaks," Mr. Grady wrote in a Dec. 20, 2001 e-mail to a UnitedHealth employee. "We'll have those on Christmas Eve." (*Wall Street Journal,* September 18, 2006, p. A1)

Steaks and an occasional bottle of wine might be understandable, but they were not the only extra benefits Mr. Grady got from UnitedHealth. He also received $517,138 in monetary compensation from that company over a two-year period, from 2001 when he recommended the switch in health insurance coverage, to 2003, when the school district learned of these payments, apparently from a dissatisfied employee at UnitedHealth. It quickly became apparent, as a result of the lawsuit filed by the Columbus public schools in an attempt to recover the funds that it claimed were inappropriately paid, that this was not at all an isolated occurrence:

> The episode spotlights a widespread and largely invisible practice that critics say boosts the costs of health care. Many consultants and brokers who are hired to help employers get the best deal on health insurance or prescription-drug coverage have significant financial ties with the health vendors they are supposed to be scrutinizing. The ties may take the form of bonuses for bringing in business, or commissions and consulting fees. Often they are disclosed only partly or not at all. (*Wall Street Journal,* September 18, 2006, p. A1)

Few of the consulting firms or insurance companies appeared to think of these bonuses, commissions, and fees as inappropriate or improper. Instead—when contacted, and found willing to respond—their spokespersons tended to explain that the practice of making these payments was widespread and accepted, and they generally went on to emphasize that the payments were intended to foster cooperation between consulting firms and insurance companies, and help to control the spiraling costs of health care within the United States:

> "All [insurance] companies offer bonuses" says Joe Grady [president of the local consulting firm that hired his father]. "It's a way to sell the product and saves them [the insurance companies] from hiring 20,000 agents." He denies that his father pushed the district to choose UnitedHealth and contends the district knew all along about the payments. (*Wall Street Journal,* September 18, 2006, p. A1)

> "Health care finance and delivery are not the core mission of most employers", says Robert O'Brien, the head of health and benefits consulting at Mercer [a large general insurance consultant, with annual revenues from their health care division of $526 million]. "We help employers manage the expense and complexity of their health and benefits programs in a way that maximizes their value for employees." (*Wall Street Journal,* September 18, 2006, p. A1)

In court documents that were filed in conjunction with other payment cases, it was found that UnitedHealth typically offered a commission of 1 percent of the premium dollars paid by the client. Aetna Inc., another of the very large health care insurance companies, located in Hartford, Connecticut, computed payments to consulting firms based upon a different formula. If a consultant kept 90 percent of his/her clients loyal to Aetna when their contacts came up for re-bidding, generally every three years, the consulting firm received a "retention bonus" of 0.75 percent of the client's premium payments over the life of the contract; if the consultant were able to keep 100 percent of his/her clients loyal to the firm, the bonus rose to 1.25 percent. WellPoint of Indianapolis Inc., the third of the three largest health care insurance companies within the United States, declined to offer details on the formula by which their payments were computed, but did admit that "they continued to offer contingent commissions" (*Wall Street Journal,* September 18, 2006, p. A1).

Class Assignment

Firstly, think of yourself as a senior executive within one of those three large health care insurance companies: UnitedHealth, Aetna, or WellPoint. Let us say that you are the chief financial officer. You clearly know about these payments. Would you just accept them as a normal and understood cost of doing business, or would you object to them? Let us further say that an outside member of the board of directors has just heard of the payments, and does object. You know that when he or she raises the issue at the next board meeting, others at that meeting will turn to you. You are known as an intelligent and articulate executive, next in line for promotion to chief executive officer. A major argument of this text is that managers at all levels of an organization should decide for themselves, through analysis, the moral stand they believe to be most appropriate, *but they must be able to logically convince others.* How would you logically convince the others at that board meeting?

Secondly, put yourself in what probably will be a more realistic situation. Assume that you have worked in whatever functional field you are now pursuing—accounting, finance, marketing, human relations, etc.—at one of those large insurance companies for two years, ever since you graduated from your college or MBA program. Assume that not only have you just heard of these payments, but that you have also been asked to participate, perhaps as the person authorizing a series of payments to a new consulting firm. Does this involvement disturb you? Assume that the president of your company has what is termed an "open door" policy; that is, employees at any level can make an appointment and come to see him or her about any issue that they believe to be important. Now, what are the risks to your career if you take advantage of that policy, and do go to see the president? What are the risks to your career if you do not? Assume in this case that you truly like your job, and your life outside of work. Also recognize that it is always easy to say, "Oh, I wouldn't worry about the risks; I could always just leave and find another job," but understand that it may not be easy to find another job. Potential employers will generally contact past employers, and the indifferent response from a past employer that "It is our policy not to comment on the reasons an employee left, or on the performance of that employee while at our firm" is considered a black mark.

Chapter 1

The Nature of Moral Problems in Management

Accounts of corporate wrong-doing have always been with us. Certainly most of the railroad barons and the steel magnates of the late 1800s were not examples of financial rectitude, and the years prior to the Great Depression were filled with stories of manipulative dealings in business firms ranging from street railways to insurance companies and savings banks. Then, during the late 1990s, it was found that senior executives at a number of very large companies—Enron, Tyco and WorldCom—had deliberately caused the falsification of the income statements and balances sheets of their firms in order to report much greater profits, gain much higher stock prices, and receive much larger bonuses. Executives at all three of those firms were later convicted and sentenced to jail.

Now, a number of years later as I write this chapter, the nature of moral problems in management has changed from the deliberate actions of senior executives for personal gain to the continual pressures on managers at all levels throughout the firm for improved performance in an increasingly complex and competitive global environment. It is not possible to change the degree of complexity or the extent of competition. Those are now givens. Instead, it is going to be necessary to deal directly with the moral problems brought about by the risk and reward pressures experienced by all, and therefore open to resolution by all. These moral problems are—to repeat the earlier definition from the Preface for emphasis—situations in which the financial performance of the firm (measured by revenues costs and profits) is in conflict with the social performance (difficult to measure but represented by the overall well-being and general satisfaction of those associated with the firm as employees, customers, suppliers, distributors, creditors, stockholders, local residents, national citizens, and global inhabitants) of that firm. There are three premises or requirements for resolving these moral problems, also repeated from the Preface for emphasis:

1. Recognize that moral problems in business are complex and difficult to resolve. Moral problems in business inherently involve some individuals, groups, or organizations associated with the firm who are going to be hurt or harmed in ways outside their own control, while others will be benefited or helped. Further, some of those individuals, groups, or organizations associated with the firm will have their rights ignored or denied, while others will have their rights recognized and extended. There

is a mixture of benefits and harms, of rights exercised and rights denied, in the moral problems of management, and this mixture makes it very difficult for managers to decide upon a course of action that they can confidently say is the right or fair or proper course of action when faced with a moral problem.

2. Understand that business managers cannot rely upon their moral standards of behavior, or the intuitive ways they just automatically feel about which actions they believe to be right and fair and proper and which they believe to be not, when faced with a moral problem. Moral standards of behavior differ between people, depending upon their personal goals, norms, beliefs, and values, which in turn are dependent upon their cultural and religious traditions and their economic and social situations. The individuals and groups in a global economy come from very different cultural and religious traditions and live in very different economic and social situations; consequently, their moral standards of behavior, being subjective, are bound to differ substantially. Business managers have to understand, and deal with, those differences.
3. Accept that it is not enough for a manager to simply reach a decision on what he or she believes to be a right and fair and proper balance of benefits for some and harms for others, of rights recognized for some and rights denied for others, in any given situation. Managers have to go further, and *be able to convincingly explain why that balance should be viewed as best.* A convincing explanation requires objective methods of analysis rather than subjective standards of behavior. These objective methods of analysis include: (a) economic outcomes based upon impersonal market forces; (b) legal requirements based upon impartial social and political processes, and (c) ethical duties based upon universal ethical principles. This logical decision process starts with a listing of the benefits and harms, together with an accounting of the rights exercised and the rights denied, for each of the involved individuals, groups, and organizations to make certain that everyone understands the magnitude of the problem, despite their differences in their personal standards of behavior, and then moves on to the tripartite economic, legal, and ethical analysis. This logical process is shown graphically in Figure 1.1. The balance of this chapter will explain each of the seven elements within Figure 1.1, in sequence.

FIGURE 1.1 The Application of Objective Methods of Moral Analysis in Management

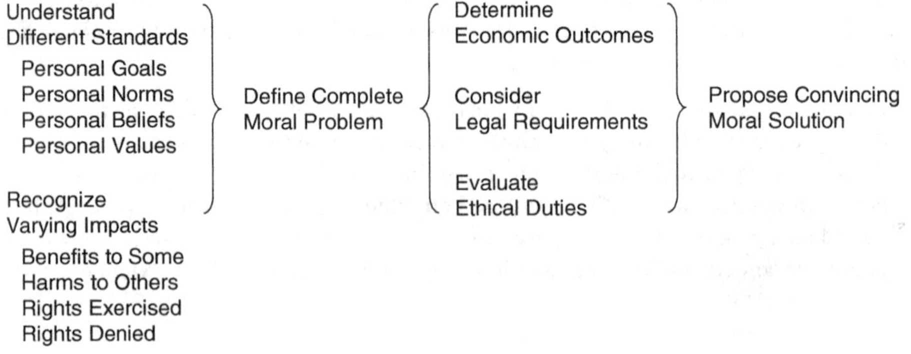

Understand the Different Standards

Most people, when they first encounter a situation in which the interests of some individuals or groups are going to be hurt or harmed in some way, or in which the rights of those individuals or groups are going to be ignored or compromised in some other way, turn first to their moral standards of behavior. Moral standards of behavior are our intuitive gauges for decisions and actions. They are the means we all use when we first encounter a moral problem in which some people are going to be injured to decide whether our actions, and/or those of the other people and other groups with whom we live and work, can be judged to be proper.

The problem is that our moral standards of behavior are subjective. They are personal. They are the way each of us intuitively feels about our actions and those of our neighbors, friends, and associates, but we can't really justify those feelings. You may feel that lying is wrong under any and all circumstances. I may feel that lying to avoid causing embarrassment or anguish to a close friend is perfectly all right. We can't or at least we generally don't resolve those differences, and so we usually just agree to disagree on the question. Such an understanding is perfectly acceptable when we are dealing with a minor moral problem such as lying to avoid causing discomfort to a friend. Such an understanding—to agree to disagree—is not acceptable when we are concerned with a major moral problem such as lying to substantial numbers of the stockholders in a company, or to even larger numbers of the customers of that firm.

For a major moral problem, we have to decide the issue, not ignore the conflict, and the first step is to understand that moral standards are not an adequate framework for decision because they are variable as well as personal. They vary by individual, by group, by region, by country, by culture, and by time. We all have evidence of that variation. Business managers in South and Central America and large parts of Africa and Asia think that it is perfectly acceptable to make small payments to government officials to facilitate needed documents and permits. That is termed *bribery* in the United States. Government officials in the United States feel that it is perfectly acceptable to consult with and be paid by foreign firms that have business relationships with the government after they retire. That is termed *treason* in South and Central America and large parts of Africa and Asia.

Moral standards of behavior differ between peoples because the goals, norms, beliefs, and values upon which they depend also differ, and those goals, norms, beliefs, and values in turn differ because of variations in the religious and cultural traditions and the economic and social situations in which the individuals are immersed. These relationships are shown in Figure 1.2.

Now we will take up each of the elements in Figure 1.2 in sequence—starting with the personal goals, norms, beliefs, and values—and show their derivation from the religious and cultural traditions and the economic and social situations of each individual:

- *Personal goals.* Goals are our expectations of outcomes. They are the things we want out of life and the things we expect others probably want out of life as well. They include material possessions (cars, homes, boats, and vacations), lifestyle preferences (money, position, workload, and power), personal goods (family, friends, health, and respect), and social aims (justice, equality, a clean environment, and a

FIGURE 1.2 Individual Determinants of Moral Standards

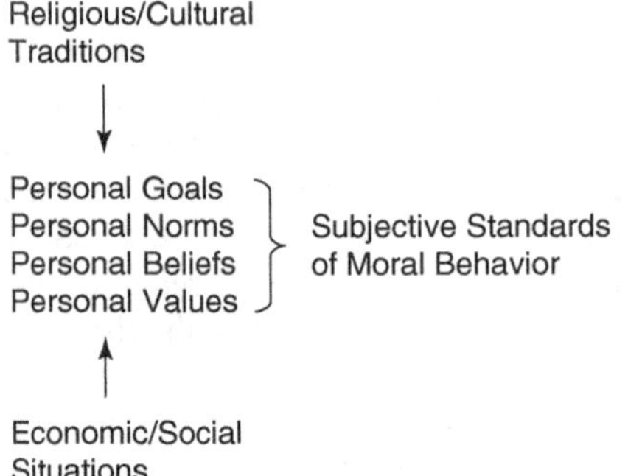

world at peace). If I want more money and power and you want greater justice and equality, then probably we are going to differ on what we think is right or wrong.

- *Personal norms.* Norms are our expectations of behavior. They are the ways we expect to act and the ways in which we expect others to act in given situations. Norms differ from moral standards in that they have no close association with judgments about right or wrong. Norms are expectations of behavior; morals are gauges of behavior. I expect you to drive on the right-hand side of the road; that is a norm. If you persist on driving on the left-hand (in the United States), I will say that you are wrong; that is a moral standard.
- *Personal beliefs.* Beliefs are our expectations of thought. They are the ways we expect to think, and the ways in which we expect others to think, about given situations. Our beliefs generally support our norms, and our norms usually lead toward our goals. For example, I believe that cigarette smoke causes cancer, and consequently I expect you not to smoke in my presence because one of my goals is good health. If you persist in smoking, despite my repeated (and heated) objections, I am going to say that you are wrong for you have acted against my moral standard derived from those goals, norms, and beliefs.
- *Personal values.* Values are our priorities among goals, norms, and beliefs. They are the ways we judge the relative importance of what we want to have, how we want to act, and why we believe as we do. Most people do not consider that all of their goals, norms, and beliefs are of equal importance. Generally there are some that seem more important, more "valued" than others. Let us say that you and I value democracy (a belief) very highly; if someone offers to give the both of us money (a goal) to vote a given way (a norm), we are going to say that such a person is wrong.

The goals, norms, beliefs, and values of a person will vary depending upon the cultural and religious tradition of that person, and those variations will in turn affect the moral standards. Clearly, many of the cultural and religious traditions of people living in the economically advanced regions of North America and Western Europe differ from those living in the developing regions of Southeast Asia and Central Africa. If we assume that all of these groups hold their religious beliefs and cultural norms in equally high esteem, then their differing goals, norms, beliefs, and values are going to affect the ways in which members of each group view a given moral issue in which some people are going to be hurt or harmed, while others will be benefited or helped, and/or in which some people have their rights ignored, while others find their rights acknowledged.

The goals, norms, beliefs, and values of a person will also vary depending upon the economic and social situation of that person. The economic situation includes the relative income and living standards of the individual. The social situation does not mean the social status of the person; instead it refers to his or her membership in different organizations whose members can influence his or her goals, norms, beliefs, values, and—ultimately—his or her moral standards. Clearly once again, the relative incomes and the organizational memberships of people living in North America and Western Europe are going to differ from those living in Southeast Asia and Central Africa, and here also the differing goals, norms, beliefs, and values are going to affect the ways in which each group views a given moral issue in which some people are going to be hurt or harmed, and/or have their rights ignored or dismissed.

How should you attempt to bridge those different moral standards, and arrive at an ethical solution that you believe to be proper given the circumstances, *and that you think you could logically explain to all of the other groups involved in the decision or action in order to reach a morally acceptable solution?* The argument of this book is that you work through each of the next six stages in the moral analysis in sequence, starting with an explicit recognition of the moral impacts.

Recognize the Moral Impacts

Moral problems have earlier been described as being complex because they result in benefits for some and harms for others and because they recognize the rights of some and ignore the rights of others. Those benefits and harms, these rights and wrongs, together compose the "impacts" of the problem. The impacts are the relative outcomes that people think about when they first begin to consider a morally controversial decision or action such as the one that was described in the first case in this text: "Health Care Insurance Companies and Payments to Customer Consultants."

In that case it was explained that large health care insurance companies had promised substantial cash payments to the consultants who were advising small business firms and public organizations (school districts, police departments, firefighters, etc.) on the best health care insurance policies to purchase for their employees. Health care insurance policies tend to be complex. Those policies vary in terms of the conditions covered, the treatments offered, and the co-payments required, and most small firms and public organizations don't have the staff to properly evaluate these variations.

The health care insurance companies benefited from the payment of cash bonuses to the health care consultants by not having to hire large numbers of sale personnel to explain their policies to their small business and public organization customers; instead, they could rely upon the consultants to provide those explanations. The health care consultants benefited from the receipt of the cash payments. The small business firms and public organizations, however, were harmed because the amount of those bonuses was hidden in the invoices sent to the business firms and public organizations as part of general overhead costs, and many of the employees in those firms and organizations, once this practice became known, felt strongly that they had been harmed because they did not get the combination of coverage, treatment, or co-payment options that most benefited themselves and their employees. Instead, they feared that they likely got the combination that most benefited the insurance companies. And, the business firms and public organizations felt that they had a right to know about the payments by the insurance firms—and a right to unbiased advice from the consulting firms.

Consequently, it is strongly recommended that you start your analysis of the problem, and your determination of the solution, by firstly identifying exactly who is going to be benefited and who is going to be harmed, and then who is going to be able to freely exercise their rights and who is going to be prevented from an equally free exercise of their rights. People feel strongly about being harmed. People feel even more strongly about being deprived of their rights. Your first step then is to make certain that everyone involved in the moral problem understands what is happening to everyone else, following these general formats:

- *Benefits.* Whose well-being will be substantially improved by the present or proposed action (what is being done, or what is planned to be done) either by yourself or by the organization to which you belong? Focus on material or financial or personal benefits to identifiable groups of people, not to inanimate companies or communities or countries. Moral problems involve a mixture of outcomes. List the positive outcomes of that mixture. Specifically, identify the major groups of people whose well-being you believe will be improved, and give a short description of the nature of that improvement for each group.
- *Harms.* Whose well-being will be substantially harmed by the present or proposed action (what is being done, or what is planned to be done) either by yourself or by the organization to which you belong? Focus on material or financial or personal harms to identifiable groups of people, not to inanimate companies or communities or countries. Moral problems, once again, constitute a mixture of outcome. List the negative outcomes of that mixture. Identify the major groups of people whose well-being you believe will be damaged, and give once again a short description of the nature of that damage for each group.
- *Rights.* Whose rights will be exercised and made more certain by the present or proposed action either by yourself or by the organization to which you belong? Focus on the rights of identifiable groups of people, not of inanimate companies or communities or countries. Be selective. Make certain that there is a clear right or claim of a privilege to do something important that is being exercised, not just a general desire to do something beneficial. Identify the major groups of people whose rights you believe will be sustained or expanded in some way, and give some indication of the nature of those rights.
- *Wrongs.* Whose rights will be denied and made less certain by the present or proposed action either by yourself or by the organization to which you belong? Focus on the wrongs of identifiable groups of people, not of inanimate companies or communities or countries. Again, be selective. Make certain that there is a clear right or claim of someone to do something important that is being denied, not just a general desire to do something beneficial. Identify the major groups of these people whose rights you believe will be denied or reduced in some way, and give an indication of the nature of those rights.

State the Moral Problem

If your listed balance of benefits received and harms imposed, and your described contrast of rights exercised and rights denied, conflicts with your personal moral standards, then clearly you have what you believe to be a moral problem. But, remember that—due to the differences in moral standards that come from variations in goals, norms, beliefs, and values, and from the contrasts in religious and cultural traditions and economic and social situations—not everyone will agree with you.

To reach a solution, you want to get everyone to fully comprehend your view of the issue. Doubtless other groups will want to get everyone—including you—to fully comprehend their understanding of the issue as well. If all groups fully comprehend all sides, clearly and accurately, then a compromise that meets the tests of economic benefits, legal requirements, and ethical duties is possible. That is why you want to first define and then state the moral problem as clearly as you can. Get agreement here, and the rest of the decision process will be far easier.

It is strongly suggested that you state the moral problem in the form of an extended question. A question is much less threatening and far more considerate than a statement. And, the question format explicitly recognizes the concerns of others and makes it possible to include those concerns in the subsequent analysis, discussion, and conclusion:

> Is it "right" that the health care insurance companies within the United States make substantial cash payments to the health care consulting firms that advise the customers of the health care insurers—the small businesses and public organizations—on the comparative advantages and disadvantages of the policies offered by those insurers? Certainly those payments work out to the benefit of the insurers who are more likely retain their customers without the expense of employing a large sales force, and also to the benefit of the consultants who receive greater revenues and record higher profits. But, the small businesses and public organizations are forced to pay more for their insurance policies, as the cash payments are added to the policy invoices in the form of general overhead, and thus probably lower the amount of health care received by the employees of the small businesses and public organizations. Further, the small businesses and public organizations and their employees can certainly claim that they have a right to know about the cash payments, and that withholding that knowledge results in an obvious conflict of interest.

In this particular example, just the statement of the moral problem went a long ways toward resolving that conflict of interest. Senior executives at the insurance companies, and sales personnel at the consulting firms, both believed that the cash payments were simply a tradition within their industry and that their customers knew about them, and thus tolerated if not approved of the long-standing practice. When they realized that the managers and employees of the small businesses and public organizations did not know about them, and definitely did not approve of them, they understood that a lawsuit was coming and quickly reached a settlement. The court has closed the transcript of the judicial hearing that eliminated the need for a trial, so the terms of that settlement are not known.

Many if not most employees at companies such as the health care insurers and health care consultants described in this case believe that bringing a moral problem to the attention of senior executives within their firms can be very detrimental to their careers. Consequently, they "get along by going along." But, here was an example where it would have paid to "stand out by standing up."

Determine the Economic Outcomes

"Economic outcomes" in moral analysis refers to the net balance of benefits over costs for the full society, given that the values of those benefits and costs are determined by all of the people within that full society, acting through open and free markets. This is the concept known as *Pareto Optimality*. The underlying belief is that people, through output product markets, express their preferences for the goods and services they most want to buy, and through input factor markets, express their preferences for the capital (money), labor (time), and land (raw materials) they most want to sell. Producing firms purchase or rent that capital, labor, and material at the lowest possible costs; convert those factors of production into products with the greatest possible efficiencies; and then sell the output goods and services at the highest possible prices. Competition in the output product markets keeps the prices from becoming improperly high, and competition in the input factor markets keeps the costs from becoming unfairly low. The full society, then, gets as many as possible of the products they most want to have while giving up as few as possible of the factors they least want to own.

This analytical method of "economic outcomes" can also be expressed as three easily understood dictums: (1) More is better than less. (2) Specifically, more is better than less when that "more" consists of what people really want, as expressed through their preferences in the product markets. (3) And even more specifically, that more of what people really want is better than less when that "more" is produced as efficiently as possible by using as little as possible of what people least want, as expressed by their preferences in the factor markets.

The concept of the greatest possible economic benefit at the least possible economic cost, which is the "more is better than less" argument or the Pareto Optimality theory, is considered to be a valid means of morally evaluating the benefits and harms of a moral problem as long as three conditions are met:

- *All market must be competitive.* Open and competitive product markets must exist for all output goods and services, and open and competitive factor markets must exist for all input capital, labor, and material to generate a true net benefit for society. Without fully competitive markets, the preferences of the members of that society cannot be rationally expressed.
- *All customers and all suppliers must be informed.* All customers in the output product markets and all suppliers in the input factor markets must be knowledgeable about the features of the products and the standards of the supplies. Without full information, the customers and suppliers cannot make rational choices and express true market preferences.
- *All costs must be included.* External costs are those outside the productive process; they are frequently ignored because no one in the producing firm has to write out

> a check as they must to purchase capital, labor, and material. Again, for customers and suppliers to express true market preferences, those external costs must be recognized, computed, and then either deducted from the prices of the input factors or included in the prices of the output products.

The cash payments from the health care insurers to the health care consultants certainly limited the competitiveness of the output product market for health insurance, and the lack of information about those payments among the small business and public organization customers certainly limited their ability to make rational choices and express their true market preferences for health insurance. It would be difficult to argue that the economic outcomes of those cash payments provided a net or Pareto Optimal benefit to society.

Consider the Legal Requirements

"Legal requirements" in moral analysis refer to the laws adopted by members of society to regulate the behavior of members of that society. Clearly, some regulation is needed. If everyone pursued their own self-interests, without regard to the self-interests of others, there would be disruption and chaos, and no economic benefits would be possible for anyone. The problem is that every regulation protects—to some extent—the rights of some individuals and groups within society even while it limits—also to some extent—the rights of other individuals and groups within that same society. Legal requirements, in one sense, are very similar to economic outcomes. Both result in a balance. Economic outcomes in moral analysis focus upon a balance between benefits and harms. Legal requirements in moral analysis also focus upon a balance, though in this instance it is a balance between an increase in rights for some and a decrease in rights for others.

The issue in moral analysis, of course, is how those balances are to be determined. The economic balance between benefits distributed and harms allocated is theoretically determined by impartial markets, and most people accept that approach as long as (1) the input factor and output product markets are fully open and competitive, (2) the factor owners and product customers are fully informed, and (3) the external costs are fully included. The legal balance between rights exercised and rights denied is theoretically determined by impartial elections, and many people accept that approach as long as (1) all elections are open and competitive, (2) all citizens can freely participate, and (3) all participants are fully informed. But, there can be problems here because elections are often subject to unrecognized influences and unusual circumstances, and thus are less than truly impartial.

Let me give a hypothetical example of unrecognized influences and unusual circumstances that can affect the outcome of competitive elections. Assume that I own a considerable amount of land in a rapidly growing residential community. Perhaps that land was my family's farm, which I inherited but have not yet subdivided for housing. You and hundreds of other families bought homes that were built on land that had been sold and then subdivided by other farm families within the area. You had assumed that there were zoning restrictions so that my acreage, which is the only vacant property left, would also be used for housing. But, you were wrong. The original farm acreage had been excluded from zoning restrictions by the town council when development first started.

I own my land outright and, consequently, I think that I have a right to do what I please with that land and make as large a profit as possible from its sale. A real estate developer offers me a very high price to build a very large shopping center. My right to sell what I own without interference will be exercised. Your right to live quietly, in your own home on your own land, without commercial intrusions, will be denied. That denial will be particularly irksome given (1) that your home site is directly adjacent to the rear of my property so that the unattractive loading docks and rubbish containers of the stores will be close to your outdoor patio grill; and (2) that the developer readily admits that the large chain stores his or her firm has already signed to long-term leases expect to stay open until 10:00 every night, and that they will occasionally sponsor rock concerts to draw their wanted younger customers.

How do we determine what would be equitable under those circumstances? You and the other homeowners could ask the town council to schedule a special election, but because generally there are far more residents who want the twin conveniences of close location and broad selection provided by a new mall, but don't live close enough to suffer the twin inconveniences of more traffic and greater noise, you will probably lose. You will be even more likely to lose if the developer takes a financial interest in the outcome and begins running well-designed ads on television stations extolling not only the retail benefits the mall will bring to local customers but also the tax contributions mall will make to local schools.

The hypothetical example I posed is not truly realistic because it presupposes that there are no existing laws regulating development. Generally there are, even in areas undergoing recent development from long-held farm land, but in many instances the laws that do exist have not been kept up to date, and also in many specific situations those laws may favor one party at the expense of others. Let us assume that the court system that can adjudicate conflicts between parties is impartial, but here the party with greater resources to hire experienced attorneys and continue expensive claims often has a decided advantage. One of the major themes of this book is that we need to look at economic outcomes, legal requirements, *and* ethical duties to reach a truly equitable balance between benefits for some and harms for others or between rights recognized for some and rights denied for others. We now turn to those ethical duties.

Evaluate the Ethical Duties

"Ethical duties" in moral analysis refers to the obligations owed by members of society to other members of that society. Clearly, some obligations do exist. We ought not to lie to each other, or agreements will not be possible. We ought not to cheat each other, or contracts will not be possible. And we ought not to steal from each other, or communities will not be possible. A society without agreements, without contracts, and without communities would be impossible to sustain. The problem is that if I could lie just a little bit, cheat just a little bit, and steal just a little bit, the society could still be maintained—weakened but still in existence—and I would be advantaged, though you—the truthful, honest, and honorable one—would be harmed. Once again, the focus in moral analysis is on the balance between self-interest and social interest.

But, there is a difference here. The doctrine of economic outcomes attempts to find an *equitable* balance between benefits for some people within society and harms for others that will result in an overall improvement for the full society. The doctrine of legal requirements similarly attempts to find an *equitable* balance between rights for some people and wrongs (deprivation of right) for others that also will result in an overall improvement for our society. The doctrine of ethical duties does not look for a balance between duties. Instead, it attempts to define what is meant by *equitable,* and it attempts to reach that definition through a logic that everyone within society can logically understand and hopefully accept. In short, ethical duties attempt to set the rules or conditions that should govern the operations of markets and the applications of laws.

Everyone within society may logically understand the series of ethical duties that will be briefly summarized later in this chapter, but of course not everyone will accept them. That should not surprise us. Life is a conflict between self-interest and social interest. But, as long as the readers of this book remember (1) that ethical duties attempt to define what is equitable when applied to markets and laws, (2) that equitable means "fair to all and just for everyone," and (3) that if you are able to logically show that certain economic outcomes and/or legal requirements truly were equitable in that sense of fair to all and just for everyone, then (4) you would be close to reaching an acceptable solution to the given moral problem you were addressing. That is the purpose of this book: how to reach equitable, and therefore acceptable, solutions to moral problems in which some individuals, groups, or organizations will be benefited, while others will be harmed, or in which some individuals, groups, or organizations will have their rights accepted, while others will see their rights dismissed.

Now, on to a brief summary of these ethical duties, described in the historical sequence of their initial formulation. There are, in my view, eight of them. All have a logical base. If you can explain the logical basis of economic outcomes, legal requirements, *and* ethical duties, then you are well on your way to resolving moral problems, and assuming the role of leader, not manager, within an organization:

1. *Long-term interests* (Protagoras, 490–422 BC). The goal of the Pre-Socratic Greek philosophers was to define the behaviors that would lead to an enjoyable life. A balanced pursuit of accomplishments and pleasures was said to be the means to that goal, but this had to be moderated to avoid provoking others. An enjoyable life required a stable and friendly society with no one seeking retribution or revenge, and that in turn meant taking the interests of others into account. The resulting principle can be expressed in modern terms as "Never take any action that will bring immediate benefits to you now, but that is likely to provoke adverse reactions in the future." This rule is now referred to as "enlightened self-interest."
2. *Personal virtues* (Aristotle, 384–322 BC). The argument here is that we can do as we like, and follow our own self-interests, as long as we adopt a set of standards for our treatment of others. Those standards form our character. We have to be honest, open, and truthful to eliminate distrust, and we should live temperately so as not to incite

envy. In short, we have to be proud of our actions and of our character, because it is hard to be proud of actions that exploit or diminish others. The principle, then, can be expressed, again in modern terms, as "Never take any action that is not honest, open, and truthful, and that you would not feel pride to see reported widely in national newspapers and on network newscasts."

3. *Religious injunctions* (St. Augustine, 354–403 AD, and St. Thomas Aquinas, 1225–1274). Honesty, truthfulness, and temperance are not enough; we also have to have some degree of compassion and kindness toward each other to form a truly good society. Compassion and kindness are best expressed in the Golden Rule, which is not limited to the Judeo-Christian tradition, but is part of almost all of the world's religions. Reciprocity and compassion together build a sense of community. The principle, then, can be expressed as "Never take any action that is not kind and compassionate, and that does not build a sense of community, a sense of all of us working together for commonly accepted goals."
4. *Government requirements* (Hobbes, 1588–1679, and Locke, 1632–1704). Compassion, kindness, and a sense of community would be ideal if everyone shared those characteristics, but everyone doesn't. Instead, people compete for property and position, and that competition, unrestrained, can bring chaos. To avoid that chaos, we need a Social Contract, or a set of rules that everyone could logically accept. This set of rules, the authors proposed, was that everyone should obey a central authority as long as that authority respected each individual's rights to life, liberty, and property. This principle then can be expressed as "Never take any action that violates the law because law respects the basic rights of life, liberty, and property."
5. *Utilitarian benefits* (Bentham, 1747–1832, and Mill, 1806–1873). Common obedience to the law would work well if the people associated with the central authority did not have self-interests of their own that then could shape the law. Consequently, we need a means of evaluating the laws of our government, and that same means can be used to evaluate the actions of ourselves. The authors then proposed that a law, or an action, would be right if it led to greater social benefits than social harms. This is the rule that is often summarized as "greatest good for the greatest number," though in reality the society, not the majority, has to benefit. The principle can be summarized as "Never take any action that does not result in greater good than harm for the society of which you are a part."
6. *Universal rules* (Kant, 1724–1804). Net social benefit is elegant in theory, but the theory does not say anything about how we should measure either the benefits or the harms—what is your life or health or well-being worth?—nor does it explain how we should distribute those benefits or allocate those harms. What we need is a rule to eliminate the self-interest of the person who decides in any given situation, and we can do that by universalizing the decision process. The principle, then, can be expressed as "Never take any action that you would not be willing to see others, faced with the same or a closely similar situation, also be free and even forced to take."
7. *Distributive justice* (Rawls, 1921–2002). The problem with the "willingness to see others be free and even forced to take" rule for actions that allegedly come from a good intent to promote social interest rather than a selfish desire to advance self-interest is that people differ in their social and economic situations. People have

different social and economic wants. We need a rule to protect the poor and the uneducated who lack the power and position to achieve those wants. If we did not know who among us would be poor and uneducated—the Social Contract—everyone would be in favor of such a rule. The principle, then, can be expressed as "Never take any action in which the least among us will be harmed in any way."

8. *Contributive liberty* (Nozick, 1938–2002). Perhaps liberty, the freedom to follow one's own self-interest within the constraints of the law and the markets, is more important than justice, the right to be protected from extremes of that law and those markets. If so, then the only agreement that could be made under the conditions of the Social Contract—in which people do not know who would be rich or poor, who powerful or weak—would be that no one should interfere with the rights of anyone else to improve their legal abilities and marketable skills. The principle, then, can be expressed as "Never take any action that will interfere with the rights of others for self-development and self-improvement."

The method of moral analysis recommended in this text is that you look first at *your* moral standards of behavior—what do *you* intuitively believe to be proper decisions and actions, based upon *your* goals, norms, beliefs and values. Then, look at the situation that you have encountered. Who will be benefited and who will be harmed? Who will be able to exercise their rights and who will be denied an equally free exercise of their rights? If those conditions in that situation conflict with your moral standards of behavior, then you have a moral problem. Express that moral problem as clearly as you can, so that *everyone* involved will understand your concerns. Then, analyze that moral problem through the perspectives of economic outcomes, legal requirements, and ethical duties to arrive at *your* moral solution.

Chapter 2 will discuss in greater detail the analytical procedure of economic outcomes. Chapter 3 will deal with legal requirements. Chapter 4 will describe the ethical duties. Chapter 5 will focus on the reasons to be moral: the trust, commitment, and effort that frequently develop among all of the participants within an extended organization in response to decisions and actions that they perceive to be equitable, or fair and just to all. Chapter 6 will consider the managerial and organizational changes needed to achieve exactly those results, and the resultant organizational cooperation, innovation, and unification that are needed for success in our highly competitive global environment.

Case 1-1

Condominium Owners versus Condominium Employees

A condominium is a residential building in which the individual units are owned by the people living within those units, while the common spaces—the hallways, entrances, elevators, and stairways—and the physical features—the building structure and exterior surfaces, the central furnace and air conditioner, and the water and waste systems—are either owned by a corporation that is in turn jointly owned by those residents or by a trust owned by others but established for the benefit and control of those residents. In short, a condominium or "condo" is an apartment that a resident owns rather than rents and that is in a building controlled by an association of unit owners rather than by representatives of renting landlords.

Ownership of the individual units is legally confined to the interior walls and the space within those walls. Residents can do as they like to the interiors of their units, as long as they do not disturb others or harm the value of their jointly-owned or controlled building. Maintenance and repair of the common spaces and the physical features falls under the direction of an association of owners, or board, whose members are elected by all of the residents, usually on a rotating "elect a third of the board members each year" basis. The owners, and thus the elected members of the board, frequently have little in common beyond the financial resources to purchase rather than rent their living accommodations, and the resulting differences can lead to conflicts.

These conflicts often occur in connection with expenditures for the maintenance and repair of the building because those costs form a major part of the monthly fees assigned to each residential unit. An example of one of these cost-based conflicts was recently described in the *New York Times* ["Hard Times," by Randy Cohen and published in the *New York Times Magazine,* March 22, 2009, p. 18]. Mr. Cohen described a situation in which the board of a 273 unit condominium building had received a request from a group of the residents to replace the unionized cleaning contractor who had worked for the condominium for a number of years with a new, non-unionized crew for a cost savings of $35,000 per year.

This occurred during the economic downturn in the U.S. economy that began in 2007, and it can be assumed that the income levels of many of the condominium residents had been adversely affected by that downturn and so the potential saving would be appreciated by those residents. On the other hand, there had been no complaints about the quality of the cleaning service that the contractor's crew had provided—the entrance lobby, elevators, and floor hallways were felt to be clean and attractive and the exterior sidewalks and entrance steps properly swept, etc.—and here it can also be assumed that many of the workers who were to be replaced had been equally affected by the economic downturn, and needed their current jobs with regular wages.

Class Assignment

What is your view? If you were a member of the board of this condominium, would you replace the current unionized cleaning service with a new non-union group for a cost savings of $35,000 per year? You certainly can choose whatever alternative you prefer, but remember that the one of the major messages of this book is that when you address important issues in which some people will be harmed while others will be benefited, as they will in this instance, that you should take a leadership position and attempt to *logically convince* the other members of that board.

Case 1-2

Motel Rates after Hurricane Katrina

Hurricane Katrina was the costliest storm in the history of the United States. The center of that storm came ashore directly through New Orleans on the morning of August 29, 2005, and many of the levies protecting that city failed. But the damage caused by the high winds (some gusts were measured at 175 mph) and high tides (8 feet above normal) was not confined to New Orleans. The harsh effects of the storm were felt along much of the Gulf Coast, from southwestern Louisiana to southern Mississippi, Alabama, and the Florida Panhandle.

The warning system was not as good as it should have been, and few evacuation orders were issued by public officials, but many people were alerted by radio and television programs, packed their cars and drove inland, attempting to get to higher ground, beyond the reach of the expected storm surge. People who did not leave, choosing instead to "ride out the storm" in solidly constructed local schools and public buildings, found afterward that their homes had been either damaged or destroyed, that fresh food, clean water, and electric power were unavailable, and they too were forced to move inland, away from the coast.

The inland motels, grocery stores, and drug stores were overwhelmed. All of the affected states along the Gulf Coast had laws that prohibited businesses from raising prices during a period of emergency, but most of the motels had published list prices that were charged only during holidays when travel was heavy and occupancies were full. Those list prices were approximately twice as high as the amounts that were usually charged under normal conditions. It is alleged that during the emergency many motels did charge those higher published rates.

In one instance the manager at a motel that was close to the coast but undamaged and in a still functioning city received a telephone call from the owner ordering him to charge the higher rates. The owner said that they had been set a year in advance, had been published, and thus could not be considered to be part of an illegal "storm opportunity" increase. The manager conveyed the owner's instructions to all of the clerks working at the registration desk, but one of those clerks refused to comply, and voluntarily quit her job. In the trial that eventually followed, in which the clerk sued to get her job back, she testified, ". . . there was a lot going on there that I did not agree with. In my opinion I was breaking the law. I was just not treating people right." She then concluded, "I'm the one that's down there breaking the law. I'm doing it because the manager said to do it. But, it's my name on them folios. Not his." (*Sherman v. Miss. Emp. Sec. Com'n,* 989 So.2d 398, 399, Miss. 2008)

Class Assignment

The assignment here is divided into two parts. Firstly, what would you have done if you had been manager of that motel when the owner called and told you to charge the higher rates? Would you have gone along, or would you have objected? Remember, you have to be able to *logically convince* that person. You can't just express some mild disagreement, perhaps saying, "I'm not certain that's right," and expect the owner to immediately withdraw his or her instructions.

The second part of the assignment is to assume that you were a member of the jury at the trial where the desk clerk sued the motel owner to get her job back. She was the one who said in her testimony, "In my opinion I was breaking the law. I was just not treating people right." You can vote "yes" or "no" on her getting her job back, but remember to be effective you will have to be able to *logically convince* the other jury members. And, if the jury decides, "Yes, she should get her job back," the second part of the verdict will be to decide if she should receive a dollar award for feeling forced to resign. Here you can pick any amount, from none to a small figure to cover her living costs after she resigned to a much bigger number to influence the future actions of the motel owner. But again, you will have to be able to *logically convince* the other jury members that your proposed amount is proper or fair given the circumstances.

Case 1-3

Citigroup and the $100 Million Bonus

Citigroup Inc. is a very large financial conglomerate. Essentially, it is a combined commercial bank, investment bank, brokerage firm, and trust company with a number of associated trading groups. Overall, prior to the financial crisis that started in 2007, there were 12,000 offices in 140 countries, with more than 300,000 employees and more than 200 million customer accounts.

Citigroup suffered huge losses during that financial crisis, at least partially caused by its extensive participation in the sub-prime mortgage market and its active construction and sale of collateralized debt obligations based upon those mortgages. Citigroup's stock market valuation dropped from $240 billion in 2007 to just $6 billion in 2008. Bankruptcy seemed imminent.

To avoid that fate, which would have had massive global consequences, the U.S. Treasury was forced to add $45 billion of Troubled Asset Relief Program (TARP) funds to Citigroup reserves, and the Federal Deposit Insurance Corporation (FDIC) had to pledge to cover 90 percent of all future losses on Citigroup's $335 billion portfolio of securitized investments and collateralized loans. In return, Citigroup provided the government with $27 billion in preferred shares (later converted to 36 percent of Citigroup's common stock), agreed to attempt to modify the mortgages it held using standards set by the FDIC as part of an effort to help families stay in their homes, and promised to "cap" executive salaries.

Citigroup agreed to cap or limit executive salaries, and indeed Vikram Pandit, the chief executive officer, accepted a salary of just $1.00 per year until the crisis eased. But, nothing was said about executive bonuses. And here there came a very major problem.

The senior officer who headed Citigroup's energy trading group Philbro (originally named Phillips Brothers before it was purchased by Citigroup early in the acquisition spree that eventually resulted in the "too big to fail" conglomerate) was due a very large bonus. Philbro was a secretive unit that was not located on Wall Street; instead it operated on the site of a former Connecticut dairy farm that had been luxurious transformed. That senior officer, Andrew Hall, had an employment contract that guaranteed him a percentage of the trading profits of this unit. Those profits, while never disclosed by Citigroup, were said by people who were familiar with the situation to normally be very large; they also said that 2008 was not an exception to that rule. It was further said by those "in the know" people that the bonus that year would be more than $100 million, and that if the bonus was not paid, and paid promptly, Mr. Hall would leave and take all of the members of his trading staff, who also were due large bonuses though not in the same nine-figure range, with him to found a totally new operation. Someone with a bit of a sense of humor added that there are plenty of old dairy farms in Connecticut.

Class Assignment

What is your opinion? Mr. Hall has a valid contract, and he did earn a very substantial profit for the company at which he works. But that company has been subsidized by a cash payment of $45 billion and a credit pledge of $335 billion—both of which essentially come from U.S. taxpayers, most of whom have never earned more than $50,000 a year in their lives. Should the $100 million bonus be paid to Mr. Hall this year? Assume that you are a consultant on executive compensation, and have been asked to advise members of the board of directors of Citigroup. What would you say? Remember, you should be prepared to *logically convince* the members of that board.

Case 1-4

Bernard Madoff and the Largest Financial Scam in History

On March 12, 2009, Bernard L. ("Bernie") Madoff pled guilty to an 11-count criminal indictment, admitting that he had defrauded thousands of investors of billions of dollars through a Ponzi scheme that he had operated under the shelter of his asset management firm—Madoff Investment Securities—for nearly 20 years. Federal prosecutors estimated that client losses totaled $65 billion.

A Ponzi scheme is an investment fund that pays what appear to be high and steady returns to the early investors from the monies put into the fund by subsequent contributors, not from legitimate gains. The scheme is named after Charles Ponzi, who emigrated from Italy to the United States in 1908 and then became notorious for using this technique in Boston during the early 1920s. At that time, eastern Massachusetts was heavily industrialized with textile mills, shoe factories, and machinery manufacturers, all of whom were dependent upon immigrants for much of their unskilled labor force. The existing banks and investment firms focused on what was termed "old money" and did not accept deposits from working-class families. Ponzi provided the needed alternative, and for a period of time appeared to be exceedingly successful.

Most Ponzi schemes do not last very long because continuing the returns that the fund advertises widely and pays regularly requires an ever-increasing flow of money from later investors in order to keep the circle not only going but growing. Also, as more investors talk about outstanding opportunities for steadiness and growth, and as more competitors complain that something must be wrong, the more likely it is that the scheme will come to the attention of governmental agencies. Ponzi's scheme lasted for 5 years; Madoff's for approximately 20, though his operations were so secretive that it is unclear exactly when he started using the "take funds from the late comers to pay the first comers" scheme.

Madoff founded Bernard L. Madoff Investment Securities LLC in 1960 with an initial investment of just $5,000 saved from stints as a beach lifeguard and a lawn sprinkler installer. He built his firm into a successful market maker, facilitating security trades by serving as a middleman between institutional investors. He focused on low

Note: William A. L. Rodgers, University of Michigan MBA, 2010, served as co-author of this case.

volume, over-the-counter (OTC) stocks on the outskirts of traditional markets like the New York Stock Exchange (NYSE) and American Stock Exchange (ASE), and was one of the first to invest heavily in the electronic technology needed to automate the buying and selling of those stocks at reduced trading costs. Then, in the mid-1970s, he purchased a position in the Cincinnati Stock Exchange and invested $250,000 to help upgrade its computer equipment and improve its software, which enabled the exchange to report running stock quotes. Cincinnati became the first all-electronic computerized stock exchange, and eventually changed its name to the National Association of Securities Dealers Automated Quotations (NASDAQ).

By 1989, Madoff Investment Securities was handling more than 5 percent of the trading volume on the NYSE. This rapid ascent made him an unpopular target of the traditional traders on the floor of that exchange, as did a controversial practice called "payment for order flow," in which his company would pay large firms like Fidelity and Schwab to send their customer orders directly to his electronic trading desk instead of to the NYSE. Congressional hearings ensued after complaints by the floor traders, who were still primarily operating on a manual "shout and signal" system, but Madoff continued the payments and benefited from the attention that the investigation generated, which primarily served to enhance his stature on Wall Street. He became chairman of NASDAQ; was asked to take a leadership role in the Securities Industry and Financial Markets Association, Wall Street's principal lobbying arm in Washington; and served for a period of time as Chairman of the Board of Governors of the National Association of Securities Dealers (NASD).

In short, toward the end of this period of rapid growth, Bernard Madoff had become very well known within financial circles as a successful manager of stock trading operations, a senior participant in stock trading associations, and a wealthy recipient of stock trading profits. Less well known was his activity in an investment-advisory business that he had started as a low-profile adjunct to the trading operations at Madoff Investment Securities during the 1970s. Under his direction, this operation began to actively manage entrusted funds, rather than merely provide financial advice to clients, and it gradually drew in increasing amounts of money from institutional investors, wealthy individuals, private charities, and many middle-income families who invested through third-party companies or "feeder funds." Madoff focused on the internal operations of this investment-management portion of his business, and relied upon his father-in-law, Saul Alpern, for the external marketing.

Saul Alpern developed a recruiting circuit that included stops in the New York Catskills, Palm Beach, and Long Island, calling on prominent Jewish families who were familiar with the success of Alpern's son-in-law. As time passed, Madoff also began to use his personal wealth as a market-building tool, entertaining clients on his large yacht or at his numerous homes and leveraging his influence at charitable organizations to build a network of trust and an aura of integrity.

Madoff never became a household name among the majority of American investors who dealt with more established institutions. Within the Jewish philanthropic community in New York, however, Madoff's growing fortune, burgeoning reputation, generous donations, and quiet confidence made him the money manager of choice for many of the major groups. Enticed by the steady double-digit investment returns those charities reportedly received from Madoff, outsiders began desperately working connections for the opportunity to meet him and get in on the action. Through friends of friends,

Madoff's network reached well beyond New York, picking up new investors through social settings like country clubs and golf courses throughout the country and even abroad. Demand for inclusion in Madoff's fund became global.

As Madoff's profile in the hedge fund community grew, skepticism about his amazingly consistent returns grew. Rivals complained that they could not achieve the same returns when replicating his trading strategy (essentially a hedge fund, with options sold or purchased to protect, or "hedge" against losses on long-held securities), and those complaints prompted a few regulatory investigations that proved inconclusive. Madoff ran the investment management arm of his firm with great secrecy; it was totally separate from the market-making arm. The two divisions were located on different office floors and used separate computer systems, and the traders knew very little about what the hedgers did on the floor below them. The employees who worked on that lower floor remained totally loyal to Madoff and never alleged or even hinted at any improprieties. The necessary audits were performed by a small accounting firm that had worked with Madoff since the start of his company, and they also never reported any problems.

Madoff's personal privacy and constructed secrecy kept him out of the spotlight and allowed him to create a fraudulent investment program that became grotesque in its final size and investor loss. But the operations of that investment program continued without interruption or difficulty until Bernard Madoff confessed to his two sons who ran the trading floor of the firm that the entire investment program was a total sham, that no investments had ever been made, and that the consequential losses were huge. The two sons, as requested by their father, reported this to the Securities and Exchange Commission (SEC), and Barnard Madoff was arrested that afternoon.

Class Assignment

1. Why in your opinion did Bernard Madoff do this? He had been exceedingly successful in the electronic exchange trading that he had started and his firm continued, and he had clearly achieved both wealth and stature. What was it that drove him, again in your view, "off the cliff"? What does this say about human character? What does this say about the nature and/or culture of the investment community?
2. Why was it so easy for Bernard Madoff to raise so much money? The case describes a "network of trust and an aura of probity." How does a person build a network of trust and aura of probity? Give some thought here. It may help you to avoid a similar situation in the future.
3. The *Wall Street Journal* (August 20, 2009, p. B5) published three articles on the lessons that business schools should teach and business students should take away from the financial meltdown that had occurred. The huge Madoff investment losses were part of that meltdown. What are the lessons that you think are important from the Madoff investment fraud as part of that overall meltdown?
4. What would you have done differently had you been (a) an advisor to a charitable organization that was investing substantial funds through Madoff; (b) a member of a well-paid feeder fund that was collecting smaller amounts from middle income investors for transfer to Madoff; or (c) a competitor who had reported to the SEC that the investment model Madoff was using was incapable of generating such large and consistent returns, but seen little happen?

Case 1-5

Lead Paint on Children's Toys: Who Was Responsible?

RC2 Corporation of Oak Brook, Illinois, holds the relatively new position of marketing specialist in the children's toy industry. The company neither develops nor manufacturers the toys that it sells. Instead, it contracts with large media companies and publishing houses for the rights to use the characters developed by others such as Big Bird, Winnie the Pooh, Bob the Builder, and Thomas the Tank Engine. RC2 then designs wooden or stuffed toys based upon those characters; contracts with low-cost manufacturers, primarily in China, to make them; ships the finished toys in low-cost container vessels to the United States and Europe; and distributes them through low-cost retail chains such as Walmart, Kmart, and Toys "R" Us for final sale to the parents. It is a low-cost and high-volume business model that has been highly successful.

RC2 was a relatively small player in the toy market, but its revenues had more than doubled in the five years before the U.S. Consumer Product Safety Commission announced the company had been ordered to recall half a million Thomas and Friends wooden railway train sets that consisted of model engines, cars, and track sections because their paint coatings contained lead.[1]

Parents, of course, were surprised and shocked. Lead is known to be highly toxic. When ingested by young children it can cause learning disabilities, behavioral problems, and growth concerns. In older children and adults, lead poisoning can lead to high blood pressure, kidney failure, and stomach distress. The adverse effects of lead upon health had become known during the 1960s, and laws were passed in the early 1970s throughout the United States and Western Europe to restrict lead amounts in all consumer products, and over time these laws had been extended on a nearly global basis. By 2007, for example, it was illegal in China to use lead-based paint on export goods. Despite the parental concerns and the relevant laws, however, lead paint continued to be found on many children's toys. Soon, news came out that one of the bigger toy companies, Mattell, was also recalling nearly one million toys due to the discovery of lead paint used by a contract manufacturer in China.[2]

What went wrong? It was easy to blame the Chinese toy manufacturing companies, and many people did. They explained that lead paint creates brighter, shinier colors that appeal both to the children who play with the toys and the parents who purchase them. Also, lead paint flows more evenly, so that it is easier and less expensive to apply. And finally, lead paint is much cheaper; it is said to sell in China for a third of the cost of paint that would meet global standards of protection.

[1] "Train Wreck," *The New York Times,* June 19, 2007, Section C, p. 1.

[2] "The Little Engine That Could Poison," *The New York Times,* June 22, p. 22.

The general conclusion of those on this side of "it's their fault" argument was that the Chinese manufacturers had deliberately disregarded both the standards in their purchase contracts and the laws in their country in search of high profits. There were others, however, who disagreed, believing some of the responsibility should be shared by American and European multinational companies that put too much pressure on Chinese companies to supply cheap products in the interest of increasing profit margins.[3]

Those who believed that the responsibility extended beyond the Chinese manufacturers, who admittedly had applied the lead-based paint for reasons of appearance and profit, cited a recent change in the competitive structure of the children's toy industry. Traditionally, this industry had three participants: small manufacturing companies who designed and made toys, regional wholesale firms who distributed the toys, and local retail stores who sold the toys. These toys were almost always generic; that is, they were of the "If you've seen one stuffed bear, cast truck, or wooden locomotive you've seen them all" variety.

Similar to many other industries, however, the children's toy industry began to consolidate in search of the dual economies of scale and scope during the 1980s. This was at the same time that children's television programs such as *Sesame Street* began to dominate the networks with content that was both intriguing to preschool children and acceptable to their parents. The right to market toys based upon the characters popularized on these programs quickly was recognized as a huge competitive advantage by the media companies, who held the rights to those characters, the manufacturers who wanted those rights for their toys, and the retail chains who wanted the high volume sales that would result.

The manufacturers, that over this period had grown by accretion, were caught between large and well-financed media companies that wanted high royalties and the equally large and well-financed retail chains that wanted low prices. Numerous accounts have been published relating the experiences of manufacturers and importers that had come with an appointment and a proposal to the headquarter offices of one of the larger retail chains, had then been told that the chain purchasing department had analyzed the costs of producing the items on that proposal in the expected volumes, and ended by stating, "This is the price (as specific dollar figure) that you're going to have to accept."

There are far fewer anecdotal accounts of manufacturers and/or importers going similarly hat-in-hand to the headquarter offices of the large media companies (generally in New York or Los Angeles, not in Arkansas), but it can be assumed that they also encountered a similar "This is the price you're going to have to pay" rigidity. There was limited bargaining at either end of the value chain in the children's toy industry because both the media companies and retail chains, equally large and well-financed players, held the pricing power.

The manufacturers, given those limits, quickly arranged for far less expensive production abroad and turned themselves into marketing specialists. These changes in the

[3] *The New York Times,* August 25, 2007.

competitive structure of the preschool toy industry, from the traditional to the consolidated, are shown in the following graphic:

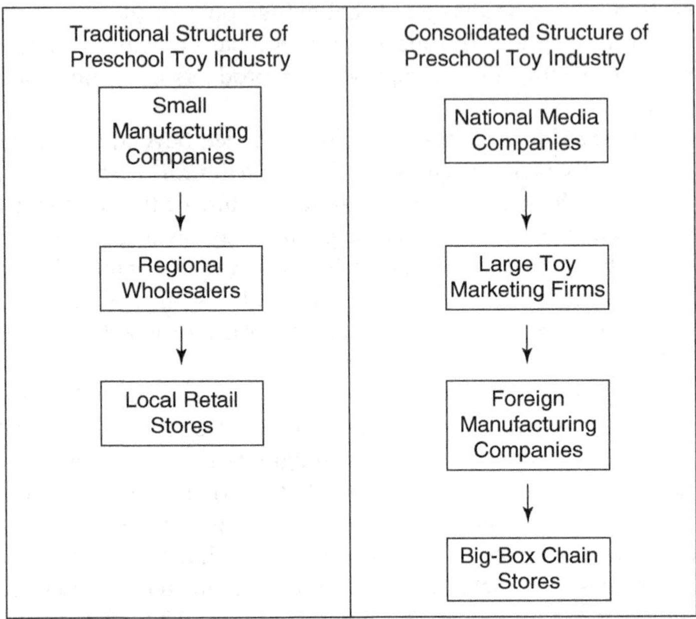

In the traditional structure of the preschool toy industry, it would seem clear who was responsible for the use of lead-based paint upon the children's toys, had such an event occurred. It would have been the small manufacturing firms that designed and made the toys they sold to the regional wholesale firms that, in turn, sold to the local retail stores that then sold to the public. The final price to the public was the one that determined the overall demand, and the three participants had approximately equal power to divide the profits.

In the consolidated structure, however, the responsibility for the lead paint on the children's toys is not so clear. Obviously, the foreign manufacturers were the ones that actually put the lead paint on the children's toys—but here the industry participants did not share equal size and power: the two on the ends held very dominate positions. Without the consent of the national media companies, toys based upon their popular television characters could not be manufactured and sold, and high royalty payments were required to gain that consent. Similarly, without acceptance by the big-box chain stores, toys based upon those characters could not have been sold in the volumes needed to pay the high royalties that had been charged, and low unit costs were needed to obtain that acceptance.

Class Assignment

After an exceedingly harmful event occurs and the results become widely known, it is always easy to say what should have been done to prevent that event from occurring. In this case, despite the legal contracts that the marketing specialist firms, RC2 and

Mattel, had with their Chinese suppliers that clearly stated that *no* lead paint should ever be used, one fairly obvious preventive measure would have been to test on a regular basis each shipment of wooden toys for lead in the paint. In the famous words of President Ronald Reagan when speaking about an atomic weapons treaty his administration had reached with the government of Russia, "Trust, but verify."

1. Why, in your opinion, did the senior executives at RC2 and Mattel not set up a statistically reliable sampling program to check for all of the obvious safety hazards that can appear on wooden toys for young children: small parts that can be swallowed, sharp edges that could cut, or toxic chemicals that might be present in the wood or have been added to the paint? Those marketing specialist firms had already been forced, by recent changes in U.S. law, to inspect the operations of their Chinese suppliers for unsafe working conditions and improper employment practices. Why did they not begin inspecting those suppliers' products when they arrived in the United States?
2. Who, in your opinion, should bear the costs of such an inspection program? Should it be the federal government (to protect U.S. citizens), the marketing specialist firms (to protect their own interests), or all of the members of the toys for young children value chain, from the national media companies to the big box retailers (to protect their customers)? Remember, the last two participants named have strong economic clout at each end of this value chain. How would you convince them to join in the effort?
3. Are there any good alternatives to an inspection program? Inspecting what someone else has already done is totally inefficient in any economic sense—and it eventually led to inspection of the inspectors. It would be far better to get it done right the first time. Getting it done right the first time should be the primary task of management. Members of this class are, it is easy to assume, in a program on management. How would you get it done right the first time?
4. Lastly, what exactly changed in the children's toy industry that brought about this outcome in which an unknown and unknowable number of very young children were badly hurt? So far as is known, after lead paint had been found to be so harmful to the mental and physical development of children, there had been no use of that paint on preschool toys until the consolidation occurred in the 1990s. Were the managers in that new industry structure, both American and Chinese, simply less concerned about the impact of their actions upon others, or was there something more basic going on? If so, what was the more basic something, and how would you have dealt with it?

Chapter 2

Moral Analysis and Economic Outcomes

We are concerned in this book with moral problems. These are the decisions and actions faced by managers in which their firm's financial performance (measured by revenues, costs, and profits) and social performance (difficult to measure, but represented by the overall well-being and satisfaction of the population) are in conflict. These are the situations in which some individuals and groups to whom the organization has some form of obligation—employees, customers, suppliers, distributors, creditors, stockholders, local residents, national citizens, and global inhabitants—are going to be hurt or harmed in some way outside their own control, while others will be benefited and helped. These are also the situations in which some of those individuals or groups are going to see their rights ignored or perhaps diminished, while others will see their rights accepted and even expanded. The question then is how to find a equitable balance between economic performance and social performance when faced with those conditions *and how to logically convince others to accept that balance.*

One of the most basic premises of this book is that this logical conviction of others is key. To place this in personal terms, it is key not only to the future of your employer and your society but also to the future of your career. In the previous chapter, it was suggested that you reach for this logical conviction by first understanding the differences between the moral standards—the intuitive judgment of proper versus improper actions that we all make, often on a daily basis—of the individuals and groups who will be either involved in or affected by the proposed decision or action. Then, it was suggested that you continue your analysis by recognizing the moral impacts—the mixture of benefits and harms, the contrast between rights recognized and rights denied—upon those same individuals and groups.

People's moral standards are bound to differ, due to differences in their religious and cultural traditions and their economic and social situations, and these differences have become far more pronounced in our highly competitive global economy. Not everyone will agree with your intuitive viewpoint. To get widespread understanding—and the hoped-for conviction—you will have to address their legitimate moral concerns. It was suggested that you do this by next stating, as clearly as possible, the moral problem in a way that obviously recognizes those concerns, and then examining those concerns though the analytical methods of economic outcomes, legal requirements, and ethical duties. The intent—once again—is to reach a decision, or strike a balance, that can be

FIGURE 2.1 The Logical Analysis of Moral Issues in Management

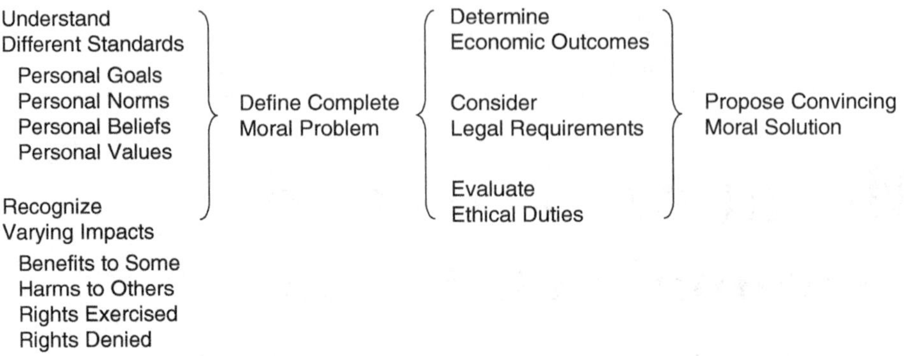

understood and—hopefully—accepted by all. The process of reaching this decision, or striking that balance, is repeated in Figure 2.1.

"Economic outcomes," the first evaluative means in moral analysis, does not refer just to the net balance of revenues over costs for the company that has proposed a given decision or action. *Economic outcomes in economic theory refer to the net balance of benefits over harms for the full society* as a result of that decision or action. This, as was described very briefly in the prior chapter, is the concept known as Pareto Optimality. It forms the moral basis of economic theory.

The Moral Basis of Economic Theory

For many persons, the concept of a moral basis for economic theory is a contradiction in terms. They learned the theory as a logical and mathematical approach to markets and prices and production, devoid of moral substance. As a result of this education, most non-economists, and more than a few economists as well, appear to focus almost entirely on profit maximization. They view the theory of the firm as descriptive, designed to rationalize the behavior of business managers, and believe that such single-minded pursuit of profit automatically excludes any consideration of environmental health, worker safety, consumer interests, or other "side issues."

An excessive concentration on profits doubtless has resulted in these and other problems within our society, but that is neither a consequence nor a corollary of economic theory. Economic theory, in its more complete form, addresses these issues and includes ethical as well as economic precepts. *Economic theory in its complete form is more a normative theory of society than a descriptive theory of the firm.* Profit maximization is a part of that theory, but it is only a part, and certainly not the central focus, though it must be admitted, and this adds to the lack of understanding, that techniques for profit maximization occupy a central portion of the curriculum at most schools of business administration.

The central focus of the larger theory of society is the efficient utilization of resources to satisfy consumer wants and needs. At economic equilibrium—and an essential element in reaching equilibrium throughout the entire economic system is the effort by business managers to balance marginal increases in revenues against marginal increases in costs, which automatically results in maximum profits for the firm within market and resource constraints—it is theoretically possible to achieve Pareto Optimality.

Pareto Optimality refers to a condition in which the scarce resources of society are being used so efficiently by the producing firms, and the goods and services are being distributed so effectively by the competitive markets, that it would be impossible to make any single person better off without harming some other person. Remember this phrase: "It would be impossible to make any single person better off without making some other person worse off." This is the ethical substance of economic theory encapsulated in Pareto Optimality: produce the maximum economic benefits for society, recognizing the full personal and social costs of that production, and rely on impartial markets for the equitable distribution of those benefits.

Pareto Optimality provides the ethical content of economic theory. Without this concept of maximum social benefit at minimal social cost, the theory deteriorates into a simple prescription for individual gain and corporate profit. With this concept, the theory becomes a means of achieving a social goal: maximum benefits of most wanted goods and services produced at minimum costs of least wanted resources.

The theory requires that every business manager attempt to optimize profits. Consequently, the decision rule that a concerned economist would propose for finding the proper balance between the economic and social performance of a business firm would be to always be truthful (don't mislead), honorable (observe contracts), and competitive (set prices and costs at marginal levels), and always decide for the greatest financial return. The question of this chapter is: Can we use this decision rule when faced with an obvious moral problem in which some people are going to be benefited and others harmed?

For many economists, the concept of Pareto Optimality excludes any need to consider moral problems in management. This view is very direct and can be summarized very simply. "Ethical duties are not relevant in business, beyond the normal standards not to lie, cheat, or steal. All that is necessary is to maintain price-competitive markets and recognize the full costs of production in those prices, and then the market system will ensure that scarce resources are used to optimally satisfy consumer needs. A firm that is optimally satisfying consumer needs, to the limit of the available resources, is operating most efficiently and most profitably. Consequently, business managers should act to maximize profits, while following legal requirements of non-collusion and equal opportunity and adhering to personal standards of truthfulness and honesty. Profit maximization, according to economic theory, leads automatically from the satisfaction of individual consumer wants to the generation of maximum social benefits."

Is this summary an overstatement of the microeconomic view of ethics and management? Probably not. The belief that profit maximization leads inexorably to the well-being of society is a central tenet of economic theory and has been stated very succinctly, very clearly, and very often by, among others, James McKie of the Brookings Institution and Milton Friedman of the University of Chicago:

> The primary goal and motivating force for business organizations is profit. The firm attempts to make as large a profit as it can, thereby maintaining its efficiency and taking advantage of available opportunities to innovate and contribute to growth. Profits are kept to reasonable or appropriate levels by market competition, which leads the firm pursuing

> its own self-interest to an end that is not part of its conscious intention: enhancement of the public welfare. (James McKie, "Changing Views" in *Social Responsibility and the Business Predicament,* Brookings Institute, 1974, p. 19)
>
> The view has been gaining widespread acceptance that corporate officials . . . have a "social responsibility" that goes beyond serving the interest of their stockholders or their members. This view shows a fundamental misconception of the character and nature of a free economy. In such an economy, there is one and only one social responsibility of business—to use its resources and engage in activities designed to increase its profits, so long as it stays within the rules of the game, which is to say, engages in open and free competition, without deception or fraud. . . . Few trends could so thoroughly undermine the very foundations of our free society as the acceptance by corporate officials of a social responsibility other than to make as much money for their stockholders as possible. (Milton Friedman, *Capitalism and Freedom,* University of Chicago Press, 1962, p. 133)

The statement by Milton Friedman was expanded into an article, "The Social Responsibility of Business Is to Increase Its Profits," that was published in the *New York Times Magazine* a number of years ago (September 13, 1970. p. 32f). This article is often assigned for students at business schools in classes on business ethics or corporate social responsibility. It is a frustrating article to read and then to discuss in class because it never makes clear the theoretical basis of Pareto Optimality. Professor Friedman assumed that readers would recognize and understand that basis of his contention.

The purpose of this chapter is to explain the theoretical basis of Professor Friedman's and Professor McKie's very similar contentions. It will be necessary to describe in some detail both the structural components of economic theory and the logical interrelationships that exist among those components. Doubtless an explanation of this nature will be dull for those with a good grasp of economic theory, and trying for all others, but a full explanation is needed to deal with the "equitable when applied to all" implications of the theory in a meaningful way. If you truly are bored with economic theory, and willing to accept the rationality of the structure, skip ahead a few pages and dive directly into the section titled "The Moral Claims of Economic Theory."

The Logical Structure of Economic Theory

Economic theory is complex. Perhaps, to make this planned explanation more comprehensible, it would be well to start with an overall summary. The focus of the theory, as stated previously, is the efficient utilization of scarce resources to maximize the production of wanted goods and services. The mechanism of the theory is the market structure. Each firm is located midway between "factor" markets for the input factors of production (labor, material, and capital) and "product" markets for the output goods and services. The demand for each good or service is aggregated from the preference functions of individual consumers, who act to maximize their satisfactions from a limited mix of products. The supply of each good or service is aggregated from the production schedules of individual firms, which act to balance their marginal revenues and marginal costs at a given level of capacity.

The production of goods and services creates derived demands for the input factors of labor, material, and capital. These factors are substitutable—can be interchanged—so the derived demands vary with the costs. These costs, of course, reflect the constrained supplies in the different factor markets. A firm attempting to minimize costs and maximize revenues will therefore use the most available resources to produce the most wanted products, generating not only the greatest profits for itself but the greatest benefits for society. The components of the theory, and the relationships among these components, which together produce corporate profits and social benefits, may be more understandable in graphic form, as shown in Figure 2.2.

Now it is necessary to work through each of the six sections in the Figure 2.2 graphic in greater detail so that the relationships among revenues, costs, and social benefits will be clear. Those relationships, and their consequent outcomes, constitute the ethical content of economic theory.

Individual Consumers

Each consumer has a slightly different set of preferences for the various goods and services that are available, and these preferences can be expressed as "utilities," or quantitative measures of the relative usefulness of a given product or service to a specific customer. The "marginal utility," or extra usefulness, of one additional unit of that product or service to that customer tends to decline, because eventually the person will have a surfeit of the good. The price that the person is willing to pay for the good also declines along with the marginal utility or degree of surfeit. Price relative to the number

FIGURE 2.2 **Graphic Summary of Economic Theory**

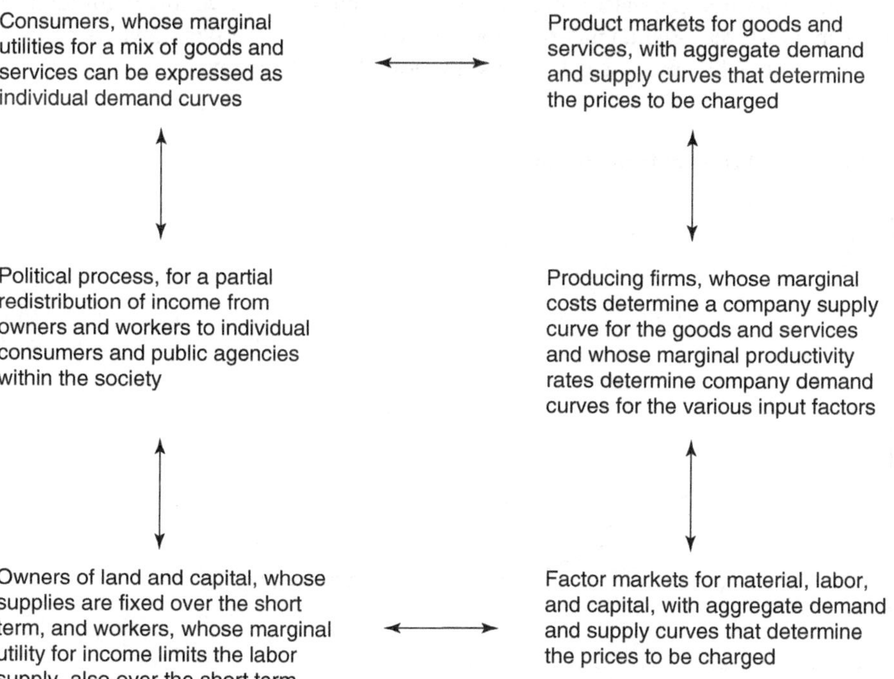

of units that will be purchased by a given person at a given time forms the individual demand curve, as shown in Figure 2.3.

Price can also be used to compare the relative usefulness of different goods and services to an individual. It can be expected that a person selecting a mix of products will choose an assortment of goods and services such that marginal utility per monetary unit would be equal for all the items at a given level of spending for this individual. Each good would be demanded up to the point where the marginal utility per dollar would be exactly the same as the marginal utility per dollar for any other good. If a customer had a higher marginal utility relative to price for any particular good, he or she would doubtless substitute more of that good for some of the others to achieve a better balance among his or her preferences. The final balance or mix, where the marginal utilities per monetary unit are equal for all products and services, can be termed the point of equilibrium for that customer.

The concept of consumer equilibrium is an important element in the structure of the economic condition termed Pareto Optimality. A customer with balanced marginal utilities per monetary unit for all available goods and services cannot be made better off at his or her level of spending, according to his or her standards of preference. The customer may buy hamburgers, french fries, and beer, and we may think that he or she should be buying fish, fresh vegetables, and fruit, but that person is satisfying his or her standards, not our own, and they are being satisfied up to the limits of his or her ceiling on expenditures. Consequently, that person cannot be made better off without an increase in disposable income. Now, let us look at the determination of the level of disposable income in microeconomic theory. This is more complex than the determination of the mix of desired purchases, but the logical structure can be followed through the product markets, the producing firms, the factor markets, the private owners of those factors, and the public processes for redistribution of factor income.

FIGURE 2.3 Personal Demand Curve

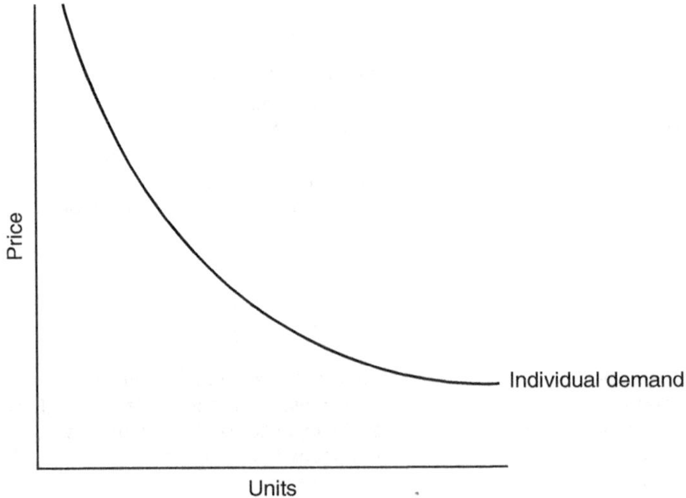

Product Markets

A product market consists of all the individual customers for a given good or service, together with all the producing firms that supply that good or service. The demand curves of all those customers can be aggregated to form a market demand curve. This market demand curve reflects the total demand for a good or service, relative to price. If price is the vertical axis and demand the horizontal axis, the market demand curve will generally slope downward and toward the right, indicating increased total purchases by all customers at the lower price levels.

Crossing this market demand curve is a market supply curve that portrays the total available supply, again relative to price. The market supply curve generally slopes upward and toward the right, for the higher the price, the more units in total most companies can be expected to produce, until they reach their limit of capacity. The market price, of course, is set at the intersection of the curves representing aggregate demand and aggregate supply, as shown in Figure 2.4.

Producing Firms

The aggregate supply curve, the "other half" of each product market relationship, is formed by adding together the individual supply curves of all the producing firms. These individual supply curves are generated by the cost structures of those firms at different levels of production, while the actual level of production for each firm is determined by a comparison of "marginal revenues" and "marginal costs."

The marginal revenue of a producing firm is the extra revenue that the firm would receive by selling one additional unit of the good or service. To sell that additional unit in a fully price-competitive market, it is necessary to move down the aggregate demand curve to a slightly lower price level. To sell that additional unit in a non-price-competitive market, it is necessary to spend greater amounts on advertising and

FIGURE 2.4 Market Demand and Supply Curves

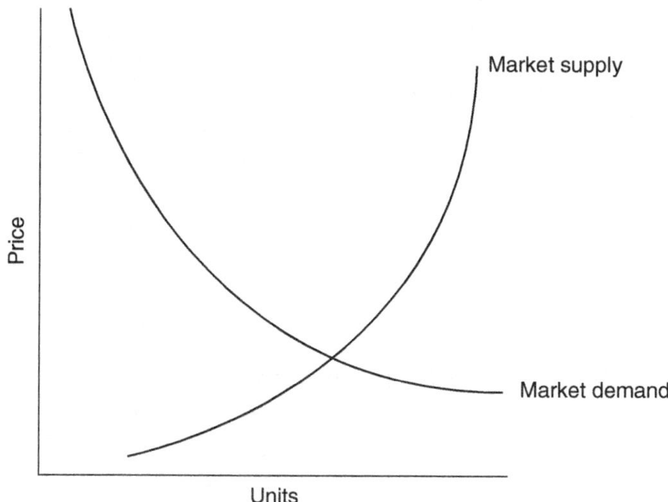

promotion to differentiate the product from those manufactured by other firms. Under either alternative, the marginal revenue from selling the last unit will be less than the average revenue from selling all other units. Marginal revenues inevitably decrease with volume.

The marginal cost of the producing firm is the obverse of the marginal revenue. Marginal cost is the extra expense that the firm would incur by producing one additional unit of the product or service. Marginal costs initially decline with volume due to economies of scale and learning curve effects, but they eventually rise due to diminishing returns as the physical capacity of the plant is approached. The rising portion of the marginal cost curve forms the supply curve of the firm; it represents the number of units that the firm should produce and supply to the market at each price level, as shown in Figure 2.5.

The producing firm achieves equilibrium when marginal costs are equal to marginal revenues. At the intersection of the marginal cost and marginal revenue curves, the profits of the firm are maximized. The firm can increase profits only by improving its technology; this would change the marginal costs and, consequently, the supply curve. However, over the long term, all firms would adopt the new technology and achieve the same cost structure. Production equilibrium would be reestablished at the new intersections of the marginal cost and marginal revenue curves for all firms within the industry.

All the costs of production have to be included in computing the marginal cost curve for a firm. This is the second of the ethical constructs in microeconomic theory, along with the individual selection of goods and services according to private preference standards, or "utilities." The internal personal costs (e.g., hazardous working conditions) and the external social costs (e.g., harmful environmental discharges) have to be computed so that customers pay the full costs of production. The technology, of course, can be changed to improve working conditions and reduce environmental discharges,

FIGURE 2.5 Marginal Cost and Revenue Curves

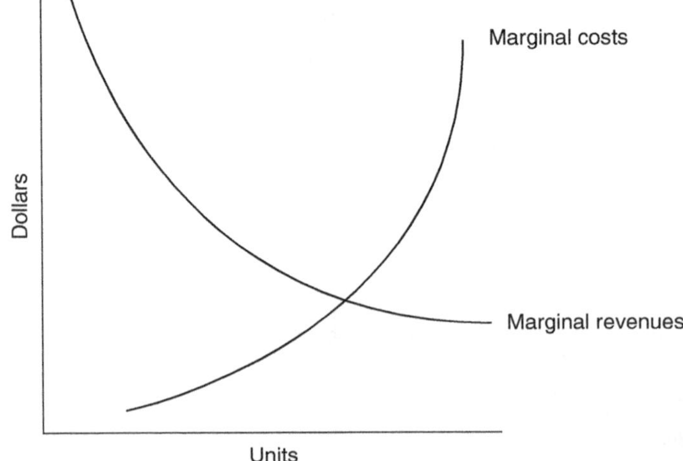

and this should be done to bring marginal costs down to marginal revenues at a new, non-hazardous and nonpolluting equilibrium, but *it is an essential element in economic theory that product-market prices reflect the full costs of production.*

Factor Markets

The technology of the producing firm determines the maximum output of goods and services that can be achieved for a given mix of input factors. The input factors of production are land (an apparently obsolete term that, instead, refers to all of the basic raw materials), labor (also perhaps an obsolete term, because it includes both salaries for office employees and wages for factory workers), and capital. Charges for the input factors are rents for the land and other basic resources, wages for the labor, and interest for the capital. These charges are interdependent because the factors are interrelated; that is, one factor may be substituted for others in the production function.

The relationships among these input factors, and the amount of one that would have to be used to substitute for another, are determined by the technology of the production function and by the "marginal productivity" of each factor for a given technology. The marginal productivity of a factor of production is the additional output generated by adding one more unit of that factor while keeping all others constant. For example, it would be possible to add one additional worker to a production line without changing the capital investments in the line or the material components of the product. There should then be an increase in the physical output of that production line, and that increase—measured in units or portions of units—would be the marginal productivity of that worker. To maximize profits, a company should increase the use of each factor of production until the value of its marginal product (the increase in unit output, or productivity, times the price of those units) equals the cost of the input factor.

Factor Owners

The aggregate demand for each factor of production is equal to the proportion of that factor used in the production function of each firm times the output of those firms that is supplied to meet the product market demand. The demand for each factor of production, therefore, is "derived" from the primary markets for goods and services.

The aggregate supply of each factor of production, however, is limited. Over the long term, stocks of the basic materials may be expanded by bringing into production marginal agricultural lands, oil fields, and ore mines, while the reserves of investment capital may be increased by raising the rate of capital formation. Over the short term, however, the supply amounts are fixed. Aggregate supplies of labor are also limited, though for a different cause: each worker has a marginal utility for income that decreases and becomes negative as his or her desire for greater leisure exceeds his or her preference for further work. This negative utility function creates a "backward sloping" supply curve for labor and sharply limits the amounts available at the higher wage rates, as shown in Figure 2.6.

The price system in the different factor markets, therefore, ensures that the limited factors of production will be used in the most economically effective manner to produce the goods and services to be sold in the product markets and that the rents, wages, and interest paid for these factors will reflect both the productivity of the factor and the derived demand of the goods.

FIGURE 2.6 Factor Supply Curves

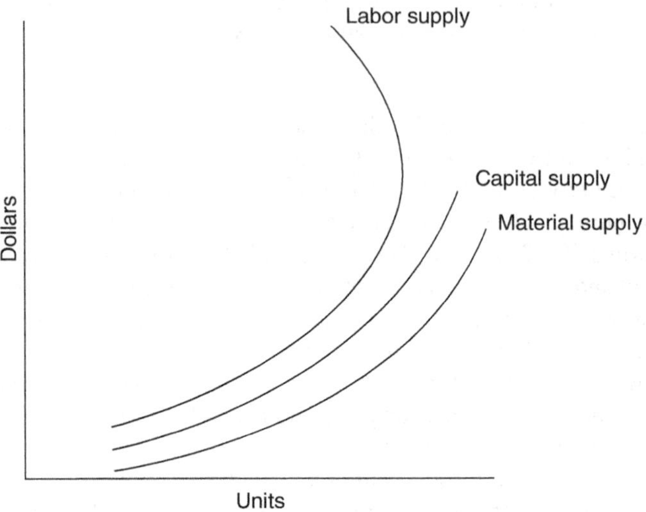

Overall Society

The owners of the factors of production, within a capitalistic economy, are also the customers for the products and services generated by the production functions at the various firms within that economy. The owners receive the rents, the wages, and the interest payments for the use of the resources they want to sell, and then purchase the goods and services they want to buy, following their personal preferences or utilities.

There is a political process for the redistribution of the rents, wages, and interest payments, through both tax provisions and welfare allocations, so that all individuals and groups within a given society have an ability to participate in the product markets for the various goods and services to the extent determined by the members of that society. This political process is the third ethical construct in microeconomic theory. It ensures that the distribution of the revenues for material, capital, and labor will be "equitable," following a democratically determined definition of equity.

The Moral Claims of Economic Theory

Now that there is a common understanding of the basic structure of economic theory, or the logical system of relationships among individual customers, product markets, producing firms, factor markets, resource owners, and political processes, it is possible to look at the claims of that theory relative to the social welfare. There are five explicit assertions:

1. *Effective use of resources.* The price mechanisms of the factor markets allocate the scarce resources of society to their most effective uses. The marginal productivity of each factor, together with the cost (reflecting supply versus demand), determines the

relative usage of the factors by the producing firms. At factor equilibrium, it would be impossible to expand total production without an increase in resource supply.

2. *Efficient conversion of resources into products.* The production functions of the producing firms convert the limited input factors into the wanted output goods and services by the most effective methods (process technologies) and at the most efficient rates (output amounts). A firm's technology and capacity are long-term decisions, while the operating rate is a short-term choice, but all are based upon the balance between marginal revenues and marginal costs. Internal personal harms and external social damages are included in the marginal costs. At process equilibrium, it would be impossible to convert resources into products more efficiently and with less personal harm or social damage without an advance in technology.
3. *Effective distribution of products.* The price mechanisms of the product markets distribute the wanted goods and services of society to their most effective uses. The marginal utilities of each customer together with the prices (again reflecting supply versus demand) for the various products determine the relative consumption of the goods and services. At market equilibrium, it would be impossible to improve consumer satisfaction without an increase in personal income.
4. *Complete inclusion of costs.* All costs that are external to the production process have to be identified, computed, and then included in either an increased price for the output product or service or a decreased payment for the input resource. If consumers are willing to pay that increased price as part of their selection of most wanted goods, or if suppliers are willing to accept that decreased payment as part of their selection of least wanted resources, then it would be hard to claim that those choices do not reflect the overall values of society.
5. *Political adjustment of inequalities.* If, for some reason, it is thought that the combined choices of all consumers in the output product markets and of all suppliers in the input factor markets, despite the inclusion of all external costs, do not reflect the overall values of society, then political adjustment of personal incomes may be needed. The political processes of a democratic society should reflect, or at least approximate, the social values of that society. Personal incomes might be redistributed according to ownership of the factors of production, or according to each individual's need, effort, contribution, or competence. Redistribution of the overall benefits of the economic system is a political, not an economic, process.

Pragmatic Objections to Economic Theory

The usual objections to microeconomic theory are pragmatic in nature, based upon very obvious problems in our national society, and they generally include the following issues that have been widely discussed in the Business Ethics literature:

1. *Exclusion of segments of society.* It is alleged that the minorities and the poor, because they lack ownership of any of the factors of production beyond their unskilled labor, receive inadequate income to participate in the product markets and consequently cannot maximize their own satisfactions in any meaningful way. The microeconomic response is quite obvious. "We grant you that this happens, but it is

the fault of the political process and not of the economic system. You develop logically attractive political decision rules for the more equitable division of the benefits, and we will work to economically maximize the production of those benefits within market and resource constraints."

2. *Presence of injurious practices.* It is also alleged that managers of productive firms, because of an excessive concern with maximizing profits, have permitted or even encouraged some practices that are injurious to some members of society (through workplace dangers or environmental pollution) or that are destructive to the market system (through purchase bribes or employment discrimination). Here, the response of most economists would be that these problems occur, but that they would not occur under the strict application of the theory. Let us look at five of these claimed moral problems and their presumed theoretical solutions:

    - Purchase bribes. Personal payments to influence purchase decisions are evidently common overseas, and not unknown within the United States. In an efficient market, however, bribes would be futile; they would raise the cost function by an amount equivalent to the payment so that non-bribing competitors would have a definite price advantage. The microeconomic response is obvious: Insist that purchase decisions be open and subject to public comparison of the bids, to ensure the selection of the lowest-priced proposal to supply comparative goods and services. The lowest-priced proposal would necessarily come from a non-bribing competitor.
    - Process pollutants. Many industrial processes result in toxic residues and inert materials as by-products, which are now either discharged as air or water pollutants or buried as liquid or solid wastes. The toxic by-products have an obvious social cost, both immediate and long term. The microeconomic response has been clearly stated many times: Companies should recognize these non-factor costs that are external to the productive process and include them in the pricing function. It might be expected, were these external costs accurately computed, that investments in proper disposal equipment would become clearly beneficial for the firm, or if they were fully included in the price, the product would become overly expensive for the customer to buy. Under either alternative, the amount of pollution would be substantially reduced.
    - Workplace hazards. It would appear that many of the mechanical hazards of industrial processing have been eliminated. Forty years of state and federal labor laws have removed most of the unprotected belts, open gearing, and non-shielded presses. Chemical risks still remain, however, and physiological and psychological problems will probably always be a part of mass manufacturing, due to the repetitive nature of the tasks and the time constraints of the process. The microeconomic response to workplace hazards is similar to that for process pollutants: The non-factor costs of production should be recognized and included in the final price. Certainly, if markets are to operate efficiently to allocate resources within the society, customers have to pay the full costs of production, not partial costs subsidized by the physical or mental health of the workers.
    - Product dangers. The press has recently reported numerous instances of unsafe products, particularly in the automobile industry. Gas tanks poorly located, radial tires poorly fabricated, and automatic transmissions poorly designed have all been

mentioned, together with such non-automotive products as hair dryers (containing asbestos), teddy bears (containing sharp objects), and packaged foods (containing non-nutrients). I think it is safe to assume that the economic response would be that a product offered for sale within a competitive market should perform the function for which it was designed, and that many of the reported failures and hazards come from decisions to differentiate products in slight or artificial ways to avoid the discipline of price competition. Whatever the cause of product failures and hazards, the costs of improper design are now being charged back against the manufacturing firms through liability suits and jury awards, and it can be assumed that product safety will soon be improved as a result of objective economic analysis.

- Minority employment. Racial or sexual discrimination in employment, in an efficient labor market, would be self-defeating; a workforce limited to young or middle-aged white males would raise the cost of labor in the productive function and provide the non-discriminating employer with a cost advantage. It is assumed in economic analysis that all groups are equal in performance capabilities. Training might be needed to justify that assumption, but the microeconomic response would be that training to correct social injustices should be provided as a public investment, determined by the political processes. Cost-benefit analysis would—in the view of most economists—assuredly show an economic return on that investment, as well as a social gain.

3. *Absence of competitive markets.* Lastly, it is often claimed that the product markets for consumer goods and services are not price competitive because of oligopolistic (dominance by a limited number of large companies) practices among the producing firms serving those markets. Companies have become much larger recently, doubtless due to economies of scale and scope in production and distribution, while products have become more "differentiated," marked by slight distinctions in performance and design but supported by heavy promotion. The dominance of large firms in each market, and the inability of customers to judge the relative worth of products in those markets, is said to lead toward "administered" rather than competitive prices. Administered pricing, where the price level is set by the company to provide a set return above costs without reference to either supply or demand, of course destroys the efficiency of the market. The economic response, however, is very simple. "Oh, we grant you that market structures are not truly competitive, and that market processes are not actually efficient under current conditions. However, no one is advocating limited competition or inadequate information. Public policy changes to restrict competitor size and to ensure consumer information are needed to reestablish the discipline of the market."

Theoretical Objections to Economic Theory

Economic theory is awesomely complete. There are few operating decisions in business to which it could not be applied—from hiring workers, purchasing supplies, and borrowing money to selecting technologies, establishing capacities, and setting prices. Likewise, there are few moral problems to which microeconomic theory is not applicable, whether it be purchasing bribes or processing pollutants or in reference to workplace hazards, product dangers, or racial discrimination. It is very difficult to say,

"Here is a managerial decision or action with definite equitable implications that is not included in the theory."

Economic theory is also enviably unified. All the managerial decisions and actions work together, through a system of explicit market relationships, to create a socially desirable goal: maximum output of wanted goods and services at a minimum input of limited material, capital, and labor. It is very difficult to say, "Here is a managerial decision or action following microeconomic theory that does not lead to a socially beneficial outcome."

Where does this discussion lead us? Are we forced to accept economic theory as an ethical system of belief for business management because of the complete and unified nature of the paradigm? Should we always act to maximize profits, as long as we are truthful, honest, and competitive, and use the concept of Pareto Optimality as the means of resolving our moral concerns? Or, is there a theoretical problem with that paradigm?

Most non-economists are intuitively distressed by the proposal that business managers have no moral responsibilities to other members of society, outside of fiduciary duties to a small circle of corporate owners. Most non-economists are equally distressed by the proposal that business managers are also governed by no moral requirements of behavior beyond adhering to personal standards of honesty and truthfulness, observing legal statutes for contracts and against collusion, and computing accurate costs for personal harms and social dangers. Why is this distressing, and what are the arguments against the microeconomic model that can be expressed on a theoretic rather than a pragmatic or intuitive basis? There are two major arguments. One pertains to the assumptions about human nature and the second centers on the beliefs about human worth that are both part of the theory.

Assumptions about the Nature of Human Beings

The economic model is utilitarian; that is, it is a philosophical system of belief that focuses on outcomes rather than duties, with the understanding that larger outcomes are invariably better than lesser ones. Utilitarianism has often been roughly translated as "the greatest good for the greatest number." The economic model follows this doctrine. It takes the position that the ultimate end is the greatest general good, and it defines that good as the maximum benefits of consumer products and services at the minimum costs of labor, capital, and material. The problem, as with all utilitarian theories, is that the distribution of the benefits and the imposition of the costs may be unjust. Consequently, it is necessary to add a political process to the economic paradigm to ensure an equitable distribution of benefits and the allocation of costs.

But, "equitable" is defined in the theory as a democratically determined pattern of distribution and imposition. This pattern does not follow a rule—such as to each person equally, or to each according to his or her need, to his or her effort, to his or her contribution, to his or her competence, or even to his or her ownership of the factors of production. Instead, the pattern varies with the collective opinions of the members of society. This requires all members of society to be generously concerned with the charitable distribution of social benefits and the considerate imposition of social costs at the same time as they are selfishly concerned with the personal maximization of material goods and services in the product markets and of financial wages, rents, and interest payments in the factor markets.

I think that we can safely say that human nature exhibits both selfish and generous traits. We can doubtless go further and accept that human beings can perform selfish and then generous acts alternately. But, it would seem an extreme assumption to believe that people can concurrently be generously attentive to others in all political decisions and selfishly attentive to themselves in all economic activities, and never confuse the two roles. The microeconomic model would appear to be based upon an exceedingly complex and unlikely view of the nature of human beings.

Assumptions about the Value of Human Beings

The microeconomic model is impersonal, because it requires that everyone be treated as a means to an end and not as an end in and by himself or herself. Customers for goods and services are people who maximize material satisfactions as a means of determining product demand curves. Owners of land, capital, and labor are people who maximize financial revenues as a means of determining factor-supply curves. Company managers are people who maximize corporate profits as a means of balancing market demands and factor supplies. No one acts as an individual human being, pursuing personal goals that move beyond economic outcomes to personal desires for liberty, opportunity, dignity, worth, and pride.

This denial of worth can be seen particularly clearly in the position of managers within a firm, who, in economic theory, must act solely as agents for the financial interests of the stockholders. What does this do to their self-esteem and self-respect? How can managers live worthwhile lives when always being treated as a means to other people's ends or, perhaps even worse, when always treating other people as means to their own ends? Even though the society as an economic system may have achieved Pareto Optimality with maximal benefits at minimal costs, does the individual develop any sense of dignity and pride? The microeconomic model would appear to be based upon an exceedingly low and narrow view of the worth of human beings.

Conclusion

The focus of this book is on the moral problems faced by managers. These are the situations in which a firm's financial performance (measured by revenues, costs, and profits) and social performance (difficult to measure, but represented by the overall well-being and general satisfaction of the full population) are in conflict. Specifically, these are the occasions in which some individuals and groups to whom the organization has some form of obligation—employees, customers, suppliers, distributors, creditors, stockholders, local residents, national citizens, and global inhabitants—are going to be hurt or harmed in some way outside their own control, while others will be benefited and helped. These are also the occasions in which some of those individuals or groups are going to see their rights ignored or perhaps diminished, while others will see their rights recognized and even expanded. The question then is to decide how to find a equitable balance between economic performance and social performance when faced with those conditions, *and how to logically convince others to approve or accept that balance.*

The focus of this chapter is on the economic outcomes of managerial decisions and actions as a means to find that equitable balance and to reach that logical conviction. Economic theory postulates an automatic balance between financial well-being for the firm and material well-being for the society. In short, there is a definite moral content to economic theory. The question is where did the discussion of that moral content in this chapter lead us? There would seem to be two major conclusions:

1. If we look at economic theory as a structured pattern of relationships explaining the optimal inputs of scarce material, capital, and labor to produce the optimal outputs of desired goods and services, then our first conclusion has to be that it is a logically complete and intellectually satisfying view of the world as a productive system. An economically efficient productive system certainly produces more of the products people most want at less use of the resources people least value—and that is of definite value to society.
2. This economically efficient productive system, however, is dependent upon the underlying assumptions that (a) all markets are competitive, (b) all customers are informed, and (c) all external costs are included. The problem is that most markets vary in their degree of competition; most customers vary in their extent of information, and almost all external costs vary in their scope of inclusion. Consequently, our second conclusion is that we need something more to ensure that competition, to guarantee that information, and to require that inclusion, and that something more consists of the legal requirements of the law. Chapter 3 will look at these legal requirements as the next phase of moral analysis.

Case 2-1

Goldman Sachs and Information Advantages for Major Clients

The *Wall Street Journal* in a lengthy front page article (August 24, 2009, p. A1) reported that Goldman Sachs, one of the largest and most successful investment banking houses on Wall Street, had started a new policy that called for their research analysts to meet once a week with their stock traders. These meetings were called "trading huddles." The purpose of each huddle was to discuss changes in earning forecasts or market conditions that might bring short-term price movements in the stocks of specific companies. All of these companies were covered on a continual basis by the analysts, and their long-term recommendations to "buy," "hold," or "sell" were distributed to all clients who requested them. But, the analysts' forecasts discussed in these meetings were much shorter term in nature, and they focused more on anticipated market movements of a company's stock price than on the strengths and weaknesses of that company's competitive strategy. The words that were used here also had a short-term orientation; they were "up," "neutral," or "down," and the analysts expectations were openly called "tips." These tips were then transmitted by the traders to a small group of mutual funds, pension funds, university and charity endowments, and other large investors that in return would frequently place purchase/sale orders for immediate action. Many of the traders also acted on the analysts' advice, using Goldman corporate funds to purchase options on the selected or "tipped"—equities for Goldman internal accounts. It should be understood that short-term trading of this nature, while high risk, often is highly profitable both for the firm doing the trading and for its clients.

The *Wall Street Journal* article continued that, "Critics complain that Goldman's distribution of its trading ideas only to it own traders and key clients hurts other customers who aren't given the opportunity to trade on the information" (Ibid.). A senior manager for Goldman Sachs was quoted in response that any analytical statement at a meeting that could result in a changed long-term rating, earning estimate or stock-price target legally had to be disclosed to all clients, but that the short-term market movement expectations that came from the trading huddles could—and should—go only to the firm's largest clients and their own trading desks.

Class Assignment

One of the most basic assumptions supporting the construct of economic efficiency is that all customers must be fully informed. What is your view? Should Goldman Sachs disclose its analysts' expectations for short-term price movements to all of its clients who requested them? What, if anything, would Goldman Sachs lose if it did?

Case 2-2

The Concept of Fairness in Economic Theory

Professor Albert Rees was an exceedingly distinguished economist. He taught Labor Economics at the University of Chicago during the 1960s and early 1970s; authored the principal textbook in that field; and then in sequence became Director of the U.S. Council on Wage and Price Stability under President Gerald Ford (1974–1978), Provost of Princeton University, President of the Alfred P. Sloan Foundation, and member of the boards of directors at two major corporations and one highly regarded academic institution. Late in life, in a speech he gave at the University of Chicago, he talked about the importance of fairness for persons who held managerial positions:

> The neoclassical theory of wage determination, which I taught for 30 years and have tried to explain in my textbook . . . has nothing to say about fairness . . . Beginning in the mid-1970s, I began to find myself in a series of roles in which I have participated in setting or controlling wages and salaries. These included sitting on three wage stabilization bodies during the Nixon and Ford Administrations, as a director of two corporations, as a provost of a private university, as a president of a foundation, and as a trustee of a liberal arts college. In one of the corporations I served as chairman of the compensation committee.
>
> In none of these roles did I find the theory that I taught so long to be the slightest help. The factors involved in the real world seemed to be very different from those specified in the neoclassical theory. The one factor that seemed to be of overwhelming importance in all these situations was fairness. (Quotation taken from Akerlof, G.A. and R. J. Shiller, *Animal Spirits,* 2009, p. 20; it should be noted that Prof. Akerlof is a Nobel Laureate.)[1]

Class Assignment

What does fairness mean to you? Write a brief definition that you can read to the class if you are called upon. Do you agree that fairness is important in managerial roles? Why? How would you tie fairness and efficiency together, or are the two concepts irreconcilably different?

Case 2-3

The University of Illinois and "Shadow Processes" for Student Admissions

The *New York Times* on August 7, 2009 reported that a state commission that had been appointed by the governor to investigate what were termed "irregularities" in student admission procedures at the University of Illinois had just published its findings. The University of Illinois is a large and distinguished academic institution; it has 70,000 students, three campuses at Chicago, Springfield, and Urbana/Champaign (the original and still major location). The report, however, was scathing.

The lead sentence in the newspaper account read: "Top officials at the University of Illinois developed a sophisticated shadow admissions process for applicants who were supported by politicians, donors and other prominent sponsors . . ." The top officials who were named in this report included the President, Chancellor, and Associate Provost of the University; the former dean of the College of Law; and the current dean of the College of Business. They were all found to have participated in the admission of hundreds of connected but borderline or unqualified students, bowing to pressures from the politicians, donors, and sponsors. One college dean openly admitted in an e-mail sent to the director of admissions at that college that he/she would probably have to ask for the admission of a particular student because the college was about to start on a major capital campaign and it was not sensible to irritate that student's father who was counted upon to be a major contributor.

Class Assignment

Certainly the money raised in major capital campaigns benefits many people associated with the University of Illinois through campus improvements and student scholarships, but should the secretive admission of borderline and unqualified students be a part of that process? It is possible to look at the fund-raising efforts at a college or university as a market for donations. What is your view? Should the University of Illinois do what it takes to compete in that market, or is "fairness" (see Case 2-2) an issue here?

Case 2-4

Countrywide Financial Corporation: What Went So Wrong, and Why?

Angelo Mozilo, the principal founder and long-serving chief executive of Countrywide Financial Corporation, grew up as part of a low-income family in New York City.

His father was a butcher who owned a small store in the Bronx. Angelo worked in that shop as a teenager, but it soon became clear that he was determined to move up in the financial world. He made a decided effort in his schoolwork, gained a scholarship to Fordham University, graduated with a Bachelor of Science in Engineering, but did not then go to work for an engineering firm. Instead, he became a commercial real estate salesman—and that turned out to be an exceedingly fortunate choice. Friends who knew him at this time say that he related well with other people, focused solely on what his customers wanted, and was inevitably well dressed when meeting with those customers. Even at rough and muddy construction sites, he would be found wearing a well-pressed suit, a well-starched shirt, and a well-chosen necktie. He wanted to appear successful even before he truly was.

He saved as much as possible from his sales commissions, found a potential partner in an older man who had specialized in finance at the real estate firm for which they both worked, and together they formed Countrywide Financial Corporation as a mortgage broker in 1972. Originally the company was located in New York City, though they primarily served customers in the expanding suburban areas across the Hudson River in New Jersey. They kept reading in industry newsletters of the extremely rapid growth in the real estate markets of southern California, and eventually decided to move their company to that region in the late 1970s.

They selected Calabasas, California, a small but scenic town located in the coastal range of mountains north of Los Angeles, and rented office space in a modern building with large windows and tremendous views. They wanted a distinctive base for their firm. Angelo Mozilo hired sales personnel while his older partner established financial contacts, and together they hit the ground running.

Their relocated and reenergized company was successful from the start, and it began to grow very rapidly. Branch offices were opened throughout the Los Angeles metropolitan area, and then new divisions were formed in other expanding California cities and other developing western states. A public issuance of stock took place in 1982 to relieve the financial strains, and that permitted even faster growth. Sales passed the $4 billion mark in 2000, hit $10.6 billion in 2002, reached $13.8 billion in 2004, and then nearly doubled to $24.2 billion in 2006.

Corporate profits and share prices kept pace with the sales increases. In 2007 Countrywide Financial was declared to have the third best stock market price performance over a 25-year period in history. From early 1982, when Countrywide's first public issuance took place, until December 2006 when a high of $42.45 per share was reached, the stock had delivered a 23,000 percent return. To clarify that figure, shareholders who in 1982 had invested $1,000 in Countrywide equity found in 2006 that their holdings were now worth $230,000. Only Warren Buffett's Berkshire Hathaway and Sam Walton's Walmart Stores had ever exceeded that posted return over an equivalent 25-year time span.

Angelo Mozilo explained that the reasons for this outstanding record of financial success were in reality very simple. Countrywide, he said, offered a wide range of innovative products that enabled large groups of low- to middle-income families to purchase new homes both as better places to live and as secure investments for the future. For years, that double appeal formed the base for an extremely successful marketing program.

But then things began to go terribly wrong. By the end of 2008—just two years after the record high price of $42.45 per share of Countrywide stock had been reached—their company had posted losses amounting to $6.6 billion, had received federal bailout loans totaling $51 billion, and had been saved from bankruptcy only by what at the time was generally considered to be a government-directed rescue plan. Bank of America, which itself was dependent upon federal funding for survival, offered to exchange 0.1822 share of its stock for each share of Countrywide equity. The Countrywide Board of Directors accepted the offer. Bank of America stock on the last trading day of 2008 was valued at $14.08; this translated into a cash value of $2.56 per share for the Countrywide stockholders. The investor whose $1,000 purchase in 1982 had grown to $230,000 in 2006 now had just $13,870.

Why did this happen? Part of the reason, of course, was the sudden and unexpected end to the housing boom, which was particularly sudden and unexpected in the southwestern United States where Countrywide had found its most eager customers. But, there were also numerous allegations by outside observers and equally plentiful admissions by inside participants that many, if not most, of those customers had been very poorly served. Sales representatives were known for telling potential customers that they wanted to make sure they were getting the "best loan possible."

The problem was that this "best loan possible" frequently turned out to be best for Countrywide, its sales representatives and senior executives, not for its customers. The *New York Times,* in the article just cited, reported that in 2006, 45 percent of the company's loans were "teaser rate" with interest charges that could be increased sharply upward if conditions changed or simply after time passed. They offered "nothing down" loans that permitted borrowers to purchase a home without investing any of their own money as a security deposit, and promoted "no verification" loans that provided 95 percent of the assessed value of a house but required no confirmation of the borrower's claimed income or assets.

> Such loans were made, former employees say, because they were so lucrative—to Countrywide. The company harvested a steady stream of fees or payments on such loans and busily repacked them as securities to sell to investors. As long as housing prices kept rising, everyone—borrowers, lenders and investors—appeared to be winners.
>
> One former employee provided documents indicating Countrywide's minimum profit margins on subprime loans of different sizes. These ranged from 5 percent on small loans of $100,000 to $200,000 to 3 percent on loans of $350,000 to $500,000. But on subprime loans that imposed heavy burdens on borrowers, like high prepayment penalties that persisted for three years [and thus prevented the borrowers from getting out of the loans for those three years], Countrywide's margins could reach 25 percent.
>
> As a result, former employees said, the company's commission structure rewarded sales representatives for making risky, high-cost loans. For example, according to another mortgage sales representative affiliated with Countrywide, adding a three-year repayment penalty to a loan would generate an extra 1 percent of the loan's value in a commission. While mortgage brokers' commissions would vary on loans that reset after a short period with a low teaser rate, the higher the rate at reset the greater the commission earned.

> The company's incentive system also encouraged brokers and sales representatives to move borrowers into the subprime category, even if their financial position meant that they belonged higher up the loan spectrum. . . . Brokers who peddled subprime loans received commissions of 0.50 percent of the loan's value, versus 0.20 percent on loans one step up the quality ladder. (*New York Times,* August 26, 2007, p. A1)[2]

Short video commercials had been used extensively to draw in potential clients for the numerous "best loans possible" salespeople to then bring into the fold. Summaries of the pictorial and verbal content of these ads were accessed on the website for VMS, formerly known as Video Monitoring Service (http://www.vmsinfo.com/2_1_advertising-monitoring.html, accessed December 29, 2008). This company provided information about and copies of televised ads to competitive firms across a range of industries; the intent was to show "what works." The Countrywide ads were among the most popular to view and to purchase because they obviously were part of that select group:

Countrywide 15-Second Advertisement Titled "Female Home Loan/New Campaign"

The back of a Black female seen walking inside a house toward the front door.

She opens the door halfway and talks to Black male standing outside. Extreme closeup of Black female saying, "You said we couldn't afford this place."

Extreme closeup of Black male. He agrees with her. She asks another question. "You said we didn't have enough for the down payment."

Again Black male agrees with her. She then asks, "Now what do you say?" He agrees that he was wrong and she was right.

Voiceover: "We're experts at finding solutions." Print message appears on screen "Countrywide First Time Buyer Loans." She welcomes him home.

Voiceover and print message on screen: "Countrywide Home Loans. Every American and Every Dream. Countrywide.com or 800-EASY-877."

Countrywide 30-Second Advertisement Titled "Men in Field, with Young Girl"

Two Hispanic males walk through a field that overlooks a suburban development. Older Hispanic male asks the other Hispanic male, "What do you see?"

Hispanic male answers, "Houses."

Older Hispanic male then asks, "Who owns them?" Hispanic male answers, "The lucky ones."

Older Hispanic male corrects him by saying, "Not lucky, smart." He says that they learn how to buy a home.

Voiceover: "We're experts at finding solutions."

Young Hispanic male asks about payments. Older Hispanic male says that they can be just about the same as rent.

Print message on screen: "Countrywide Affordable Payment Loans."

Older Hispanic male asks, "Do you want one of those for her?" Camera quickly moves down revealing a Hispanic girl holding on to Hispanic male's leg. Hispanic male nods and older Hispanic male tells him to make the call.

Voiceover and print message on screen: "Realize Your Dream at Countrywide Home Loans. 800-Easy-877, Countrywide.Com or Visit your Local Branch."

Countrywide Financial Corporation was not the only firm that took advantage of the relaxed standards that were applied and the easy credit that was available during the housing boom from 1998 to 2007. Washington Mutual, an equally fast-growing mortgage brokerage firm located in Seattle, Washington, followed a similar pattern of appealing ads, aggressive sales, rapid growth, and eventual bankruptcy. The *New York Times* on December 28, 2008, published an extensive and detailed report on this company:

As a supervisor at a Washington Mutual mortgage processing center, John D. Parsons was accustomed to seeing babysitters claiming salaries worthy of college presidents, and schoolteachers with incomes rivaling stockbrokers'. He rarely questioned them. A real estate frenzy was under way, and WaMu, as his bank was known, was all about saying yes.

Yet even by WaMu's relaxed standards, one mortgage four years ago raised eyebrows. The borrower was claiming a six-figure income and an unusual profession: mariachi singer.

Mr. Parsons could not verify the singer's income, so he had him photographed in front of his home dressed in his mariachi outfit. The photo went in a WaMu file. Approved.

"I'd lie if I said every piece of documentation was properly signed and dated," said Mr. Parsons, speaking through wire-reinforced glass at a California prison near here [San Diego], where he is serving 16 months for theft after his fourth arrest—all involving drugs.

While Mr. Parsons, whose incarceration is not related to his work for MaWu, oversaw a team screening mortgage applications, he was snorting methamphetamine daily, he said.

"In our world, it was tolerated," said Sherri Zaback, who worked for Mr. Parsons and recalls seeing drug paraphernalia on his desk. "Everybody said, 'He gets the job done.' "

At WaMu getting the job done meant lending money to nearly anyone who asked for it—the force behind the bank's meteoric rise and its precipitous collapse this year in the biggest bank failure in American history . . .

Interviews with two dozen former employees, mortgage brokers, real estate agents and appraisers reveal the relentless pressure to churn out loans that produced such results.

> While that sample may not fully represent a bank with tens of thousands of people it does reflect the views of employees in WaMu mortgage operations in California, Florida, Illinois and Texas. (*New York Times,* December 28, 2008, p. B1)[3]

The accounts from the employees at Washington Mutual were almost identical to the stories of those at Countrywide. There were allegations at each company of the pressures supervisors put upon employees to bring in more loans; of direct orders not to worry about customers' ability to repay the loan; just sell them the loan. There were reports of special incentives for obtaining inflated property values that made the loans appear less risky, and thus easier for Wall Street banks to package for sale to the ultimate investors. One appraiser described his relations with the company as the Wild West. (Ibid.)

There were other similarities between Washington Mutual and Countrywide Financial beyond the marketing policies and the financial incentives. They both ran visually appealing television ads, though with different themes. Actors playing WaMu lenders, dressed in blue jeans and short-sleeved shirts, ridiculed the loan limits of conservative bankers wearing three-piece suits. Both companies had widely quoted slogans, though at Washington Mutual it was "The power of yes," not "The best loan possible" or "Countrywide is on your side." And, they both had boiler room "get the job done" cultures that dominated operations at each of the firms. Many of the inside employees at both companies now speak of what they were doing during those boom years with vocal regrets and feelings of guilt. While many of the outside suppliers at both companies now speak of the corporate managers with whom they interacted during those boom years in very dismissive terms, calling the operation a "sham." (Ibid.)

In an even further similarity, Washington Mutual was purchased in what also appeared to be a government-directed rescue plan. JPMorgan Chase bought the company in September 2008 for $1.9 billion, and then received $25 billion in TARP (Troubled Asset Relief Program) bailout funds for help in dealing with the failed loans and recorded losses.

Then, in a final similarity, Kerry Killinger, who had been Washington Mutual's chairman and chief executive from 1990 to 2008, was forced out at the time of the sale. He had sold most of his stock holdings during the boom years, and he left with pension and benefit payments still intact and an estimated $100 million in capital gains from those sales. Angelo Mozilo, the long-term chairman of Countrywide Financial, was similarly forced to leave immediately after the sale of that company. He also had sold most of his stock holdings over the final boom years, and left with pension and benefit payments intact; though an exit bonus of $36 million was rescinded, but he did keep an alleged $425 million from the stock sales.

Class Assignment

The House Committee on Oversight and Government Reform sponsored a Congressional Hearing on the twin issues of executive compensation and pay for performance that was held on March 7, 2008. Senior executive officers from Merrill Lynch,

Citigroup, and Countrywide—three companies that had encountered severe financial difficulties during the mortgage crisis and needed substantial governmental funding to survive afterward—were called to testify. None of those three executives felt that their pay bonuses and stock options, or the pay bonuses and stock options of their subordinates, influenced in any way the aggressive policies that had been adopted or caused the substantial losses that had occurred. Those losses, all of the senior executives agreed, were the result of the unexpected economic downturn in the housing market. At the conclusion of the hearing, Henry Waxman (D–CA), who was the chair of the committee and thus presided at the hearing, addressed those three senior executives as follows:

> Now, I thank all of your for being here. And I want to say to Mr. O'Neal [Merrill Lynch] and Mr. Prince [Citigroup] and Mr. Mozilo [Countrywide] what I said in my opening statement. You're all classic American success stories. You have tremendous accomplishments. But, that is—what is also true is that you're in the middle of an enormous debacle that ended up costing your companies and shareholders billions of dollars. It cost people their homes, it cost other people their jobs. It seems like everyone is hurting except for you . . .
>
> Executives who preside over billions of dollars of losses shouldn't be getting millions in bonuses, unvested stock, and stock sales, yet this appears to be what is happening. The bottom line is there needs to be better mechanisms for accountability. Without this, our economy will remain vulnerable to the kind of economic disruptions we're now experiencing. (Statement of Rep. Henry Waxman, Chair of the House Committee on Oversight and Government Reform and Presiding Member at the House of Representatives Hearing on CEO Pay and the Mortgage Crisis held on March 7, 2008, p. 194)

1. What do you think should happen to the performance bonuses, stock options, and capital gains that had been received by the senior executives and mid-level managers at companies such as Countrywide Financial and Washington Mutual, which subsequently suffered such large losses that they had to be rescued by "too big to fail" bailout packages from the federal government? These were the people Representative Waxman was referring to when he said, "It seems that everyone is hurting except for you." Should some of those compensation payments be "clawed back"? Focus on Angelo Mozilo and Kerry Killinger, where you know the background. Would you recommend that they be required to return some of those funds to their companies, and what, if any, percentage would you suggest? Realize that this is an exceedingly contentious issue; how would you *convincingly* justify your proposed plan of action?
2. Why do you think that the lower-level office managers, marketing persons, and credit reviewers participated—apparently so willingly though later regretfully—in actions that they must have known were going to harm their firm's customers and investors? What would you have done had you been one of those employees, making really good money to pay off your college loans but concerned about the long-term consequences? What does this tell you about human nature? Cynics would say that everyone wants to follow a "get it while the getting is good" policy, but most of us never get the opportunity or lack the courage. Are those cynics right? What do you think businesspeople really want out of life?

3. Lastly, it is frequently mentioned that the typical chief executive officer at a *Fortune* 500 company was paid $800,000 in 1980, 40 times the wages of an average worker at that time. By 2006 it was claimed that the total compensation for successful CEOs had climbed to $15 million, 600 times that of the average worker. These figures are less than totally reliable for two reasons: (a) in 1980 the average workers were employed in manufacturing jobs with high, often union driven wages for their badly needed skills, and (b) chief executives in 2006 received much of their compensation in the form of unfunded stock options and crafted personal benefits that were and remain difficult to price. Accepting those uncertainties for now, what do you think would be a *just* ratio of the total payments for chief executives in comparison to the annual wages of hourly worker within a *Fortune* 500 company, and why would that be just? The "why" is important, so how would you *convincingly* support your proposed ratio?

Case 2-5

British Petroleum and the Delay of Maintenance

On March 23, 2005, a massive explosion rocked the British Petroleum refinery located in Texas City, on the Gulf of Mexico, just outside Galveston. At that time, this refinery was one of the largest in the United States; it employed 1,800 people, covered 1,200 acres, and converted 460,000 barrels of crude oil a day into gasoline and high-value petrochemical products. The explosion occurred in a unit of the refinery that produced one of those petrochemical products. Naphtha, an exceedingly volatile component of crude oil, was isolated by distillation and converted to a more usable form through isomerization (a rearrangement of the individual atoms within each molecule that changed the physical properties but not the chemical composition of the gas) in high-pressure vessels using high-temperature processes. The resultant output was then used to raise the octane level of the gasoline that was the major output of the refinery. The naphtha, the isomer derived from the naphtha, and the gasoline with the isomer additive were all highly combustible products.

The blast was strong enough to rattle windows in downtown Galveston, 20 miles away, and was even felt in Houston, 35 miles distant. Local emergency services responded quickly, but early reports indicated that 15 people had been killed and well over 150 injured, many of those seriously burned. A BP spokesperson explained that the explosion had occurred while the isomerization unit was being brought back "on stream" to full production after having been shut down for annual inspection and repair. Start-up periods were always a dangerous time, the BP spokesperson continued, especially for the high-volatility "additive" products that are an inherent part—and problem—of petroleum refining.

The immediate reaction throughout the region was, of course, sympathy for the families of those killed and offers of help to the individuals who were injured, together with pledges by BP of a "long and intensive investigation to determine the cause of the explosion" (*New York Times,* March 24, 1005, p. A14).

But then accounts of prior problems at BP refineries, where accident levels seemed to have exceeded normal industry standards, began to appear. On March 30, 2004, almost a year to the day before the most recent explosion reported here, a blast had occurred at this same gasoline processing unit of this same Texas City refinery. No deaths or injuries had resulted, but a subsequent investigation by the U.S. Occupational Health and Safety Administration resulted in citations for 14 alleged violations of standard operating procedures (*Wall Street Journal,* March 24, 2005, p. A6). And then, just a week prior to the March 24 explosion at Texas City, BP was reported to have settled a large California lawsuit claiming that it had (1) failed to properly maintain the huge storage tanks that are a common sight at most crude oil refineries, and (2) that it had improperly falsified the maintenance records for those storage tanks, at its largest refinery within California. BP agreed in this case to pay a fine of $81 million for these documented errors. And finally, in September 2004, six months before the explosion that forms the topic of this case, an accidental release of superheated steam at the Texas City refinery had scalded two workers to death and seriously injured a third. The Occupational Health and Safety Administration in this instance charged BP with "intentional disregard of or plain indifference to" OHSA rules (*Wall Street Journal,* March 25, 2005, p. A3). These earlier events expanded the concerns of local residents, state regulators, and federal authorities alike:

> [The] deadly explosion at a Texas refinery has increased scrutiny of the safety record at BP PLC, which has been dogged by a spate of recent incidents in the U.S., including several at the site of Wednesday's explosion. (*Wall Street Journal,* March 25, 2005. p. A3)

These concerns were further magnified by a rather unusual factor associated with the most recent explosion. Four of the victims were women who worked in an office trailer located only 50 yards from the blast site. There was no official explanation why a wooden office trailer housing clerical personnel had been placed in such close proximity to potentially the most dangerous processing unit within the refinery (*New York Times,* March 15, 2005, p. A3).

In May 2005, two months after the March 25 explosion, BP issued an interim report that laid most of the blame on a small number of employees for "operational and supervisory mistakes." The company did, however, accept overall responsibility for the accident, and said that it had set aside $700 million to compensate all of the victims (*Wall Street Journal,* December 10, 2005, p. A9).

In September 2005, seven months after the March 25 explosion, the Occupational Health and Safety Administration issued a far more condemning report. This governmental agency found hundreds of safety violations that it called "egregious and willful," and levied a fine of $21.4 million. Most of the safety violations were related to a venting system at the isomerization unit that should have captured and "flared off" (harmlessly incinerated) all leaking gases and sent all leaking fluids to an underground and airproof (and therefore flameproof) storage tank. That safety system—with its interrelated valves, controls, tanks, flares, and alarms—was found not to have been working properly.

The $21.4 million fine, though a record size for the agency, was much more a minor matter for BP, which had reported an after-tax profit of $15.7 billion for the prior year. Far more important to the company, doubtless, were the terms of a three-year probationary period imposed by OHSA. BP had to (1) request permission from the agency before starting up the totally destroyed isomerization unit after rebuilding was completed; (2) report all accidents and all injuries, regardless of cause, to the agency on a regular basis; and (3) hire outside professionals to review all refinery safety programs and management communication procedures (*Wall Street Journal,* September 23, 2005; p. B1).

All of these events, reports, fines, and requirements came as a surprise to most investors, competitors, and even environmentalists. British Petroleum, long considered a laggard in the global petroleum industry, had apparently been almost totally rejuvenated starting in 1995 by the appointment of John Browne, a Cambridge University–educated physicist, art collector, and opera buff who differed markedly from the traditional image of rough-and-tumble petroleum industry executives, as CEO. The new appointee, however, did have extensive oil field experience. He had joined BP in 1966, shortly after graduation, and then lobbied extensively to be detached from the London headquarters office, which was the traditional training ground for new university hires in Britain, and sent to the North Slope of Alaska. The North Slope at this time was a cold and inhospitable place that was in the midst of an active drilling and development program to gather new supplies to meet the oil shocks and shortages of the 1970s and 1980s caused by two sequential Arab oil embargoes.

John Browne did both manual and managerial work in Alaska for eight years and then, buoyed by that experience on his résumé, rapidly moved up the corporate promotion ladder. He became manager of North American operations (and gained an MBA from Stanford while stationed in San Francisco), vice president for global development, executive vice president for global operations and then, in 1995, at 52 years of age, was appointed president and chief executive officer. BP was a traditional British company, and part of that tradition was the rule that the chairman of the board of directors had to serve in a non-executive position. The chairman oversaw operations; he or she did not direct them.

As president, John Browne quickly began directing operations in a forceful yet urbane way. In 1995, oil prices had fallen from the high levels of the 1980s when there were continual shortages of most petroleum products due to the Arab embargoes. The new supplies from Alaska, South America, and Africa had ended those shortages, created surpluses, lowered the market price for crude oil to $10 per barrel, and created a totally new set of problems for senior oil company executives.

John Browne convinced members of the board of directors that acquisitions to gain economies of scale and investments to get efficiencies of operation were the only means of survival for an underperforming company under those changed conditions. He quickly negotiated the acquisition of Amoco Oil Company, a midsized firm headquartered in Chicago with refining and retail operations in the Midwest, and then a merger with Atlantic Richfield, a somewhat larger Los Angeles firm with extensive holdings in southern California. At the same time, he endeared himself, and his company, to environmentalists when he became the first oil company executive to agree, in 1997, that global warming was real, adopted the "Beyond Petroleum" slogan for BP, and announced active programs to develop less environmentally harmful sources of energy.

The timing for all of these moves could not have been better. BP earnings expanded rapidly as industrial development in China and India created new demands for petroleum products and raised price levels for crude oil over the next seven years from $10 per barrel to $160 per barrel. BP had secure supplies of that oil, in the United States and the Arab Emirates, and was able to report record profits starting in 1998. John Browne became known as the man who had transformed BP from an also-ran into a global powerhouse. He was knighted in 1998 by Queen Elizabeth; in 2001 the government awarded him a life peerage with the title Lord Brown of Madingley.

Lord Browne's record of continual success began falling apart in late 2005. The March 25 explosion at Texas City started the decline, and the subsequent accounts of unreported or underreported accidents at other locations accelerated the process.

In December 2005, BP published its final report on the Texas City explosion. Here it accepted wider managerial responsibilities than previously acknowledged. The report explained that there were underlying causes that included a poor working environment at the facility, poor priority-setting among managers, and a lack of clear accountability at all levels. This report concluded with a plan to spend more than $1 billion over the following five years to replace older equipment and improve maintenance procedures (*Wall Street Journal,* December 10, 2005, p. A9).

The greatly increased level of spending was quickly said to be needed. There had not been a new oil refinery built in the United States since 1975 due to strict environmental laws that made it less expensive to operate abroad—particularly in smaller nations and less developed regions, where new investments, even in the so-called dirty industries, were warmly welcomed. The old U.S. plants continued to operate, however, partially because the technology of petroleum refining had not changed very much so they were still fairly efficient, but primarily because they were fully depreciated and thus highly profitable. Federal regulators and company officials alike claimed that these older U.S. plants did not pose unusual dangers, as long as effective safety and maintenance programs were in place (*Wall Street Journal,* July 27, 2005, p. A1).

Additional problems and damaging disclosures kept appearing, however. In March 2006, BP was responsible for the largest oil spill on the North Slope of Alaska since the active development of that area had started. Oil spills were greatly feared in that region as the permafrost made full remediation almost impossible. The cause was quickly determined to be the rupture of the major BP pipeline that served their gathering fields; it was found to have been poorly maintained, to be badly rusted, and to require total replacement (*New York Times,* July 27, p. C2).

Then, in October 2006 the consulting firm that BP had been required to hire to review all of their worker safety and management communication procedures by the Occupational Health and Safety Administration as one of the conclusions to their earlier study on the causes of the March 25 explosion, issued its first report. It was disclosed that the isomerization tower that had leaked the flammable gases and fluids that caused the deadly explosion on March 25 had leaked those same gases and fluids not once before, as reported by the company, but eight times. On two of those eight occasions, the safety systems had failed and serious fires had occurred, though without casualties. The investigator leading this inquiry found that BP managers were focusing on "high-frequency, low-consequence events" such as accidents to individual workers, not on the mechanical integrity of processing equipment that could result in major harms to many persons. The OSHA statement that accompanied the release of this consultant's report charged that BP's continual demands for substantial reductions in fixed costs adversely impacted both infrastructure maintenance and worker training.

It had been found, for example, that the refinery's central training staff had been reduced from 30 in 1998 (the year of the purchase from Amoco) to 8 in 2004 (*New York Times,* October 31, 2006, p. C3).

Senior BP officials objected to these findings. They claimed that budgetary decisions did not play a crucial role in the March 25 explosion that had resulted in a final toll of 15 killed and 170 injured. But that claim was at least partially overridden by a series of statements from local managers that were recorded during an internal accountability review conducted by BP, and either leaked or distributed to the press. The manager of the Texas City refinery was reported to have claimed that he had been ordered to cut costs by 25 percent in early 2005, just months before the deadly accident. He added that he had pleaded for additional funds, citing problem areas such as the poor condition of the processing equipment, but had been denied. The claim of this manager of the Texas City refinery was supported by a statement of the BP executive in charge of North American operations that he had been directed to keep maintenance expenditures low because of "10 years of lousy refinery margins." Both men's statements, however, were refuted by the BP vice president for global refining, who said that he had never received a request for additional funds for maintenance at Texas City.

Class Assignment

All management debacles, whether at the industrial or governmental level, are followed almost immediately by denials of responsibility and allegations of blame. Managers within British Petroleum at almost all levels certainly seemed to follow that pattern. The important issue, however, in the case of the explosion at the BP refinery in Texas City was not who was responsible but how it should have been prevented.

Prevention, in this instance, would have meant logically convincing the senior executives based in London, particularly the vice president for global refining quoted at the end of the case, that increased expenditures for refinery maintenance truly were needed. How does one logically convince senior corporate executives of actions that seem initially to be counter to the financial interests of their company? The recommendation of this book is that managers should start by (1) recognizing that individuals differ in their standards of behavior and (2) understanding that situations differ in their impacts upon people. A decision or action that one person might believe to be fully appropriate might strike another as totally wrong. It is necessary for a thoughtful manager to deal with these conflicts in a logically convincing manner, and that manner is portrayed below:

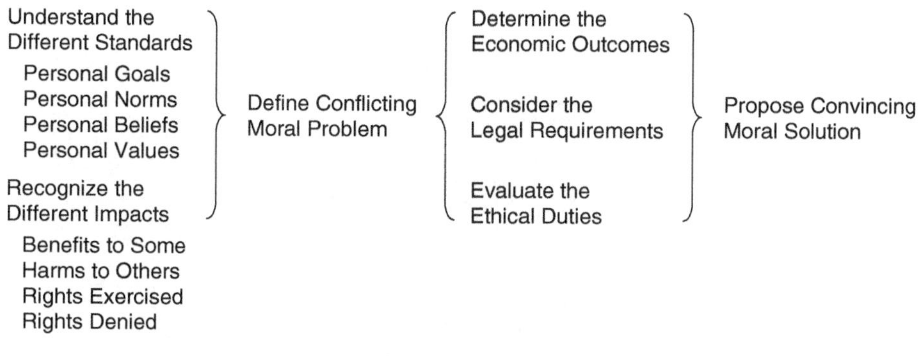

1. Put together the outline of the presentation you would recommend if you were asked to be a member of the group that was to go to London and not only request but expect to receive a substantial increase in funding for the physical maintenance of the American refineries *before the March 23, 2005, explosion.* After that explosion, making such a request would have been easy; you would have found the senior executives standing in line, waiting to hand over the company's checks.
2. Earlier in the case, it was reported that the isomerization tower that had leaked the flammable gases and fluids that caused the deadly explosion on March 25 had leaked those same gases and fluids not once before, as reported by the company, but eight times. On two of those eight occasions, the safety systems had failed and serious fires had occurred, though without casualties. Workers at the plant, particularly the clerical personnel in the wooden office trailer only 50 yards away from that tower, must have known of those leaks and fires and the danger to their safety, but they apparently said nothing. Why was that? Had you been an office worker in that trailer, would you have voiced your concerns,? How would you have done so to be effective?

Chapter 3

Moral Analysis and Legal Requirements

We are concerned in this book with moral problems. These are the decisions and actions faced by managers in which their firm's financial performance (measured by revenues, costs, and profits) and social performance (difficult to measure, but represented by the overall well-being and satisfaction level of the general population) are in conflict. These are the situations in which some individuals and groups to whom the organization has some form of obligation—employees, customers, suppliers, distributors, creditors, stockholders, local residents, national citizens, and global inhabitants—are going to be hurt or harmed in some way outside their own control, while others will be benefited and helped. These are also the situations in which some of those individuals or groups are going to see their rights ignored or perhaps diminished, while others will see their rights endorsed and even expanded. The question is how to find an equitable, fair-to-all balance between financial performance and social performance when faced with those conditions, and then *how to logically convince others to both understand and accept that balance.* Let me again emphasize my view that this understanding and approval of a fair-to-all balance is key not only to the future of your firm, but also to the future of your society and of your career. The three do go together.

In Chapter 1 it was suggested that you attempt to gain this understanding and approval by first recognizing that the moral standards of the individuals and groups who are associated with the firm, and who may well be affected by the decision or action proposed by the firm, are bound to differ. People's moral standards differ because of differences in their religious and cultural traditions and in their economic and social situations. You probably can't understand the exact nature of those differences without considerable study, but you certainly need to recognize that they do exist.

Then, you list the expected moral impacts—the mixture of benefits and harms, the contrast between rights exercised and rights denied—of the proposed decision or action, and compare those impacts to the probable moral standards of the individuals and groups who are associated with the firm. All of those people will not view the same situation in the same way. But, to get understanding and agreement, you have to be certain to address the moral concerns of the large majority of those involved.

Next, you clearly state the moral problem in a way that explicitly recognizes the probable moral concerns of that large majority. It is recommended that you state this moral problem in the form of a question: "Is it right that . . .?" As suggested in Chapter 1, a question is far less threatening than a declaration, and leads to discussion rather than conflict. Finally, examine your proposed balance of the financial outcomes and social outcomes of the decision or action, and alternative balances proposed by others, through the analytical methods of economic outcomes, legal requirements, and ethical duties. This approach was earlier portrayed as a graphic, which is repeated in Figure 3.1.

In Chapter 2 we looked at economic outcomes as one means of determining what is an equitable balance of a firm's financial performance and social performance in order to resolve a given moral problem and reach an acceptable moral solution. Economic outcomes are not just the financial consequences of the company's decision or action for the firm alone. Instead, they combine financial and social consequences for the members of the full society, due to the economic relationships that exist between a producing firm and individual consumers and product markets on the demand side and between the firm and individual suppliers and factor markets on the supply side. The political processes "in the middle" connect those two sides. According to economic theory, those market-based relationships should distribute the benefits and harms of the corporate decision or action throughout society in a way that reflects everyone's utility preferences for both product purchases and factor sales, while the political processes should ensure that all issues are considered and no individuals are left out. The result is greater output at lesser input for the full society—with that output distributed and that input selected by impartial market forces and supervised by participative social and political processes. The resulting condition, known as a Pareto Optimal Solution, in theory should work out to benefit all members of the society.

The conclusion of Chapter 2 was that maximizing economic outcomes for the full society, and distributing those outcomes by impartial markets and participative processes, is a legitimate way of beginning to address the moral problems of management. It is not, however, a complete and conclusive way of addressing those problems. There are underlying assumptions that (1) all of the product and factor markets are competitive, (2) all of the product customers and factor suppliers are informed, and (3) all of the external and internal costs have been included. But, we all know that there are variations in the degree of competition in most markets, variations in the extent of information among many customers and suppliers, and frequent lacks of inclusion for almost all external costs. Something more is needed to ensure that competition, to guarantee that

FIGURE 3.1 **Analytical Process for the Resolution of Moral Problems**

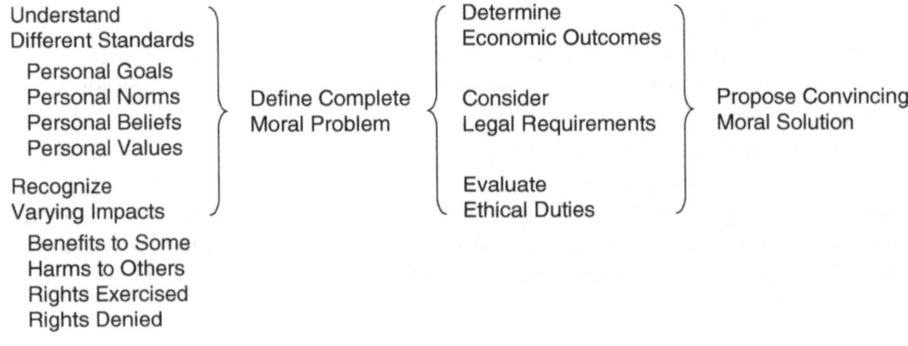

information, and to improve that conclusion—and much of that something more can be found in the legal requirements of the law.

The analytical method of legal requirements can be summarized very simply in the proposal that everyone should always obey the law. The law in a democratic society can be said to represent the minimal moral standards of that society, and those minimal moral standards should recognize the nature and understand the worth of individual human beings. You may or may not agree with the extent of those standards, or the degree of that recognition and scope of understanding, but you cannot really fault a person who obeys the law.

You may feel that a person within an organization who faces a complex moral problem in which some people are going to be harmed and harmed badly, or have their rights eroded and eroded harshly, should go beyond the law. That person, however, may well disagree with you. He or she may say, "We plan to optimize returns for our firm and benefits for our society. If you don't like that outcome, get together with a majority of your fellow citizens and pass a new law, which more fully recognizes the nature and understands the worth of other people, and we will obey the provisions of that new law. But, until that happens please do not lecture us on the superiority of your moral standards. We see nothing wrong with what we are doing, and evidently other people don't either, for what we are doing is currently legal and approved by a majority of our citizens."

This "always obey the law as written and fully meet all legal requirements" method of moral analysis has a lengthy historical base. Thomas Hobbes (1588–1679) was the originator of the proposal that the sole moral obligation of men and women was to obey the law, or the supreme governmental authority that set the law. It is necessary to recognize that Hobbes lived during the end of the Middle Ages in England. This was a time of intellectual ferment as the feudal class structure was breaking down into a more open and equal society, but it was also an era of rebellion, conflict, and crime. Homes of the nobles had to be protected by deep moats and strong walls. Travels of the merchants had to be escorted by armed guards. Hobbes explained that this was a natural outcome of every person looking after his (at this time there was little gender equality, and consequently an added "or her" would have been considered superfluous) self-interests. This, he said, led to a presence of chaos, a lack of security, and a block to progress. There are four major points in his reasoning:

1. *Equal ability.* Men, he wrote, are equals in their strength of body and mind despite their differences in class and position. Equality of ability leads to an equality of ambition, and therefore to a constant struggle by everyone for material gain and personal safety.
2. *Continual war.* The individual struggles between equals eventually become a war, and here there is a famous quotation: "And such a war as is every man against every man." This war, he wrote, was continual like bad weather, not intermittent like a shower.
3. *Depressed economy.* This continual war where "every man is enemy to every man" resulted in a lack of security, and the lack of security led to a decline in industry, and here again there is a famous quotation: "And the life of man: solitary, poor, nasty, brutish, and short."

4. *Proposed solution.* To stop this continual war, Hobbes said it is necessary to think of a "state of nature," a free association of equal individuals that would propose two "Natural Laws":

    - Men who are engaged in a continual war, in order to gain the benefits of an enforced peace, will seek it by all means available to them.
    - The only true means available to them is for all men to surrender their rights to a central authority who will establish peace by force and decree.

What does all this mean for the analytical method of legal requirements and a convincing solution of moral problems? At the simplest level, the proposal from Hobbes comes across as the rule that everyone should always obey the law because it is in everyone's self-interest to have a stable and orderly society even though they have to give up their rights to obtain that stability and order. This, essentially, is very similar to the analytical method of economic outcomes in which the proposal from Milton Friedman is that everyone should always act to maximize returns because it is in everyone's self-interest to have a productive and efficient society.

In the economic argument by Friedman, you may not like the products that are produced or the resources that are consumed, but to get productivity and efficiency, you have to accept them. In the legal instance by Hobbes, you may not like the laws that are generated, particularly when those laws are established by autocratic dictum on the part of a central authority rather than by a democratic vote through the full society, but to avoid the continual war of all against all, you have to accept them. At this level, both the economic outcomes and legal requirements for a society are based upon the enlightened self-interests of members of that society.

At a more complex level, however, the proposal from Hobbes comes forth as the legal requirement that all laws should reflect what people living in a state of nature would accept as the governing rules of society. This is not enlightened self-interest. This is impartial self-interest. This is the idea of the "Social Contract": When people don't know what position they will hold in the eventual society that is to be formed, they don't know their self-interests. This Social Contract lack of knowledge about self-interests is a very important and very basic concept in moral analysis and needs to be further explained.

If you were to take 100 people, somehow separated from all prior economic, political, and social institutions, and put them on an island, would that society be idyllic or chaotic? Let us assume that it would be idyllic as long as there was enough food, fuel, clothing, and shelter for everyone. But suppose there was a shortage; then what would happen? You might well have the war of "every man against every man" that Hobbes predicted.

A "contractarian"—that is, a person who believes in the analytical worth of the concept of the Social Contract—would argue that whatever agreement those 100 people would make to stop the conflict and end the shortage would be the most rigorous definition you could find as to what was considered to be equitable—that is, what was fair to all and just for everyone—for that society at that time. This could then be translated into legal requirements that every member of that society should follow to ensure the maintenance of their society, guide the production and distribution of their goods, and improve the conditions of their lives.

The contractarian would say that the people on the island, being free and equal but facing chaos and loss, would first discuss the distribution of benefits, the allocation of harms, the acceptance of some rights, and the denial of others. The agreement that they then reached—which would have to be unanimous to be effective; one person holding out would make the agreement non-binding in any Natural Law sense—would be totally without the material self-interests of individuals because no one at the time would be concerned with those self-interests (their positions and possessions versus those of others); they would be concerned only with their social interests (an end to the conflict and a resupply of goods). This Social Contract would be the way in which members of that society *theoretically* should distribute their benefits, allocate their harms, and ensure or deny their rights, from that time forward. Why? Because *this would be the way that had been determined by all to be best for all when all were absolutely equal in position and property.*

Obviously, you cannot put 100 people who are ignorant of their position and property on an island, and record their decision on the distribution of the benefits and harms and the acceptance and denial of rights. But, you and others can *imagine* what would happen if you put everyone involved in a moral problem—those benefited and those harmed, those with rights recognized and those with rights denied—in a room under the condition that they should think about the solution to that problem as if they did not know what position or property they would hold when they left that room.

Or, and doubtless this is a more realistic approach, it would be possible to put executives, employees, customers, suppliers, distributors, creditors, owners, local residents, national citizens, and global inhabitants in a room and assign roles. That is, some executives would be asked to think and act as if they were customers, others as suppliers. A few customers and suppliers would be asked to address the issues as if they were executives, while others would think of themselves as owners. The advantage of the Social Contract, or—as it has become better known in more recent years—the "Veil of Ignorance," is that it forces people to think about issues from different perspectives, and those different perspectives often lead to equitable solutions that are more in the social interests of the full community rather than in the material interests of the individual persons, groups, or organizations.

The primacy of community interests is the reason that the concept of legal requirements—always obey all provisions of the law—can be used as a method of moral analysis. The idea is that there is a set of rules, established by the full society, that recognize those community interests. Why not, then, fall back upon those rules when faced with a conflict between the financial performance of an organization and the social performance of that organization? Why not let the law decide, particularly in a democratic society where the argument can easily be made that the rules within the law represent the collective moral judgments made by members of the full society? Why not follow these collective moral judgments, instead of trying to establish our individual moral opinions?

There are numerous examples of laws that do reflect collective moral judgments. Almost everybody within the United States would agree that unprovoked assaults are wrong; we have laws against assault. Almost everybody would agree that toxic chemical discharges are wrong; we have laws against pollution. Almost all of us would agree that charitable giving is right; we have no laws against charitable giving. Instead, we have laws—provisions within the tax code—that encourage gifts of money, food, and clothing to the poor and to organizations that work to help the poor. The question of this chapter is whether we can use this set of rules—generally complex, frequently obsolete, and continually changing—to form equitable judgments about the balance between the financial performance and the social performance of our organizations.

Numerous attorneys and business executives believe that you can base equitable decisions and actions on the requirements of the law. These people would say that if a law can be shown to be wrong it should be changed, but that until it is changed it provides a meaningful guide for action. It provides this guide for action, they would add, because each law comes as close as possible within a democratic society to representing a combined moral judgment by all of the members of that democratic society on a given issue or problem. They will concede that you and I might not agree personally with that combined moral judgment on that particular issue or problem. But, they would add, if managers follow the law on that issue, those managers cannot truly be said to be wrong in any moral sense because they are following the probable moral standards of a majority of their peers.

How do we respond to those claims? And if it is not possible to respond logically and convincingly, are we then forced to accept those claims that the rule of law should be determinant in resolving moral problems, even though some people may be hurt or harmed, or have their rights ignored or restricted, in ways that they themselves believe to be unfair? I think that it is necessary first to define the law, so that all of us will recognize that we are discussing the same set of concepts, and then to examine the processes that are involved in formulating the law. This examination will be generally the same as in Chapter 2, in which we looked at market forces as the determinants for managerial decisions in moral problems. However, legal theory is much *less complete* and much *less explicit* than economic theory, and there are far more alternative interpretations that will have to be considered. First, however, let us define the law and expand on what is meant by the "rule of law."

Definition of the Law

The law can be defined as a consistent set of universal rules that are widely published, generally accepted, and usually enforced. These rules describe the ways in which people are required to act in their relationships with other people within a society. They are requirements to act in a given way, not just expectations or suggestions or petitions to act in that way. There is an aura of insistency about the law; it defines what theoretically you *must* do.

These requirements to act, or more generally requirements *not to act* in a given way—most laws are negative commandments, telling us what we should not do in given situations—have a set of characteristics that was partially described briefly earlier. In a more complete form, the law can be defined as a consistent, universal, published, accepted, and enforced set of rules. Each of those five terms needs to be further defined:

1. *Consistent.* The requirements to act or not to act have to be consistent to be considered part of the law. That is, if two requirements contradict each other, both cannot be termed a law because obviously people cannot obey both.
2. *Universal.* The requirements to act or not to act also have to be universal, or applicable to everyone with similar characteristics facing the same set of circumstances,

to be considered part of the law. People tend not to obey rules that they believe are applied only to themselves and not to others.

3. *Published.* The requirements to act or not to act have to be published, in written form, so that they are accessible to everyone within the society, to be considered part of the law. Everyone may not have the time to read or be able to understand those rules, which tend to be complex due to the need to precisely define what constitute similar characteristics and the same set of circumstances. However, trained professionals—attorneys—are available to interpret and explain the law, so that ignorance of the published rules is not considered to be a valid excuse.
4. *Accepted.* The requirements to act or not to act in a given way have to be in large measure obeyed. If most members of the society do not voluntarily obey the law, too great a burden will be placed on the last provision, that of enforcement.
5. *Enforced.* The requirements to act or not to act in a given way have to be enforced. Members of society have to understand that they will be compelled to obey the law if they do not choose to do so voluntarily. People have to recognize that if they disobey the law, and if that disobedience is noted and can be proven, they will suffer some loss of convenience, time, money, freedom, or life. There is, it was earlier noted, an aura of insistency about the law. There is also, or should be also, an aura of inevitability; law should define what will happen if you don't follow the rules.

This set of rules that are consistent, universal, published, accepted, and enforced—what we call law—is supported by a framework of highly specialized social institutions. There are legislatures and councils to form the law; attorneys and paralegal personnel to explain the law; courts and agencies to interpret the law; sheriffs and police to enforce the law. These social institutions often change people's perception of the law because the institutions are obviously not perfect, and often in conflict.

The adversarial relationships within a trial court frequently seem to ignore the provisions of consistency and universality and to focus on winning rather than on justice. The enforcement actions of the police also often seem to be arbitrary and to concentrate on keeping the peace rather than maintaining equity. Let us admit that enforcing the law, on the street, is a difficult and occasionally dangerous task. Police do not always act in the interests of the full society. Let us also admit that interpreting the law, in the court, is a complex and frequently tempting activity. Attorneys, also, do not always act in the interests of the full society. Indeed, they are required instead by the codes of their profession to act in the interests of their clients, because it is assumed that adjudged conflicts between the interests of different clients represented by separate attorneys will result in just verdicts. But overall, within this chapter, it is necessary to remember that we are looking at the law as an ideal concept of consistent and universal rules to guide human actions and managerial decisions and actions within a society, not as a flawed reality.

The Law as Collective Moral Standards

If the law is viewed in ideal terms as a set of universal and consistent rules to govern human actions and management decisions within society, the question is whether we can accept these rules—flawed though they may be by pragmatic problems in interpretation and enforcement—as representing the collective moral judgments of members of our society. If we can, then we have the standards to guide managerial decisions and actions even though these standards may be at a minimal level. If we cannot accept the set of rules as representing the collective moral judgment of our society, then we will have to look elsewhere for our standards. In considering the possible relationship between moral judgments and legal requirements, there would seem to be three conclusions that can be reached fairly quickly:

1. *Considerable overlap.* The published requirements of the law overlap to a considerable extent but do not duplicate exactly the probable moral standards of society. Clearly, a person who violates the federal law against bank robbery also violates the moral standard against theft. And it is easy to show that the laws governing sexual conduct, narcotics usage, product liability, and contract adherence are similar to the moral beliefs that are probably held by a majority of people in our society. I think that we can fairly readily agree that in a democratic society, the legal requirements do reflect many of the basic values of the citizens and that there is a considerable area of overlap between the law and morality, as shown in Figure 3.2.

   But the area of overlap is not complete. There are some laws that are morally inert, with no ethical content whatever. The requirement that we drive on the right-hand side of the road, for example, is neither inherently right nor inherently wrong; it is just essential that we all agree on which side we are going to drive. There are also some laws that are morally repugnant. Until the early 1960s, some areas of the United States legally required racial discrimination (segregated education, housing, and travel accommodations), and even slavery was legally condoned just 100 years earlier. Finally, there are some moral standards that have no legal standing whatever. We all object to lying, but truthfulness is not required by law except in a court, under oath, and in a few other specific instances such as accounting records and financial contracts.

   People who believe in the rule of law and accept legal regulations as the best means of governing human conduct within society would respond by saying that it is not at all clear that racial segregation was deplored by a majority of the population prior to 1962, or even that slavery was considered unconscionable before 1862. In a much lighter vein, concerning lying, they might even claim that most people have become accustomed to, and perhaps are somewhat amused by, a reasonable lack of truthfulness in advertising messages and political discourse. Moral standards, they

FIGURE 3.2 Overlap between Moral Standards and Legal Requirements

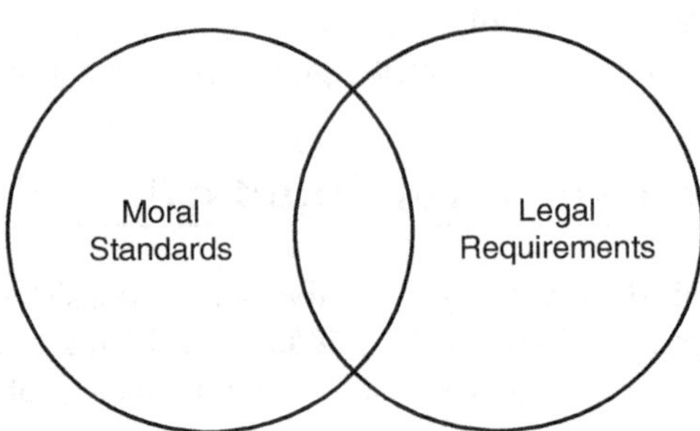

would say, are difficult to determine, and we must be careful not to infer that our standards represent those held by a majority of the population.

2. *Negative injunctions.* The requirements of the law tend to be negative, while the standards of morality more often are positive. In the law, we are forbidden to assault, rob, or defame each other, but we are not required to help people, even in extreme situations. There is no law, for example, that we must go to the aid of a drowning child. Here, we do have a situation where the moral standards of the majority can be inferred, for doubtless 99.9 percent of the adult population within the United States would go to the aid of a drowning child, to the limit of their ability. People who support the rule of law, however, would say that this instance does not indicate a lack of relationship between moral standards and legal requirements; it only indicates the difficulty of translating one into the other when a positive, compassionate, or charitable act is needed. How, they would question, can you define—in consistent and universal terms—what is meant by assistance, the characteristics of the person who is to provide that assistance, and the circumstances under which it will be required? This, they would conclude, is just another illustration that the law represents the minimum set of standards to govern behavior in society and that actions beyond that minimum have to come from individual initiative, not legal force.
3. *Lengthy delays.* The requirements of the law tend to lag behind the apparent moral standards of society. Slavery, of course, is the most odious example, but sexual and racial discrimination, environmental pollution, and foreign bribery can all be cited as moral problems that were belatedly addressed by legislation. Advocates of the rule of law would say, however, that the evidence of a delay between apparent moral consensus and enacted legal duty does not necessarily indicate a lack of relationship between legal requirements and moral standards. It only serves to confirm that relationship, they would claim, for laws controlling discrimination, pollution, and bribery were eventually passed.

None of these arguments—that legal requirements are not fully consistent (overlap rather than duplicate) with moral standards, or that the legal requirements appear in different forms (negative rather than positive) and at different times (sequential rather than concurrent) than moral standards—seems truly decisive. None of these arguments really helps to determine whether a given legal requirement does indeed represent a collective moral judgment by members of a specific society and consequently can serve as means to analyze the managerial decisions and actions of a company within that society. We can easily say that the law does not represent *our* moral judgment in a given situation, but how can we say that the law in that instance does not represent the moral judgment of a majority of our peers? For that, I think, we have to follow through the process by which our society has developed the law as a universal and consistent set of rules to govern human conduct.

The Process for the Formulation of the Law

Law is obviously a dynamic entity, because the rules change over time. Think of the changes that have occurred in the laws governing employment, for example, or pollution. This is essentially the same point that was made previously: that there seems to be a time lag between changes in moral standards and subsequent changes in legal requirements. Actions that 20 years ago were considered to be fully legal—such as racial and gender discrimination in hiring, or the discharge of chemical wastes into lakes and streams—are now clearly illegal. The question is whether these changes in the law came from changes in the moral standards of a majority of our population through participative social and political processes and, consequently, whether the law does indeed come close to representing the collective moral standards of our society. The social and political processes by which the changing moral standards of individual human beings are alleged to become institutionalized into the formal legal frameworks of their societies are lengthy and complex, but a simplified version is shown in graphic form in Figure 3.3.

There are four stages in the proposed formation of explicit legal requirements through the inclusion of collective moral standards. These are the stages of (1) individual persons, (2) small groups, (3) formal organizations, and (4) political institutions. Each will be addressed in sequence. Some of the material in the first or "individual person" stage has been covered in an earlier chapter, but it is repeated here for emphasis and understanding.

1. *Individual persons.* Each individual within society has, as was described in the first chapter, a set of goals, norms, beliefs, and values that together form his or her moral standards. Goals, also as described in that chapter, are what we want out of life. They include material possessions (cars, homes, boats, and vacations), lifestyle preferences (security, position, leisure, and power), personal goods (family, friends, health,

FIGURE 3.3 Process by which Individual Norms, Beliefs and Values Are Institutionalized into Law

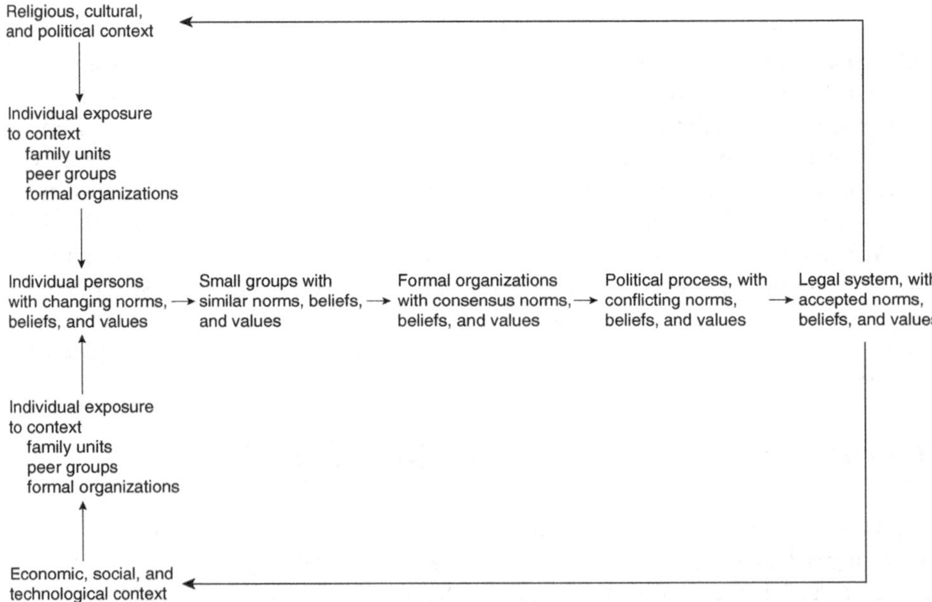

and respect), and social aims (justice, equality, a clean environment, and a world at peace. Clearly, these goals differ between people. Equally clearly, they influence the norms, beliefs, and values that those individuals hold, and consequently the moral standards that they profess and allegedly the laws that they wish to see enacted.

Norms, once more as described in the earlier chapter, are criteria of behavior. They are the ways an individual expects others to act, when faced with given situations. Foreign students from certain Asiatic countries, for example, used to bow slightly when addressing a university professor; the bow was their norm or expectation of behavior given that situation. University faculty members within the United States, however, were usually somewhat annoyed when that occurs; their norm or expectation of behavior in that situation was considerably less formal and generally more egalitarian. The depth of the bow and the degree of annoyance both declined over time as the expectations of behavior on both sides were modified through learning.

Another example of a norm of behavior is far less facetious and much more relevant to the discussion of moral standards and the law. Most people expect that others, when they meet them, should not cause them injury. Norms are expectations of the ways people ideally should act, not anticipations of the ways people really will act. A person who holds a norm against assault and robbery—as most of us do—will not ordinarily walk down a dark street in the warehouse district of a big city at three in the morning; he or she feels that people should not assault and rob each other, not that they will not do so.

Norms are expectations of desired behavior, not requirements for that behavior. This is the major difference between a norm and a law. A norm is not published, may not be obeyed, and cannot be enforced except by the sanctions of a small group whose members hold similar norms and use such penalties as disapproval or exclusion. Norms also are often neither consistent nor universal. The person who actually commits a crime in the warehouse district at three in the morning, feeling it permissible to assault and rob someone else given his or her situation and need upon that particular night, doubtless would feel outraged and unfairly treated if assaulted and robbed in the same place and at the same time the following night. Norms are just the way we feel about behavior; often they are neither logically consistent nor universally applied because we have never thought through the reasons we hold them.

Beliefs are criteria of thought; they are the ways an individual expects other people to think about given concepts and to support specific norms. I believe in participatory democracy, for example, and I expect others to recognize the worth of that concept and support my norm of free elections. You may believe in environmental preservation, and expect other people to recognize the importance of that idea and support your norm against the improper disposal of harmful chemicals.

Beliefs are different from norms in that they involve no action—no overt behavior toward others—just an abstract way of thinking that tends to support an individual's goals and norms. Asiatic students who used to bow to American professors believed, it is alleged, in a hierarchical society based upon age, not position, with definite gradations between older faculty and younger students. People who hold the norm that others should not assault and rob them, even on darkened streets and in deserted neighborhoods, generally believe in the worth of human beings and the preservation of personal property. In one last example, the norm that a company should not bury toxic wastes in leaking 55-gallon drums is associated with beliefs about the public benefits of a clean environment and the adverse effects of chemical pollution upon family health.

Values, the fourth and last of this pattern of personal criteria that together form the moral standards of an individual, are the rankings or priorities that a person establishes for his or her goals, norms and beliefs. Most people do not consider that all their goals, norms, and beliefs are equal in importance; generally, there are some that seem much more important than others. The important goals, norms, and beliefs are the ones that a person "values," or holds in high esteem.

Values, of course, are often controversial. Why? Because a goal, norm, or belief that one person holds in high esteem can conflict with a different goal, norm, or belief that another person holds in equally high esteem. Generally, there will be little accommodation or compromise, because each person attaches great importance to his or her goals of what people should want to achieve, to his or her norms of how people should want to act, and to his or her beliefs of why people should want to have certain goals and norms. We live in a pluralistic society, with numerous cultural traditions, and in a secular nation, with no endorsed religious doctrines; consequently, we have to live with the fact that goals, norms, beliefs, and values will differ among individuals. These differences can and do lead to conflicts. Similarities, however, can and do lead to people associating in small groups. Those small groups are important in the formation of the law.

2. *Small groups.* People with similar goals, norms, beliefs, and values tend to associate with each other. This is partially the result of those similarities; we all like to be with other people who tend to accept our views on the important issues of life. But, it is also partially the result of the influence of our religious and cultural traditions and our economic and social situations upon our goals, norms, beliefs, and values. We also all like to associate with others who tend to share our traditions and situations. These associations, over time, lead to the formation of small and informal groups of like-minded individuals.

These small and informal groups of like-minded individuals do, through a process called accretion of power, have an apparent though delayed and indirect impact upon the legal requirements in a democratic society. People with closely similar goals, norms, beliefs, and values, and from nearly identical traditions and situations, tend to rely upon the groups to which they belong to forward their views and respect their backgrounds in their interactions with the larger formal organizations and political institutions.

It has to be admitted that these tendencies toward conformity can—and frequently do—lead to exclusion and discrimination. This, we will find, is one of the reasons that the legal requirements of a society cannot be said to be fully based upon the moral standards of all of the members of that society. There frequently has been some ostracism of people who hold diverse standards. But, it also has to be admitted that these small and informal groups of people who share parallel views and compatible backgrounds do wield considerable influence through social and political processes upon the viewpoints of organizations and the requirements of societies. Groups of people, even though their numbers are small and their structures informal, are generally more powerful in changing organizational policies and societal laws than are single individuals.

There are exceptions to this "groups are more powerful than individuals" dictum, of course. Some individuals are particularly articulate. Some individuals are exceptionally adept. Some individuals are unusually charismatic. And, some individuals are abundantly wealthy. But, in general, it can be said that coherent groups generate greater influence on organizational policies and societal laws than do independent persons, for most of us are not "particularly articulate," "exceptionally adept," "unusually charismatic," or "abundantly wealthy."

3. *Large organizations.* Small, informal groups usually become part of larger, more formal organizations. These larger, formal organizations can be of many different types: business firms, labor unions, political parties, charitable agencies, religious institutions, and veterans' associations. They all share—and this is the reason for the "formal" classification—accepted goals, stated policies, and structured positions. People know why they exist, or claim to exist; how they act, or claim to act; and who's in charge, or claims to be in charge. There are exceptions here, of course. The accepted goals of some organizations tend to get lost over time. The stated policies ("policies" are explicit statements as to what should be done in given situations, and are thus related to norms) tend to get forgotten, and the structured positions ("structure" refers to the hierarchical ranking, or authoritative power, of those positions) tend to get supplanted. But generally, the goals, the policies, and the positions are dominant in the management of large, formal organizations.

   The small informal groups that are part of each large and formal organization frequently come into conflict with each other over their distinctive goals, norms, beliefs, and values. Over time, the larger organizations and the small groups either achieve an acceptable compromise on these issues and their resultant standards or split into smaller organizations that can achieve such a compromise. There are alternative theories on the means by which these compromises are formed: autocratic decisions, bureaucratic adjustments, coalition bargains, or leadership influences. Doubtless all these methods are employed to different degrees in different organizations, but the outcome that can be most frequently observed is that many large organizations do eventually display a culture of shared goals, norms, beliefs, and values that do lead to accepted standards of decision and action. Organizations that display such a coherent culture—and remember that these are not just business firms; they include labor unions, political parties, charitable agencies, religious groups, and industrial associations as well—do thus tend to have considerable power in the political institutions that formulate the laws and establish the legal requirements of the society.

4. *Political institutions.* The political institutions—governmental units at federal, state, and local levels—are the means by which the goals, norms, beliefs, and values, and the resultant moral standards, of individuals persons, small groups, and larger organizations are formalized into law. The political process by which this transmission occurs can, once again, be seen basically as a means of resolving conflict. Individuals, groups, and organizations obviously have different opinions on what should be achieved in the future (goals), what should be done now (norms), what should be the supporting rationale (beliefs), what should be the order of priority (values), and what are the standards that should be applied (morals). These different views have to be

reconciled into consistent, universal, published, accepted, and enforced set of rules (the definition of the law) to be effective. This is—or theoretically should be—the function of the political institutions.

Again, there are alternative theories on the ways by which this is done: presidential leadership, institutional compromise, congressional bargaining, and constituent pressure. The terms would differ at the federal, state, and local levels, but the process doubtless remains approximately the same. The important issue is that all of the institutional participants in this process are influenced by votes, surveys, contributions, reports, messages, and—to some extent—threats from private individuals, small groups, and large organizations. The accretion of power means that the groups are more effective than the individuals, and the organizations more effective than the groups, in wielding this influence.

The actual process by which laws are enacted represents a complex series of interactions. Doubtless no one except a member of Congress or a representative in one of the state legislatures fully appreciates the extent and time demands of the formal hearings, office meetings, and committee reports, with their constant interruptions. There are also informal exchanges that occur in hallways, parking lots, and evening receptions, supplemented by genuinely open efforts to summarize opinions from typical voters expressed in personal letters, telephone calls, and media reports, and frequently hidden programs to include viewpoints of special interests reinforced by campaign contributions. All of these help to form the opinions of the legislators. It is easy to be cynical while thinking of these political processes, particularly when the high costs of election campaigning are considered and the need to raise funds to finance those campaigns is included, but it is difficult to invent a better process than participative democracy. Indeed, it is often remarked that democratic processes constitute the worst political system possible, except for all of the others.

The Problems in the Formulation of the Law

The question now is whether this sequence of private individuals to small groups to large organizations to political institutions, lengthy and complex though it may be, truly does serve to combine the personal moral standards of a majority of our population, slowly and gradually, into the universal legal requirements of our full society. That is, does the law actually represent the collective moral judgment of our citizens, or does this cumulative process break down at some point? The proposal that the laws of a democratic society do indeed represent the collective moral judgments of the members of that society is certainly appealing. However, there would seem to be five major problems in the transfer from individual moral standards to universal legal requirements through the various stages of the social and political process:

1. *Inadequate information.* The goals, norms, beliefs, and values, and consequently the moral standards, of the members of society may be based upon a lack of information relative to issues of importance. Most people in central Ohio, where the payments by health care insurance companies to the consultants who advised small- to medium-sized companies and public organizations on the purchase of health care policies originally came to light (described in the first case in this book, following

the Preface) were ignorant of this practice, even though it directly affected their well-being and that of their families and institutions. It is difficult for personal moral standards to actively influence the formation of the law if some information is missing.

2. *Incomplete participation.* The moral standards of some members of society may not be included in the formation of the small groups that subsequently influence the formal organizations and the legal institutions. People with similar goals, norms, beliefs, and values, and from identical religious/cultural traditions and economic social situations, tend to become associated in small groups, but those similarities and identities also tend to exclude other members of society from different traditions and alternative situations. Goals, norms, beliefs, and values often lead to conflicts as well as to associations. It is difficult for personal moral standards to actively influence the formation of the law if some viewpoints are excluded.
3. *Inarticulate representation.* The moral standards of some groups within society may not be fully represented in the consensus of the formal organizations that subsequently influence the legal institutions. Many organizations do share goals, norms, beliefs, and values, but there is no evidence that each group within each organization has an equal ability or opportunity to express their preferences. This can be seen in the goals, norms, beliefs, and values of many nonprofit organizations such as hospitals and universities; the standards of the professional personnel—the physicians in one instance and the faculty in the other—often seem to predominate. It is difficult for personal moral standards to actively influence the formation of the law if some groups can't convey their preferences effectively.
4. *Inconsistent formulation.* The moral standards of some organizations within society may not be equally considered in the agreements of the political institutions that result, or should result, in the formulation of the law. This is the same point that was made above in shaping the consensus of an organization, though on a much larger scale. There is no guarantee that all organizations have equal influence, or even equal influence weighted by size or need, in determining the final provisions of the law. This can be seen in much tax legislation; certain organizations always seem to be favored. It is difficult for personal moral standards to actively influence the formation of the law if some organizations are given preference.
5. *Indefinite wording.* The wording of legal requirements, of laws and contracts, is not a theoretical problem. It has nothing to do with the proposition that laws should be obeyed because they either represent or should represent the minimal moral standards of a large percentage of the population. Instead, this is a very practical issue. Many law firms now practice what is termed "positive" law; they view their primary professional duty as one of representing to the best of their ability the interests of their clients. One way to do this is to look for omissions in the provisions of the law; these frequently occur due to delays and pressures in the formulation of the law and often work to the advantage of specific clients.

Conclusion

What can we say in summary? We can observe that there obviously is some overlap between the moral standards of our citizens and the legal requirements of our society. The moral standards against stealing and the legal requirements against robbery serve as an obvious example. And we see that some changes in the goals, norms, beliefs, and values of individual members of society do eventually make it through the small group, formal organization, and political institution processes and then are reflected by changes in the law. The Foreign Corrupt Practices Act and the Federal Equal Employment Act are examples here.

But we will have to admit that there is no direct relationship in all instances. The social and political processes by which the law is formulated are too complex and too cumbersome—and perhaps too subject to manipulation—for changes in people's goals, norms, beliefs, and values to be directly translated into changes in that set of universal and consistent rules that we call law. Consequently, we cannot view this set of rules as representing the collective moral judgments of our society, and therefore we cannot rely totally on this set of rules when confronted by a moral problem.

Legal requirements can serve as a guide to managerial decisions and actions, but as in the case of economic outcomes, they are not enough. They don't include the full range of personal goals, norms, beliefs, and values and consequently—once again, as in economic outcomes—don't represent the true nature and actual worth of individual human beings. Legal requirements are useful. They provide an approximation of that nature, and they approach that worth by recognizing the value of liberty, opportunity, dignity, and respect. But, we need something more to fully include those values. In the next chapter we will look at the fundamental norms and absolute values of ethical duties as a third means of providing that "something more."

Case 3-1

Credit Card Companies and Mandatory Arbitration

Most credit card holders do not realize that there is a clause in the contract they signed when they first obtained their card that requires them to settle any future disputes with the issuer through arbitration, not through trial. Arbitration is a form of alternative dispute resolution (ADR) in which an allegedly neutral person evaluates the claims of the conflicting parties and then issues a resolution that is legally binding on both sides. It is very different from mediation, in which the neutral person encourages negotiations between the conflicting parties in an effort to reach a compromise; if he or she does suggest a solution here, it is not legally binding on anyone.

Credit card companies are said to like the mandatory arbitration procedures to settle disputes because they are far less expensive and much more prompt than court trials, and the companies assume that credit card users prefer them for the same reasons. The problem, of course, comes in the neutrality of the arbitrators who conduct the hearings and issue the verdicts. Arbitrators are normally employed on a part-time basis by for-profit companies such as the National Arbitration Forum or non-profit groups such as the American Arbitration Association. The credit card companies contract with one of the companies or groups to assign and compensate the arbitrators, most of whom are lawyers who are frequently retired but looking for additional income. The *New York Times* (July 22, 2009) reported that most arbitrators earn about $400 per hour, though some are paid as much as $10,000 per day. The *New York Times* also said, in that same article, that in cases where the arbitrators had been assigned and paid by the National Arbitration Forum to settle disputes between business firms and individual creditors, the rulings favored the business firms 94 percent of the time.

The *New York Times* article was apparently published in anticipation of a hearing by a congressional committee on a proposal to ban compulsory arbitration clauses from all credit card contracts as part of a push for more consumer protection. Earlier in the summer of 2009, Congress had passed, and President Obama had signed, new financial regulations that banned interest rate hikes or penalty fee increases on personal credit cards without an adequate (45-day) notice. The proposed ban on compulsory arbitration clauses was said by advocates to be the needed third leg for that stool.

The credit card companies and the banks that issued those cards objected strongly. They claimed that not only would this new requirement drive up the costs and delays of reaching settlements, it would also open the door for class-action lawsuits that could drag on for years, and result in unfair awards by inflamed juries.

Class Assignment

The assignment for this short case is divided into two parts: First, what is your view of compulsory arbitration requirements: should they be permitted or banned, and why? Structure your decision so that you can convince others. Second, have you had any disputes with your credit card company that proved difficult to resolve, and what changes in the law would you recommend to avoid that type of dispute or to facilitate the sort of resolution you believe to be needed?

Case 3-2

Law Firms and Aggressive Advice to Clients

One of the most famous statements by a practicing lawyer on the duties of attorneys came from Elihu Root (1845–1937). Mr. Root worked in New York City and specialized in corporate law, but he frequently left for high-level positions in Washington, DC. He served as Secretary of War under President William McKinley (1899–1901), as Secretary of State for President Theodore Roosevelt (1905–1909), and as U.S. Senator for the state of New York (1910–1916). He then returned to his corporate law practice. His statement shortly thereafter was, "Half the practice of a decent attorney consists of telling clients they are damned fools and should stop" (Mary Ann Glendon, *A Nation Under Lawyers,* Harvard University Press, 1994, p. 37).

Had Mr. Root been still living and working in 2007, he doubtless would have been tempted to convey that same advice to the partners of a major law firm located in what was once one of the most heavily industrialized and prosperous cities in the northeast. This firm apparently believed that its function was to represent the interests of its corporate clients as zealously as possible, and consequently it put together a seminar that was essentially on the topic, "How Not to Hire Americans." Many of the larger companies within this manufacturing-based city had suffered from foreign competition—and been forced to close. New companies were emerging, primarily in digital and medical technology. But it was hard to find truly competent scientists and engineers locally.

Most of the younger ones wanted to move to Route 128 around Boston or to the Silicon Valley south of San Francisco, where the living was thought to be livelier, while many of the older and established ones were said to be non-current in their thinking.

There were lots of fully current younger engineers and scientists working in India, graduates of the very advanced Indian Institutes of Technology, many of whom wanted to come to the United States because of higher salaries and greater opportunities. But, for those qualified candidates to work in the United States, a potential employer had to obtain a "PERM" or a certificate issued by the Employment and Training Administration (ETA) of the Department of Labor stating that there were no qualified U.S. workers able, willing, qualified, and available to fill the position at the prevailing wage in the area of intended employment. The PERM would then be sent to the Customs and Immigration Service (CIS), which would issue the immigration permit, often termed a "green card."

The essential part of this typically complex governmental process was the need to demonstrate that there were no qualified U.S. workers available to fill the position. The law firm that is being discussed in this short case put together a seminar that it offered to clients and potential clients at a downtown hotel on how *not* to find qualified and available U.S. workers. Their advice was to advertise in newspapers that technically trained people tended not to read, go to job fairs that they tended not to attend, recruit at colleges where they normally did not study, and evaluate any résumés that were received, despite these precautions, looking for possible defects in training or experience. The law firm videotaped the seminar and mistakenly posted it on its website, where it was found by a browser who perhaps was alerted by one of the attendees. That browser selected the most inflammatory scenes and statements and placed an edited version on YouTube. It created an immediate firestorm of protest.

The law firm in question practiced what it termed "positive law." This meant that it actively looked for opportunities within existing laws that would advance the interests of its clients. The opportunity in this instance was the difficulty in defining exactly what was meant by a "qualified" U.S. candidate in the rapidly advancing fields of digital and medical technology. The partners in this law firm, had you been able to interview them at the time, doubtless would have defended their actions by saying that the foreign candidates would work for lower wages and bring better ideas and thus improve the competitive positions of the local companies, which in turn would benefit the full community. Those partners doubtless also would have claimed—and this is the central argument in what is said to make the positive law doctrine morally permissible—that if some of those overlooked scientists and engineers within the region felt that they had been harmed economically or had their rights ignored, all they had to do was to go to an equally competent law firm whose duty it would then be to represent those individuals as zealously as possible. Two sides, each represented by competent attorneys acting zealously in the interests of their clients, in a trial to be held before an impartial judge and jury, is claimed to result in justice.

Class Assignment

The class assignment for this case is divided into three parts:

1. What do you think of the argument that positive law results in justice because two sides, each represented by competent attorneys acting aggressively in the interests

of their clients with a formal courtroom, receive a full hearing and get an impartial decision?

2. How would you define justice? What does justice mean to you? Write out a statement that you would be proud to read if called upon in class. Then, what do you believe should be the proper function of a law firm? Should it be just to resolve conflicts in ways that benefit the firm's clients, or is something more involved?
3. Lastly, could an attorney make a decent living today if he of she told half of his or her clients that they were damned fools and should stop? What has changed from the days of Elihu Root, or do you assume that his statement was just a boastful but inaccurate claim?

Case 3-3

The Fight over Proxy Access

The term "proxy," when used in business, refers both to the person who acts legally on behalf of someone else at stockholder meetings and to the document that conveys that legal authority to act. Most stockholders in publicly held corporations vote by proxy for two reasons: (1) they don't want to take the time to attend the annual meetings of the companies whose stock they hold, and (2) the range of issues upon which they will be able to vote is usually severely limited by the senior executives and board members of those companies.

The proxies mailed to stockholders by most companies consist solely of a list of candidates for election to the board of directors and the name of the accounting firm that is to conduct the audit of the company's books for the next fiscal year. The candidates for the board and the accounting firm for the audit generally were nominated by the senior executives of the company and approved by the board of that company, and no alternatives or options are listed. That is, if the board of directors consists of 12 members, only 12 candidates will be shown on the ballot. It is possible for dissenting stockholders to submit different proxies, but the costs of mailing the proxies and of campaigning for the positions have to be borne by those stockholders. This seldom happens, except in the instance of hostile acquisitions where the acquiring firm has plenty of money and lots of time.

The financial crisis that started in 2007 and grew steadily worse through 2008 raised serious concerns among many stockholders about the responsibility of board members to actively, rather than just passively, oversee the operations of their company, and the accountability of senior executives for the outcomes of their major decisions. As a consequence, many of the nation's largest mutual funds, pension funds, and private capital groups have petitioned the Securities and Exchange Committee (SEC) to change to a more democratic process for the election of board members.

The petition to the SEC essentially proposed that any mutual fund, pension fund, private capital group, or even association of individual investors that had owned more than 1 percent of the stock of a particular company for at least one year would be permitted to nominate candidates for the board of directors of that company, and the names of those candidates nominated by those stockholders would have to be placed on the same proxy, with the same clarity and standing, as the names of the candidates nominated by company executives. The 1 percent minimum stock ownership provision was included to ensure that the proxy would not be overwhelmed by the names of candidates who had limited support and little chance of election.

Class Assignment

What would be your position on this "any mutual fund, pension fund, private capital group, etc., that held more than 1 percent of the capital stock of a company for more than one year could nominate candidates for election to the board of directors of a company" proposal to the SEC? Almost all major corporations and the law firms that represent them are actively opposed. How would you express your thoughts to those opponents (if you're on the "yes, we need this change" side) or to the advocates (if you're one of the "no, we don't want this change" people)?

Case 3-4

Charles Schwab versus Andrew Cuomo

Charles Schwab started the company that bears his name on an exceedingly small scale in 1963; his only product at the time was an investment advisory newsletter that was distributed to just 3,000 subscribers. Personal brokerage services were added in 1971, and then pushed along by a constant stream of innovations—discounted fees in 1975, computerized trades in 1978, 24-hour operations in 1980, and impartial investment recommendations from start to finish—his firm grew very rapidly. In 2009 it provided 7.5 million customers with individual brokerage accounts, served 1.5 million participants in corporate retirement programs, employed 12,500 persons, and had a widespread reputation for serving clients well. That reputation was brought into direct conflict with the Attorney General of the State of New York, Andrew Cuomo, by a suit over auction rate securities.

Auction rate securities are an innovative form of investment-grade bonds, where the interest rates are set by periodic auctions. Most bonds, both corporate and municipal, have an interest rate that is set at the time of issuance, and that interest rate lasts throughout the life of the bond. Auction rate bonds do not have a set rate. Instead, the bonds are ranked by investment quality (AAA to C+), and existing holders and potential investors submit bids for the number of bonds within each quality rank they wish to repurchase (the existing holders) or newly purchase (the potential investors) and the minimum interest rate they are willing to accept as a condition of that purchase. Those interest rates are then ranked from low to high, and the highest interest rate at which *all of the bonds* within a given quality ranking will be purchased (in finance this is known as the "market clearing rate") become the rate for those bonds. For most auction rate securities, this bidding process was to be held at the end of each month, with settlement the next day, and interest to the prior holders to be paid at the same time.

These auction rate securities became very popular with both corporate and municipal issuers because they seemed to add the flexibility of short-term bonds to the steadiness of long-term securities. Individuals were attracted by the interest rates that so clearly reflected actual market demand and the periodic opportunities to get their money back whenever they wished. By early 2008, the auction rate security market had grown to more than $200 billion. Because of the dual need to submit new bids each month and to record interest payments each month, most of the individual purchasers relied on their brokerage firms or investment houses to manage the auction rate securities they held.

What went wrong? February 2008 marked the start of the credit crunch crisis. Suddenly, there were no bidders at the regularly scheduled auctions, and so essentially the interest rates became zero, the market values became zero, and the holders were unable to dispose of their auction rate securities. Under pressure from state legal officers throughout the county, led by Andrew Cuomo, the Attorney General of the State of New York, the investment banks that had participated in the underwriting and original placement of these securities agreed to repurchase about $60 billion of the bonds. Citigroup, Morgan Chase, Goldman Sachs, UBS, and Merrill Lynch were among the investment banks that participated in this repurchase settlement. It was expected that they would attempt to rework those securities into normal or stated interest rate bonds.

Settlements with the "downstream" brokerage firms that were the marketers of the adjustable rate bonds after the original underwriting and placement had been completed were harder to reach on legal grounds. They were able to claim that they did not develop the designs, construct the bonds, or run the auctions, and thus were just marketing an innovative financial product that was developed, constructed, and serviced by others. TDAmeritrade (the unusual name refers to the Toronto Dominion Bank of Canada) was the only brokerage firm that agreed to settle and buy back $457 million in auction rate securities for which they apparently felt some element of responsibility.

On August 17, 2009 the *Wall Street Journal* reported that Andrew Cuomo planned to sue Charles Schwab Corp's brokerage division, alleging that Schwab either knew or was negligent in not knowing the dangers that a credit crunch crisis and the resultant lack of liquidity would bring to the regularly scheduled markets for auction rate securities. Essentially the lawsuit claimed that the brokers working for Schwab should have been trained to warn their clients of the dangers of a financial collapse.

Two days later, Charles Schwab responded with a letter to the editors of the *Wall Street Journal* that was published as an "op-ed" piece on August 19, 2009. That letter is reproduced here:

> A blizzard of new proposed regulation and overzealous litigation is poised to jeopardize the low-cost investing model that tens of millions of investors have enjoyed for decades. In the last 30 years, individual investors have benefitted from huge innovations, including low commissions, online investing, mutual fund supermarkets, and the advent of exchange traded funds. Individuals now have broad access to domestic and global markets at costs lower than institutions enjoyed only a few years ago. This has provided needed capital to our economy and enabled the creation of personal wealth for average Americans.
>
> But today's extraordinary regulatory and political environment is putting all of this at risk.
>
> My company, Charles Schwab, was founded 35 years ago as a reaction to the high cost and inherent exclusivity of traditional Wall Street investing. Today we serve almost 10 million accounts. The majority are what we refer to as self-directed: They make their own decisions about what to buy, sell, or hold. We provide them with an efficient platform, tools, assistance, education, and, of course, low costs.

We are not alone. Our direct competitors serve millions of other American investors who are looking for essentially the same thing: the freedom to inexpensively invest on their own.

We have never guaranteed individual success. Our investors understand that along with investing comes risk, as well as potential reward. Unfortunately, we are now seeing a conscious effort to limit—if not eliminate—all risks for the individual investor, whether through consumer "protection," fiduciary liability for brokers, or the threat of litigation that attempts to make our firm, and others like us, more like an insurance company than a broker.

As an example, Schwab is currently being sued by New York Attorney General Andrew Cuomo, who alleges that we should have known beforehand that the Auction Rate Securities market would freeze. Auction Rate Securities are generally high-quality, long-term bonds that can be bought and sold on a weekly or monthly basis through an auction process. The interest rate paid on the bonds was reset at each auction according to investor demand. The auction process has largely been frozen since February 2008, leaving investors holding quality long-term, but illiquid bonds.

Though this market operated smoothly and reliably for over 20 years, it is a market that we had no direct involvement in establishing or maintaining. It's a market where roughly 90 percent of the clients who invested in these securities came to Schwab asking us to locate and make available these investments for them. We did not create the products, actively market them, and had no involvement in the events that led to the collapse of the Auction Rate Securities market.

The implication of this lawsuit is that firms like ours should have known that the market would fail. Should we also have known that Lehman Brothers or Bear Stearns were going to go under, and compensate clients who bought their equity or debt? Should we have been able to predict which financial institutions would be the beneficiaries of government bailouts and which would not? I think it's fair to say we have all been surprised by many events this past year.

The issue at stake here is whether independent investors should be allowed the freedom to choose what they are allowed to buy, sell, or hold. Or should the government try to enforce a guarantee against market risk through regulation or lawsuits like the attorney general has brought against us?

If Schwab is going to be held responsible for guaranteeing every decision an investor makes, we'd need to severely limit what they purchase. Would we tell them they couldn't buy Google or IBM stock because regulators or politicians don't think they are smart enough to assess the risks and could hold us accountable for any losses? The logical outcome would be that individual investors would be constrained to a small set of plain vanilla investments—Treasurys for all—or would be forced to pay us a fee to manage their account.

To be sure, we are happy to manage money for our clients. But millions of investors have decided that their needs are best served when they direct their own finances. Forcing them to pay an advisory fee would be a significant new cost to them and the fees would likely shut many small investors out of the capital markets altogether.

I've always believed in the power of the market to drive innovation and drive down cost. I also believe in the individual and his or her ability to make reasoned decisions. I don't think our clients, or our competitors' clients, are looking for regulators or politicians to protect them from risk by constraining their choices.

Today Schwab clients can open an account with as little as $1,000. If they invest their $1,000 in an S&P 500 Index fund, they would pay no commission and their total cost of management would be 90 cents per annum. For 90 cents a year they can access everything Schwab has to offer including education, tools, our Web site, 24/7 live phone service, as well as support from one of our approximately 300 branches across the country.

This is an incredibly powerful model that I'm proud of, and a model that I think is good for this country and the market.

Don't let litigators and politicians jeopardize it. If they succeed, the individual investor will pay a heavy price.[1]

Class Assignment

This dispute between Charles Schwab and Andrew Cuomo goes to the heart of both our market-based economy and our law-based society. Address those issues through the following four questions:

1. Which side of the dispute between Charles Schwab and Andrew Cuomo are you on? Charles Schwab expressed his thoughts in an exceedingly articulate "op-ed" letter that was published in the *New York Times.* Andrew Cuomo did not respond because he is by tradition (don't taint the jury pool, and don't warn the opposing counsel) prevented from presenting his arguments before the formal trial. What arguments in your opinion will Andrew Cuomo make at that trial, and—if you were a member of the jury—what would be your verdict? Why?
2. What are the assumptions of a market-based economy that as an attorney for one of the sides you would be either be certain to bring before the jury or be prepared to counter if your opponent brought them before the jury?
3. What are the assumptions of a law-based society that as an attorney for one of the sides you would be either be certain to bring before the jury or be prepared to counter if your opponent brought them before the jury?
4. Lastly, go back to Chapter 1 and review the section on ethical duties. Are there any arguments expressed here that would help you to convince members of the jury that your side was the most equitable and fair-to-all?

Case 3-5

Foreign Tax Havens and U.S. Taxpayers

Foreign tax havens tend to be small independent states with stable governments, low taxes, strict privacy rules, good communication and transportation facilities, and discrete legal and financial services. They often are located in pleasant tourist destinations such as the Caribbean islands—Antigua, Bahamas, Barbados, Bermuda, etc.—or the Alpine regions of Europe that citizens from economically advanced countries could quietly visit and confidentially make arrangements for the transfer of substantial sums of money that would then be immune from all of the income, investment, and inheritance taxes of their home countries.

For years, the actual amounts of those "sizable sums" of money that had either been entrusted to discrete local bankers in the smaller tax havens or moved to equally discrete but more technically adept banking centers in larger participating countries remained unknown. There were estimates in the hundreds of billions of dollars, but the secrecy stayed firmly intact and there was no exact knowledge of the amounts or the owners.

Then, in February 2008, a former employee of the LTG Bank in Liechtenstein—a small principality located in the Alps between Switzerland and Austria with just 37,000 residents—evidently felt that he had been inappropriately discharged and proceeded to provide tax authorities around the world with the financial records he had copied of 1,400 persons who had opened accounts and deposited funds at that bank. The names of 100 U.S. citizens were on that list.

LTG Bank has long held a reputation as one of the major tax haven banks. It is owned by members of the ruling family in Liechtenstein, and consequently it was strongly protected by the laws of that country. Those laws provided no protection, however, to the U.S. citizens whose names had been revealed, particularly given that the released records of some of them indicated that they also had secretive accounts at the United Bank of Switzerland (UBS). A senior official in the private banking division of UBS, Bradley Birkenfeld, happened to be traveling in Florida at this time, visiting some of these dual clients who had been identified. Mr. Birkenfeld was arrested, his computer and other records were confiscated, and he was charged with conspiracy to defraud the Internal Revenue Service (IRS).

Some of the records seized when Mr. Birkenfeld was arrested indicated that the private banking division of UBS had 52,000 clients who held what the bank termed "undeclared accounts," meaning that neither the person owning the account nor the bank holding the account had notified the IRS of the existence of the account. Both of those actions were required by U.S. law. Consequently, the U.S. Justice Department, at the request of the IRS, filed an administrative summons against United Bank of Switzerland, demanding that the bank release the names of all U.S. citizens who owned undeclared, and therefore untaxed, accounts held by UBS in Switzerland, and report the holdings of those accounts. Both of those actions were prohibited under long-standing Swiss law.

Switzerland is a smallish country, with a population of 7.7 million people, located in the Alpine region of Europe between France, Germany, Italy, Liechtenstein, and Austria. Despite its location between historically contentious neighbors, it has carefully maintained a history of neutrality; the last war in which it was engaged took place in 1815. It is a mountainous country, so there is limited large-scale agriculture. It is a landlocked nation, so there is little global commerce. It lacks the basic resources of coal and ore, so there is almost no heavy industry. But, it is one of the most prosperous nations on earth, with a 2005 gross domestic product, converted to U.S. dollars, of $67,000 per person. That prosperity is based upon luxury resorts, high-quality textiles, the precision production of watches and scientific/medical instruments, and the ready availability of private banks.

For years, these private banks were small, family owned, and exceedingly discrete. During the 1800s, it became a criminal offense in Switzerland for bankers to reveal either the names or the holdings of their clients, and this lawful privacy brought the deposits of many wealthy families throughout Europe as frequent wars racked that region. Following World War II, however, the family-owned banks began to coalesce into publicly held institutions. By 2000, the two premier institutions, Credit Suisse and United Bank of Switzerland, were equal in size to those in New York or London and engaged in many of the same commercial banking and investment banking practices. The wealth management divisions of those large banks, and of the many smaller ones that remained active throughout Switzerland, however, maintained the traditional Swiss practices of extreme discretion and absolute privacy for their clients.

It is important at this point to understand that the U.S. distinction between tax avoidance (purchasing municipal bonds whose interest payments are tax free, or investing for capital gains which are charged a far lower rate than dividend payments) and tax evasion (failing to report income) is not as clear in Europe as in the United States. Part of the reason is that many European families, and not just those who are exceedingly wealthy, have survived based upon their undisclosed incomes during the many wars and recessions that have plagued that continent. A more important part of the reason, however, is that income taxes play a far less important role in financing governmental services in Europe than in the United States.

Most of the tax revenues collected by European nations (Great Britain is the major exception) come from "value-added" taxes that increase the retail prices of all consumer goods and services sold within each country. These increases consist of small percentages assessed at each of the sequential stages in the production and distribution of those goods and services. They are based upon the difference between the direct cost of the material and labor expended at each stage and the transfer price to the next stage. They are easily computed, firmly recorded in the accounting records of each company, reliably remitted to the government in each country by those companies, but actually paid, of course, by the final purchaser of the goods and services: the retail customer. It is still believed to be a reasonably equitable tax because the final value added to the price is far higher for luxury goods than for daily necessities.

The tax systems of the United States and Europe are clearly different, and the banking practices in Switzerland that were designed essentially for those differences have created conflicts with the United States. These conflicts primarily concern the nonpayment of U.S. taxes by U.S. citizens. The Internal Revenue Service within the United States has estimated the annual U.S. tax gap, which is the difference between what taxpayers owe and what they pay, at $345 billion. There have been numerous negotiations to close this tax gap.

Switzerland first entered into a tax treaty with the United States in 1951. Under that treaty Switzerland agreed to exchange information in criminal cases involving tax fraud, which had been defined as situations in which a taxpayer used, or intended to use, forged or falsified documents. Dissatisfied with that narrow interpretation—the U.S. Justice Department quickly found that it was necessary to produce the forged or falsified document in court, and those were generally difficult to find—the United Sates in 2000 adopted a new initiative called the Qualified Intermediary (QI) program, which was signed not by countries that traded with the United States but by "intermediaries" or banks that wished to interact with financial institutions within the United States.

This QI agreement required those banks to report all U.S. source income to the U.S. government. U.S. source income was defined as all income, whether in the form of dividends, interest, salary, bonus payments or capital gains, that came from a source within the United States and was credited to an account owned by a citizen of the United States. More than 7,000 foreign financial institutions signed the QI agreement, including most of the major banks within Switzerland, and promised to participate in the program.

Compliance, however, has been low. Some of the foreign banks that had agreed to participate in the program simply replaced the stocks and bonds of U.S.-based corporations in accounts held by U.S. citizens with stocks and bonds from non-U.S. firms. Others changed the name of the account holder from that of the U.S. citizen to the name of a newly set up foreign corporation owned by the U.S. citizen. These foreign corporations were frequently created in a complex series of interrelated corporations, trusts, and foundations to hide the true beneficial ownership, as shown in the following example that had been arranged in 1997 in anticipation of the QI program:

> Beverly Park Corporation was incorporated in Delaware on January 3, 1997 by a registered Delaware agent, Corporation Trust Company. Beverly Park is wholly owned by Cordera Holdings Pty Ltd., which is owned by Franley Holdings Pty Ltd., which is owned by LGF Holdings Pty Ltd., which is in turn owned by Frank Lowy Trust. (*Tax Haven Banks and U.S. Tax Compliance,* Staff Report of the Permanent Subcommittee on Investigations of the U.S. Senate, released on July 17, 2008, p. 54)

United Bank of Switzerland followed the more direct practice of replacing all U.S. stocks and bonds held by U.S. citizens with equivalent investments in non-U.S. firms for its existing private account clients. It also insisted that all new U.S. clients sell their U.S. holdings before opening a private account. Those policies were fully implemented by 2002, and in November of that year a letter was sent to all U.S. clients stating that UBS could not be forced to disclose a Swiss account held by a U.S. citizen as long as that account contained no U.S. securities—even if UBS knew that the account holder was a U.S. taxpayer obligated under U.S. tax law to report the account and its contents to the IRS. That letter continued that the reporting obligations applied to the account holder personally, not to UBS, and thus UBS had broken no U.S. law or QI obligation and so could not be forced to divulge any information or be subject to any legal claim.

Six years later, however, on February 18, 2009, the United Bank of Switzerland reached what was termed a "deferred prosecution agreement" with the U.S. government to (1) pay a $780 million fine for conspiring to defraud the IRS by failing to report the annual incomes of secretive accounts held by U.S. citizens and (2) to confirm the names of 270 U.S. citizens who were believed to hold some of those accounts through their ownership of intentionally constructed foreign corporations, trusts, and foundations. A deferred prosecution agreement is not a dismissal of the charges; instead, it is a formal contract not to bring those charges to trial unless the accused person or organization fails to complete the full terms of the contract.

In quick succession, on February 19, 2009, the U.S. Justice Department filed a new claim seeking to force the United Bank of Switzerland to release the names of all U.S. citizens who held unreported accounts in the private wealth management division of that bank. It was estimated that 52,000 U.S. citizens held such accounts. These two actions were major changes in the ongoing battle between Swiss banks and the U.S. government.

What happened? What forced the United Bank of Switzerland to move, in just over six years, from an assurance to its account holders that UBS had broken no U.S. laws or QI obligations and thus could never be forced to divulge any information or ever be subject to any claim to a formal agreement to pay a huge fine, to identify a small group of holders despite the elaborate disguises that had been erected, and perhaps to be forced to reveal the names of all U.S. holders of private accounts within that bank?

It was soon disclosed that bankers in the private wealth management division of UBS had not waited in Switzerland for U.S. clients to come to them; or to be referred to them from smaller banks in other tax havens; or to be sent to them by some of the many attorneys, consultants, and advisors who worked on tax matters throughout the world. Instead, many of the UBS private bankers working in Switzerland had gone to the United States looking for clients, apparently in violation of strict UBS guidelines.

The United Bank of Switzerland had issued, in 2004, a policy statement that placed very explicit restrictions on the activities of their Swiss-based bankers if they traveled to the United States:

> UBS will not advertise and market for its services with material going beyond generic information relating to the image of UBS AG and its brand in the U.S.
>
> UBS AG may not establish relationships for securities products or services with new clients resident in the U.S. with the use of U.S. jurisdictional means.
>
> UBS should ensure that:
>
> - No marketing or advertising activity targeted to U.S. persons takes place in the U.S.
> - No solicitation of account opening takes place in the United States.
> - No cold calling or prospecting into the United States takes place.
> - No negotiation or conclusion of contracts takes place within the United States.
> - No carrying or transmitting of cash or other valuables out of the United States takes place.
> - No routine certification of signatures, transmission of completed account documentation, or related administrative activity on behalf of UBS AG takes place.
> - Employees do not carry on substantial activities at fixed locations while in the United States thereby establishing an office or maintaining a place of business. (*Tax Haven Banks and U.S. Tax Compliance,* Staff Report of the Permanent Subcommittee on Investigations of the U.S. Senate, released on July 17, 2008, p. 91)

Mr. Birkenfeld, the UBS banker from Switzerland who had been arrested while visiting a UBS client in Florida (one of those who had been identified through the unauthorized distribution of the Bank of Liechtenstein documents by a dissatisfied prior employee of that bank) subsequently agreed to become a U.S. government witness to avoid criminal prosecution. He explained at the hearing of the Senate Subcommittee that he had been unaware of these restrictions until a colleague showed him a copy of the 2004 policy statement. He added that the policies described in that statement "entirely contradicted" the activities in his formal job description.

Mr. Birkenfeld went on to say that essentially his job, while on assigned visits to the United States, was to find new clients and that the more new clients he found the better he was paid:

> You might go to sporting events. You might go to car shows, wine tastings. You might deal with real estate agents. You might deal with attorneys. It's really where the rich people hang out; go and talk to them. It wasn't difficult to walk into a party with a business card, and then someone asks you, "What do you do?" and you say, Well, I work for a bank in Switzerland and we manage money there and open accounts. And people immediately would recognize, "Oh, this is someone who could open new business by opening accounts." (*Tax Haven Banks and U.S. Tax Compliance,* Staff Report of the Permanent Subcommittee on Investigations of the U.S. Senate, released on July 17, 2008, p. 91)

Travel to the United States by UBS bankers based in Switzerland not only was allowed, it was encouraged. From 2003 to 2008, roughly twenty UBS bankers made more than 300 trips to the United States; many of these bankers designated the purpose of their trips on the U.S. Custom Service port-of-entry forms as leisure. There was some truth to those claims. They attended many of the major professional golf matches, tennis tournaments, and sailing regattas. Doubtless those were pleasant events, but the job performance of the visiting Swiss bankers was measured, and rewarded, by the "net new money" (NNM) raised from the contacts each of them established during each trip.

> One client could make your numbers, or 10 to 25 could make your numbers. It's very hard to gauge that. And again, when people aren't paying tax in the three areas I told you—inheritance, income and capital gains—it's quite easy for people to bring money to you. They're very interested to bring as much money to the bank as possible. (*Tax Haven Banks and U.S. Tax Compliance,* Staff Report of the Permanent Subcommittee on Investigations of the U.S. Senate, released on July 17, 2008, p. 91)

These accounts that were designed to "bring as much money to the bank as possible" to avoid paying U.S. taxes in the three basic areas of inheritance, income, and investment gains were actually opened during subsequent visits by the client and members of his or her family to Switzerland. This was done to maintain the primacy of Swiss law. During that visit, methods for transferring funds through a series of apparently foreign-owned companies, foundations, and trusts were arranged for each client, as were also means for reporting on the performance of those funds after they had been received and invested. All reporting was done verbally, during U.S. client visits to Switzerland or Swiss banker visits to the United States, to avoid leaving written records. Income from the undisclosed and hidden investments was returned, when verbally requested, to the client and members of his or her family through the same series of apparently foreign-owned companies, foundations, and trusts that had been set up for the original funds transfer.

During trips to the United States to make those verbal reports on performance or to receive verbal requests for payment, the Swiss-based private bankers used code names for the clients; encrypted information for the reports; prepaid cell phones for contacts; and frequent changes of hotels, restaurants, and rental cars for anonymity. In short, this was a deliberately secretive but professionally run operation. No one carried suitcases of cash about, although at one time Mr. Birkenfeld did bring a small fortune in diamonds to a client in the United States; he got them through the U.S. Customs hidden in a tube of toothpaste.

Had the disgruntled former employee of LTG Bank in Liechtenstein not widely distributed copies of the client account documents he took from that bank, and had some of those documents not concerned U.S. clients, and had Bradley Birkenfeld from UBS Bank in Switzerland not been found actually visiting one of those clients, all of the current information about undeclared accounts of U.S. taxpayers held by UBS Bank would have remained hidden and confidential. But all that did happen, and some of that information has been revealed. The question is what to do now. Specifically, should the names of the 52,000 U.S. taxpayers who are believed—though this has not yet been proven—to have opened similar undeclared accounts at UBS be released? In the U.S.

Subcommittee Hearings that were held March 4, 2009, a number of different opinions were expressed on this issue:

1. Senator Carl Levin (D–MI), Chairman of the Subcommittee, believed that UBS should be forced to reveal the names and holdings of the 52,000 U.S. citizens because they essentially pushed their tax obligations onto other U.S. citizens who did pay their taxes:

> Switzerland and the United States disagree on whether tax evasion should be a crime. That has been true for decades. But here, Swiss bankers aided and abetted violations of U.S. tax law by traveling to this country, with client code names, encrypted computers, counter surveillance training, and all the rest of it, to enable U.S. residents to hide assets and money in Swiss accounts. The bankers then returned to Switzerland and treated their conduct as blameless since Swiss law says tax evasion is no crime. UBS deliberately entered U.S. territory, actively sought U.S. clients, and secretly helped those U.S. clients defraud the IRS. Bank secrecy under those conditions is not a value to be protected; it is part and parcel of a conspiracy to commit a crime under U.S. law. (*Tax Havens and U.S. Tax Compliance,* U.S. Senate Subcommittee Hearing, March 4, 2009, transcript pages not numbered)

2. Senator Tom Coburn (R–OK), Ranking Minority Member of the Subcommittee, recommended that U.S. income taxes be simplified and reduced (perhaps even replaced, though he did not suggest this, by substituting value-added taxes similar to those now used in Europe):

> We have before us significant problems. There is no question there has been fraud. There is no question there have been violations of U.S. law. But, let us be clear; there is also no question that the root of many of these problems is our country's very complex Tax Code. We need to simplify it, make it fair, make it straightforward.
>
> This country has the world's largest economy as well as the world's largest equity market. We are leaders in commodity and debt markets, as well. But our lead has definitely been shrinking as countries with more favorable tax rates and more sensible regulatory regimes attract capital that used to flow to our shores . . . U.S. tax policy puts this country's economy at a competitive disadvantage. For example, the U.S. boasts the following dubious distinctions:
>
> - The 2nd highest corporate tax rate in the world at 40 percent, which includes the 35 percent federal rate plus the average state rate. By contrast, the average corporate rate in Asia is 29 percent, in Latin American 27 percent, and in Europe 24 percent
> - The 8th highest dividend tax rate in the OECD
> - The 3rd highest estate or inheritance tax rate in the OECD
> - One of the highest tax rates in the world on corporate capital gains
> - Tax rates on individual income, capital gains, dividends and estates that are scheduled to rise in 2011 when current tax cuts expire.
>
> With such albatrosses around our neck, it is no wonder that America's share of the global equities market capitalization has plummeted from one-half in 1997 to just one-third in 2007. (*Tax Havens and U.S. Tax Compliance,* U.S. Senate Subcommittee Hearing, March 4, 2009, transcript pages not numbered)

3. Mr. Mark Branson, Chief Financial Officer of the Global Wealth Management Division of UBS, based in Zurich, Switzerland, claimed that his bank had only inadvertently—through the unknown actions of a few rouge employees—broken U.S. law, had cooperated with the U.S. government to the extent possible under Swiss law, but now could—and would—go no further:

> Mr. Chairman, we deeply regret our breaches of U.S. law. I can honestly say that what took place in one small part of our business is not representative of the firm's culture or the values of the 78,000 UBS employees around the world. These employees, including over 25,000 here in the U.S. [primarily working in commercial banking through branch offices recently opened by UBS, or in brokerage operations through Paine Webber, a securities firm recently purchased by UBS; all of which had been kept separate from UBS wealth management division] have suffered as they have seen the reputation of their firm harmed. That is very painful to me, as is the fact that the bank's behavior has brought international criticism to the country of Switzerland.
>
> Before I conclude I would like to address the recent civil action filed by the IRS. That action asks a U.S. court to compel UBS to disclose the names and account information of thousands of U.S. clients who maintained cross-border accounts with UBS in Switzerland and did not provide the bank with a form W-9. Because Swiss law prohibits UBS from producing responsive information located in Switzerland, UBS has sought to work cooperatively with the IRS to identify information responsive to the summons that is located in the U.S. We undertook substantial efforts over many months to collect and produce such U.S. based information. This was information that we could not provide to the IRS without violating Swiss law, and this process is continuing. We took these steps in a good faith effort to cooperate with the summons. But we believe that UBS has now complied to the fullest extent possible without subjecting its employees to criminal prosecution in Switzerland. (*Tax Havens and U.S. Tax Compliance,* U.S. Senate Subcommittee Hearing, March 4, 2009, transcript pages not numbered)

Class Assignment

What do you think should be done about the non-payment of U.S. taxes by U.S. citizens who have transferred some, if not much, of their money to secret accounts held in tax havens abroad? If the process of transfer is complex enough, with multiple stages in numerous countries, then the movement of those funds can probably never be traced by the IRS, and if the funds are then invested in foreign securities, the resulting dividends, interest, and capital gains will probably never be identified by the IRS. There would appear to be only five alternatives, none of them totally satisfactory. Regardless of this lack of full satisfaction, which of the five do you think should be selected, *and why*? Doing nothing is already one of the options:

1. *Do nothing.* The basic problem here is a conflict between U.S. law and foreign law, and there is no legitimate way that the U.S. law can be made to dominate companies and institutions in foreign countries. Mark Branson, the Chief Financial Officer of the Global Wealth Management Division of the UBS Central Bank located in Zurich, Switzerland, essentially—and insolently—made exactly this point in his testimony before the Congressional Committee that is quoted at the end of the case. It seems clear from his concluding statement that he and other senior executives at UBS were determined not to provide any further information under any possible

inducement. The problem from the U.S. point of view is that it can be assumed that if no remedial action is taken now, the practice of concealing substantial assets abroad can be expected to spread from the very wealth to the moderately wealthy to all "worry about yourself, not about your society" U.S. citizens who want to avoid U.S. taxes. The damage to the fiscal system of the United States would grow to be immense.

2. *Take harsh action.* It would certainly be possible to prevent foreign companies that were suspected of arranging secret investment accounts for U.S. citizens from operating any division or subsidiary within the United States. In the instance of UBS, this would involve shutting down, or threatening to shut down, all commercial offices of UBS and all investment offices of Paine Webber, a wholly owned subsidiary. The problem here is that such an action would be based upon suspicion, not proof; would adversely affect the 25,000 U.S. citizens currently employed in those offices; and could have a spreading impact across the U.S. financial system as foreign banks and governments retaliated.
3. *Revise U.S. law.* It would also be possible to change the basic framework of the U.S. tax system from the current percentage assessments on personal incomes, family inheritances, and capital gains to the European percentage additions to the sale prices of all purchased goods and services. Those additions would be both charged and recorded at the time of the sale, and thus could not be avoided. All services would be included in this fee structure, along with all goods (except for the basic foods and medicines), so the amounts raised would increase, and given that all U.S. visitors would have to pay these value added fees along with all citizens, there would be a much broader base. The problems here would be that the value-added tax is generally considered to be regressive (the poor pay a greater percentage of their income than do the wealthy) and expensive luxury goods could easily be purchased abroad in jurisdictions (Jamaica, for example) that do not have either a sales or value-added tax.
4. *Offer lenient treatment.* The United Bank of Switzerland had agreed to pay the $780 million fine for conspiring to defraud the IRS by failing to report the annual incomes of secretive accounts held by some U.S. citizens—but only after clear evidence emerged that UBS employees had contacted those citizens within the United States, counter to both U.S. law and UBS policy. Armed with that evidence, the U.S. Attorney General quickly sued UBS to force that bank to reveal the names of all 52,000 U.S. citizens who allegedly held these accounts. That figure of 52,000 suspected total holders came from the computer records seized by the IRS when UBS employee Bradley Birkenfeld was arrested while in Florida and actually visiting one of few clearly identified secretive clients of UBS. That client in turn had been identified from the Bank of Lichtenstein documents that had earlier been leaked by a disgruntled prior employee. This entire sequence was extremely fortuitous from the U.S. point of view, but it did happen and did bring about the first break in the secrecy.

It was said that following the news of the lawsuit brought by the U.S. Attorney General against UBS there was immediate consternation, close to panic, among many of the U.S. holders of these accounts, who quickly called their tax attorneys and tax accountants, asking "What should I do?" The IRS, with unusual foresight, quickly proposed a leniency program for all U.S. citizens who voluntarily acknowledged their UBS holdings and agreed to quickly pay their back taxes and fines with interest added. Final figures have not been released, but it is rumored that about 12,000 U.S. taxpayers have stepped forward and made that acknowledgment. One proposal now is to extend that leniency to all U.S. taxpayers who hold secretive foreign accounts, regardless of the bank or country in which those accounts are held. The problem here is that it is not at all certain that such an offer of leniency would be effective if there were not a solid suspicion among those accounts holders that their names were already known or likely to be discovered.

5. *Provide informant rewards.* Lastly, it would be possible for the U.S. government to offer the reward of a percentage of all back taxes and fines that could recovered from a secretive account held by a U.S. citizen in a foreign tax haven bank, using reliable evidence about that account provided by an employee of that bank. This cash award to the whistle-blower could be very substantial and might be supplemented with an immediate offer of U.S. citizenship to prevent retaliation in his or her home country. The problem here is that such an action by the U.S. government, while legal within the United States, would be totally illegal abroad. Should the U.S. government break foreign laws?

Chapter 4

Moral Analysis and Ethical Duties

We are concerned in this book with moral problems: the decisions and actions faced by managers in which their firm's financial performance (measured by the revenues, costs, and profits generated by the firm) and the social performance (difficult to measure, but represented by the overall well-being and general satisfaction level of the population) are in conflict. These are the situations in which some individuals and groups to whom the organization has some form of obligation—employees, customers, suppliers, distributors, creditors, stockholders, local residents, national citizens, and global inhabitants—are going to be hurt or harmed in ways outside their own control, while others are going to be benefited or helped. These are also the situations in which some of those same individuals or groups are going to see their rights ignored or perhaps diminished, while others will see their rights recognized and even expanded. The question is how to find an equitable balance between financial performance and social performance when faced with these conditions, *and how to logically convince others to accept or approve that balance.*

One of the basic premises of this book is that this logical conviction of others is key for managers at all levels of an organization that has encountered such a moral problem. It is key for the future of their organizations, the future of their societies, and the future of their careers. Moral problems of this "important for all" nature are becoming far more prevalent, due to the highly competitive nature of the stressed global economy. Consequently, graduates of our business schools are going to have to know how to effectively deal with the moral problems caused by that competition and that stress. The process for effectively dealing with these problems under those conditions has been graphically portrayed in each of the previous chapters, and is repeated in Figure 4.1 one last time for emphasis.

Within the diagram, there are three evaluative methods proposed to select the most equitable mix of benefits distributed, harms allocated, rights recognized, and rights denied. We can't avoid all of those harms brought to other people, or all of those rights ignored for other people, but we can evaluate them and find what we believe to be an equitable balance and then attempt to convince others that it is indeed more equitable than the alternatives. These evaluative methods consist of economic outcomes, legal requirements, and ethical duties. All have an element of impartiality to counter the usual assumptions of self-interest in management. Before moving on to the ethical

FIGURE 4.1 Analytical Process for the Resolution of Moral Problems

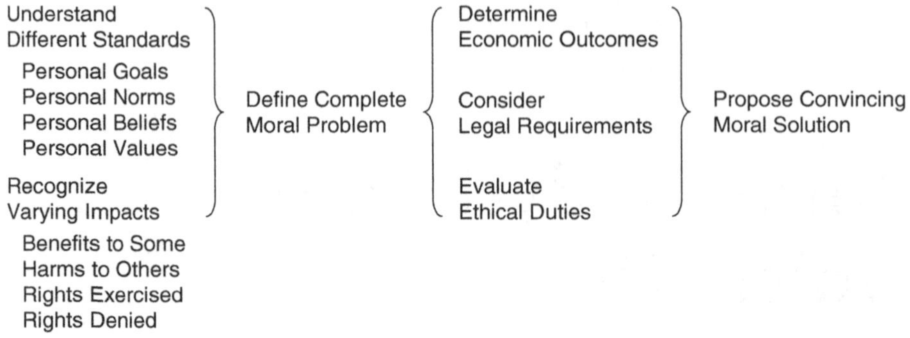

duties, which will be the subject of this chapter, let us briefly review the advantages and disadvantages of the first two, and the sources of their impartiality, to illustrate the need for the third:

1. *Economic outcomes,* based upon impartial market choices. The rule here is that managers should always use the least wanted and, therefore, the lowest cost resources owned by members of society to produce the most wanted and, therefore, the highest price products sought by members of society because this will automatically result in the greatest financial profits for the stockholders of the firm and the greatest material satisfactions for the members of society. But, there are both practical and theoretical problems with this approach; the most telling theoretical problem is that this "optimal benefits for all" outcome will occur only if (a) all input factor and output product markets are truly competitive, (b) all suppliers and all customers within those markets are fully informed, and (c) all external costs outside those markets are totally included. It certainly helps to know the economic outcomes that come from a given decision or action, but we need something more to ensure that competition, require that information, and compel that inclusion. That "something more" consists of the legal requirements of the law, based upon participative social and political processes.
2. *Legal requirements,* based upon participative social and political processes. The belief here is that managers should always obey the law, despite personal disagreements with some provisions of that law, because law can be said to represent the collective moral standards of the members of our society. Each member has a set of goals, norms, beliefs, and values that are primarily derived from his or her religious and cultural traditions and his or her economic and social situations. Combined, these goals, norms, beliefs, and values form his or her intuitive moral standards of behavior. These moral standards of citizens are aggregated into the legal requirements of society through social and political processes that move from informal groups to formal organizations to governmental institutions. Again, there are both practical and theoretical problems with this approach. The most critical practical problem is that it is difficult to write legal requirements with the precision and completeness that will cover all current and future moral problems that may come before a court. The most telling theoretical one is that most legal requirements do not combine the standards

derived from all cultural and religious traditions and all economic and social situations evenly; some are excluded. It certainly helps to know the legal requirements that apply to a given decision or action, but once again something more is needed. The "something more" in this instance are the ethical duties based upon universal principles.

Ethical duties based upon universal principles, and the application of those duties and principles in moral analysis, is the topic of this chapter. What are ethical duties? Let us be very clear here. They are duties *you* believe *you* owe to other people based upon *your* rational thought processes. No one can tell you what you ethically owe to others. You have to decide on your own. But, there are some universal principles that can help you to decide, and that you can then use to logically convince others to support your proposed solution to a given moral problem.

What are universal principles? They are rules for decisions or actions that are (1) not limited to any particular cultural or religious tradition or any specific economic or social situation, (2) are thought to lead to the overall well-being and general satisfaction of the full society, and (3) have an easily understood rationale why the application of that universal principle will lead to that beneficial result. Let me give an example. This universal principle is from Aristotle, a well-known Greek philosopher who lived 382 to 324 BC. The rule he proposed was that to ensure an overall benefit to society, a person should be open, honest, truthful, and proud of what he or she did. Why should this mix of personal characteristics ensure benefits to society? Aristotle's reasoning was that Greek society at this time was composed of groups of citizens who varied in their types of activities and that the cooperation and coordination of those groups was necessary to form a productive whole. If the members of each group knew what the members of other groups were doing, with no intentional evasion or concealment, then everyone could work together to achieve the benefits of unity. Why was pride important? This was the critical element of the rationale: If members of one group were proud of what they were doing or planned to do, they would be certain to inform others, probably even boast to others.

As an illustration of the use of this universal principle, let us go back once again to the first case in this book, the one where health care insurance companies were paying the health care consulting firms who were advising small companies and public organizations on the selection of the "best" health care policies for their employees. Those health care policies were complex and lengthy documents, and it was difficult for managers at the small companies and public organizations to tell which policy would provide the best coverage and care for any given group of employees with different health care needs When this practice of "pay to play" first became known, the executives at the health care insurance companies and the representatives of the health care consulting firms—both those who made the payments and those who received the payments—quickly made the standard proclamation: "We have done nothing wrong." But, according to Aristotle's universal principle of personal virtue they certainly had. If the payers and payees of those often substantial amounts were truly proud of what they were doing, they would been open, honest, and truthful about the practice, informing everyone they knew, and they would have been so proud that they would wanted to see this practice broadly reported in both local and national newspapers.

Aristotle's proposed principle was truly universal in that it could be applied to all and be understood by all. Those two elements—applicable to all and understandable by all—are fundamental to moral philosophy. They are the two basic points to remember as you begin the study of this often infuriating discipline.

Definition of Moral Philosophy

The universal principles that will be described in this chapter have been derived over the centuries from the study of moral philosophy. What is moral philosophy? General philosophy is the study of rational thought and conduct; that is, how people *descriptively do think* about issues that are important to them and to their society. Moral philosophy is the study of proper thought and conduct; that is, how people *normatively should think* about issues that are important to themselves and to our society. Moral philosophers have been looking at these issues of normative thought and conduct for more than 2,500 years, since the time of Protogoras who lived from 490 to 420 BC. They have attempted to establish a logical thought process, based upon an incontrovertible first principle, that would *absolutely* determine whether a given decision or action was right or wrong, just or unjust, fair or unfair.

They have not been successful in that there is no agreement on which of the proposed first principles is best, which one comes closest to *absolutely* determining the rightness or wrongness of a given decision or action. But, you will find that many of the proposed first principles from moral philosophy will help you to more clearly understand and more easily apply the earlier constructs of economic outcomes and legal requirements because they will help you to more accurately estimate the degree of rightness or wrongness of a given decision or action.

Let me provide an example here. One of the sales representatives of a health care consulting firm was reported to have received cash payments totaling $517,138 over a two-year period from one of the health care insurance companies. I think that was wrong because it was (1) not openly and proudly acknowledged and (2) not economically efficient in that it raised the costs of health care for the employees of the small companies and public organization who purchased those policies. You may or may not agree. But, let us say that the health care insurance company sent that consultant a case of quite elegant wine and a handwritten thank-you note at the end of the year instead of the cash payments. Was that right in a moral sense? In my view, maybe—if openly acknowledged. Again, you may agree or disagree.

The point that I am trying to make here is that all moral problems consist of situations in which there are benefits for some and harms for others, and in which there are rights recognized for some and denied for others. Hopefully, that idea is clear because that statement has been repeated numerous times in this book. But, *all moral solutions involve compromises on the nature and extent of those benefits and harms, and of those rights recognized and rights denied.* No one likes compromises. There should be a right, just, and fair way of doing things for all situations, but there just plain isn't. We have to make do with what we have: economic outcomes, legal requirements, and ethical duties.

Moral philosophy provides additional help in making those compromises through the universal principles that moral philosophers have developed over the centuries to define our ethical duties to each other, but that help is not as extensive or as exact as one might wish. Here, however, is a summary of those universal principles that, once again, *have to be applicable to all and understandable by all to be considered as "universal."* There are in my mind eight of these, one of which overlaps markedly with the previously discussed concept of legal requirements and another one may not overlap but certainly supports the earlier described idea of economic outcomes. All eight are explained below in the historical sequence of their development:

The Principle of Self-Interests (Protagoras, 490–420 BC, and Democritus, 460–370 BC)

The issue addressed by these early Greek philosophers was the question: "What constitutes a good life, what should a man (women were not considered important enough in Athenian society to be included in their political discussion which normally took place in a public forum) strive for?" Only fragments of their original writings remain, but these twin questions were clearly predominant. The most famous surviving quotation of Protagoras was "Man is the measure of all things." This referred to man, not men, and the usual interpretation is that the only measure that matters is the life of the individual, and the means by which that life can be made to be satisfying and fulfilling. The most famous surviving quotation of Democritus (though the accreditation and even accuracy of this statement has been questioned for years) is "Better a good life than a pleasant dinner," and the common interpretation here is that it is only the long-term goal of a good life, to be evaluated just prior to death, that matters.

Both writers agreed that the evaluative goals for that good life had to be a combination of comfortable conditions and cheerful companions and that such untroubled happiness could be achieved only by a moderation in personal lifestyles and an acceptance of public standards. Both were thought to be necessary in order to avoid irritating or provoking others. Justice was thus seen as a contract in which each citizen agreed not to harm other citizens, either by acting adversely to them or by creating envy among them, and it was proposed that all parties would accept this contract because it was in everyone's *long-term self interests* to live in a peaceful, orderly society with little probability of retribution and harm.

Here we find that 2,500 years ago two very early moral philosophers were discussing a universal principle that would tie good personal conduct to the goal of a stable, cooperative society, and they were using the *long-term* consequences of that conduct as the basis for this principle. Hopefully, it is now clearer what was meant by the earlier statement in this chapter that ethical principles have to be clearly applicable to all, and logically understandable by all. In my view, this ancient principle clearly would have been seen as applicable to every Athenian citizen attending one of the public forums within that city, and also understandable by everyone there. It can be expressed in modern terms as "Never take any decision or action that is not in the long-term, or *enlightened,* self-interests of yourself, and of the organization to which you belong, in order to avoid the possibility of future retribution and harm from others."

Principle of Personal Virtues (Socrates, 470–399 BC, Plato, 427–347 BC, and Aristotle, 384–322 BC)

The concept of moderated or enlightened self-interest was not acceptable to this remarkable series of Greek philosophers. The problem, Socrates noted early in his series of public discussions or forum teachings, was that a person could act with subterfuge or deceit and thus achieve a position of such wealth and power that he would have no fear of future retribution or harm. Socrates started the sequence of analysis to which all three moral philosophers contributed, and that ended with the principle that everyone should act in ways that conveyed a sense of honor, pride, and self-worth. We don't necessarily have to be kind and considerate to others, they concluded. We don't even have to be concerned about the reactions of others. We do, however, have to be honest, truthful, courageous, temperate, and high-minded in our own actions. Why? Because the goal of human existence is the active, rational pursuit of excellence, and excellence requires those personal virtues.

The "rational pursuit of excellence"—a goal also often termed "knowledge of the good"—is the basis of classic Greek philosophy. If you commit those two phrases firmly to your memory, all of the rest of the teachings of Socrates, Plato, and Aristotle will be crystal clear to you.

Two thousand four hundred years ago in Athens, these unusually perspicacious men began to address questions of ethical duties and moral justice and laid the foundation for the Western approach to both politics (rules for the conduct of society) and ethics (rules for the conduct of people). This sort of thinking about duties and justice, about politics and ethics, had never before been present in the ancient world. Why in Athens, and why at this time?

The reason was an unusual combination of prosperity and peace. Greece is a mountainous peninsula, with limited agricultural land suitable for growing grain, but the climate is warm and mild, ideal for olives, grapes, and livestock. There were easy "along the coast" sea routes to Egypt, then the granary of the Eastern Mediterranean. Egypt had surplus wheat and barley for export, but it needed olive oil and wine for home consumption. A very prosperous trade developed between the two regions. The defeat of the invading Persian army at Marathon in 490 BC brought a period of peace in Greece that lasted for 140 years, a time that came to be known as the "Golden Age" of Athens.

Conflicts among the nobles (the ex-warriors), the merchants (the ex-sailors), and the citizens (the current residents) brought about an interest in government within Athens. An interest in government brought about schools, first to teach rhetoric (how to talk to assembled groups of citizens) and then logic (how to convince members of those assembled groups). An interest in logic led back to the question, "What is the good life?"

Socrates addressed this question, "What is the good life," for both individuals and societies, which, at the time, meant advanced city-states such as Athens. Socrates wrote nothing, yet Plato recorded Socrates' discussions with other Athenians in the form of a set of dialogues soon after the death of the older man, and these can be assumed to be his thoughts if not his words.

The goal of Socrates was to develop the "first rule for a successful life." Successful then meant happy; it would probably now be translated as contented and prosperous. There could be no happiness in the pursuit of pleasure, Socrates continued, or in the ownership of property, unless you knew how to use each one of those well. Knowledge of the "good" was thus the goal of life. But knowledge of this good came from both the goodness/badness of the character and the wisdom/foolishness of the intellect. It was necessary to develop both so that everyone (nobles, merchants, and citizens alike) would recognize proposals that were good both for themselves (ethics) and for their society (politics). Ethics and politics were synonymous in Greek thinking; you could not have one without the other.

Plato succeeded Socrates as the major public thinker following the death of the older man in 399 BC. He focused more on politics, on the need to have a good society in order to have a good life. He wrote *The Republic,* in which he began discussing the concept of justice—what it was and how it could be achieved. Athens at the time, like the other city-states on the Greek peninsula, was divided into statesmen (the leaders of the citizens; they were men of thought), nobles (the warriors, who were men of courage), and merchants (the sailors, who were men of property). You needed all three for a good (again, contented and prosperous) society. "Justice" was defined as the harmonious union of all three groups of citizens, with each group excelling at what they did best, and with no one group interfering with the activities of any of the other groups.

Aristotle, the third in this remarkable sequence, focused on ethics, on the need to have good men in order to form a good society. The goal of a society, he wrote, had to be happiness for all of the citizens. But what is happiness? Not pleasure, wealth, or fame. People are reasoning animals, Aristotle wrote, and thus happiness has to be associated with reason. Given that the active use of reason leads to excellence, then happiness has to be the "pursuit of excellence" (again, remember this phrase; it is basic to the understanding of Aristotle's coming conclusion, and it is not a bad rule for modern life). Excellence, he continued, is focused in the character of a man and can be found on a number of different dimensions, such as openness, honesty, truthfulness, temperance (moderation), friendliness, courage, modesty, and pride. Consequently, if everyone would strive for excellence on those dimensions, then all of the elements in the diverse Athenian society—the statesmen, warriors, and merchants, each with very different goals, activities, and interests—would work together well for the benefit of all.

This ethical principle—that "we should be open, honest, truthful, moderate, and proud of what we do so that we work together well for the benefit of all"—has frequently been translated into modern terms: "Never take any decision or action that is not open, honest, and truthful, and that you would not feel proud (here the terms are very modern) to have reported on the front pages of national newspapers or the evening portions of a national news broadcasts."

The Principle of Religious Injunctions (early religious writers of numerous faiths)

The problem with the "be open, honest, truthful, and proud" rule, which clearly can be applied to all and is understandable by all, is that these personal virtues are not enough. There are lots of people who can be open, honest, truthful, and proud of decisions and actions that most of the rest of us would view as exploitive, mean, and self-centered. Something more was felt to be needed, and for many of the early religious writers that something more came from the inherent and established concepts of community (brotherhood and sisterhood) and service (kindness, compassion and help) that underlie almost all faiths.

It is always awkward to write of religious faiths, and of their injunctions to act with kindness and compassion in service to others, in a textbook because, obviously, faiths do differ, and unfortunately in the past and continuing into the present, those differences have been far more emphasized than the similarities. But, there are similarities. Let me give an example. Variations of the well-known "Do unto others as you would have others do unto you" Golden Rule of Christianity can be found in most of the other religions of the world, and many of these predate by a considerable extent the beginning of the Christian era:

> Buddhism (religious creed and ethical system of central and eastern Asia, founded about 460 BC). "Harm not others with that which pains yourself."
>
> Confucianism (ethical system added to the existing Chinese religious creed about 510 BC). "Loving kindness is the one maxim which ought to be acted upon throughout one's life."
>
> Hinduism (traditional religious creed and social system of the Indian subcontinent). "This is the sum of duty: do nothing to others which if done to you would cause you pain."
>
> Islam (religious creed of western and southeastern Asia, founded about AD 630). "Not one of you is a believer until you wish to everyone what you love for yourself."
>
> Judaism. "What is hurtful to yourself, do not do to others. That is the whole of the Torah, and the remainder is but commentary. Go and learn it."
>
> Taoism (religious creed and philosophic system of northern China, founded about 550 BC). "Regard your neighbor's gain as your gain, and regard your neighbor's loss as your loss."

The basic teachings of most religions stress a sense of community among all holders of a given faith, a belief in a common goal for that community, and a duty of kindness, compassion, and help to people, even to those outside the faith. The modern version of this ethical principle, once more applicable to all and understandable by all, can be expressed as "Never take any action that is not kind and compassionate toward others, and that does not forward a sense of true community, a belief that all of us should work jointly toward a common goal."

Principle of Government Requirements (Hobbes, 1588–1679, and Locke, 1632–1704)

Kindness, compassion, and a sense of everyone working jointly toward a common goal would be ideal if everyone would be kind, compassionate, and oriented toward the well-being of the full community, but everyone won't be. Hobbes, as was explained earlier in Chapter 3 and consequently will be summarized only briefly here, returned to the early "people truly are self-centered" assumptions of the pre-Socratic philosophers, before the "moderated" and "long-term" assumptions were added.

Hobbes proposed that people were essentially equal in strength of body and mind, and that this equality of ability lead to an equality of hope in the achievement of ends, and that in turn led to a constant struggle for gain, for safety, and for reputation. This constant struggle, he claimed, could easily become a war where "every man is enemy to every man," and the resulting chaos would probably result in a decline in science, trade and production with the final outcome: "the life of man: solitary, poor, nasty, brutish, and short."

To avoid that outcome, Hobbes proposed that men and women living in a state of nature, a free association of individuals before any corrupting political and economics institutions had been invented, would agree to surrender their most crucial right—the right to life—to a powerful central authority that would then guarantee the peace and enforce the law. Locke added the rights to liberty and property to make a trio of the rights considered most crucial.

Together these two writers developed the idea of the Social Contract. Here the question was what would free people—deciding among themselves to advance their individual self-interests but *ignorant of exactly what those self-interests really were* due to their early "state of nature" condition before any property had been divided or wealth had been created—choose as their most basic ethical principle, applicable to all and understandable by all. Hobbes and Locke both concluded that that basic ethical principle would be "obey the law to avoid chaos and loss." The modern version of this "obey the law" rule can be expressed as "Never take any action that violates the law because the law represents the agreed-up minimal moral standards of our full society, and those minimal moral standards must be observed by all to maintain the peace among all and advance the well-being of all."

The Principle of Utilitarian Benefits (Bentham, 1747–1832, and Mill, 1806–1873)

Bentham and Mill jointly made the argument that, clearly, obedience to the law was a basic requirement of a productive and pleasant society, but that specific laws could be either manipulated or misdirected for individual gain, particularly by the powerful central authority proposed by Hobbes and Locke. There had to be a means of evaluating which laws were good and consequently should be obeyed, and which were not and consequently should be replaced.

Bentham proposed that all individuals are governed by feelings of pleasure and pain, and they naturally act to increase the pleasure and decrease the pain. This net effect he termed "utility": that phrase is still in use, more than 200 years later, to refer to individual preferences in economic theory. Utility, he continued, could be defined as the benefit, advantage, or happiness of the party involved. That party could be an individual or, more frequently, a collection of individuals freely associating in an ongoing community, and then Bentham concluded that laws could be considered to be good, and therefore should be obeyed, and not replaced if they advanced the utility or the happiness of all of the persons freely associated within that full community.

Mill later formalized this concept. He started by saying that there had been little progress in the search for the true criteria that would separate right from wrong in human activities and that there had to be one fundamental principle to accomplish this; there could not be multiple competing principles. The fundamental principle he proposed was the creation of the greatest net good for the full society. This was later changed by an English clergyman to the familiar "greatest good for the greatest number," but Mill objected, saying the measure should be the net effect upon the full society, not upon a fortunate portion that society. The modern version of this ethical principle can be expressed as "Never take any action that does not result in greater net benefits than harms for the full society of which you are a part."

The Principle of Universal Duties (Kant, 1724–1804)

There are two basic problems with the principle of greater net benefits than harms for the full society as a gauge of what is right, just, and fair for that society. The first focuses on distribution. Every member of the community does not receive an absolutely equal share of the social benefits and social harms. Some may garner most of the benefits, while others may suffer almost all of the harms. The second problem concerns measurement. The benefits usually consist of desired goods and useful services; both—particularly in a market economy—can easily be expressed in financial equivalents. Harms, however, often involve the life and health of individuals or the usefulness and attractiveness of their surroundings; both are difficult to convert to a monetary scale.

Kant knew of these problems, but he did not refer to them in his writing. Kant was also focused on the search for an absolute principle that would logically separate right from wrong in all human activities (as had been Mill), but he wanted to base his reasoning on duties rather than outcomes. He started by proposing that nothing in this world could be considered to be an absolute good, except for a good will. This "good will" is usually translated as a person's positive intent, beneficial desire, or recognized duty to help others. Obviously, a person's true positive intent, beneficial desire, or recognized duty toward others cannot be directly observed because it is both internal and private.

How then can other people tell whether a particular individual's will is indeed good and reflects a true sense of obligations toward others? Kant proposed that a will could be considered to be good only if the individual involved was willing to have his or her intent made into a universal law: everyone in the same situation should then be free or even encouraged to act in exactly the same way. This was the first formulation of the universal duty, or Categorical Imperative.

The second formulation of the Categorical Imperative is derived from the first: Every person should always treat others as ends, worthy of dignity and respect, and never as means to his or her own ends. Kant maintained that this second formation had exactly the same meaning as the first, for clearly all individuals would be willing to have everyone else in the world act in exactly this categorically imperative way toward themselves, and treat them with dignity and respect. The modern version of this ethical principle then is "Never take any action that you would not be willing to see others, faced with the same or a closely similar situation, also be free or even encouraged to take, and never take any action that does not treat all others as ends, worthy of dignity and respect, and never as means to your own ends."

The Principle of Distributive Justice (Rawls, 1921–2002)

Many critics have noted that the problem with Kant's first formulation of the universal duty principle—which states that none of us should ever take any action that we would not be willing to see others free or even encouraged to take in roughly similar situations—is that it provides no means for the comparison or relative ranking of alternatives. In Kant's view, a decision or action was either morally right or morally wrong, with no possible gradations between those two extremes. The problem with his second formulation—which states that we should always treat other people as ends, worthy of dignity and respect, and never as means to our own ends—is that it is hard not to treat other people as means to our ends. Adam Smith explained in *The Wealth of Nations* (1776), while Kant was still active, that storekeepers were the means to procuring our dinners, customers were the means to earning our livelihoods, and workers were the means to staffing our factories. Almost exactly 200 years later, John Rawls thought we needed something more precise than a rule to treat everyone with dignity and respect, and he proposed an ethical principle that he believed to be both universal and applicable because it was based upon the difficult-to-deny benefits of economic efficiency.

Rawls believed that society was an association of free individuals, and that cooperation between those individuals was needed to generate social benefits in the form of marketable goods and services, but that these difficult-to-deny benefits were unjustly distributed because some people were excluded from the twin markets for output goods and services and for input material, capital, and labor. These unfortunate, left-out people owned no material or capital and had so few inherent abilities or educated skills that they were unable to find remunerative employment in the labor markets, and thus had only minimal wages to satisfy their needs in the product markets. Rawls believe that those distributive inequalities were not adequately addressed by the social and political processes that were an accepted portion of the complete economic theory.

Rawls suggested that under the conditions of the Social Contract, or—as he termed this same concept—the Veil of Ignorance (where people did not know what abilities, skills, or resources they might have, and thus their potential for earnings to satisfy their needs), they would make a single and simple agreement. This single and simple agreement would be that inequalities in the distribution of the material benefits of social cooperation would be permitted only as long as it was reasonable to assume that those inequalities would work out to the benefit of all. That is, it would be perfectly all right to pay scientists more than laborers because it would be reasonable to assume that the additional pay would attract more scientists who would invent better products that would make life more rewarding for everyone, including the laborers.

Rawls understood that it would be impossible to compute the impacts of all the inequalities in benefit distribution upon the life prospects of all of the people within society, and so he suggested that instead we could compute the impact upon the "least among us," those with the least education, the least income, and the least skills and abilities—and consequently the ones most likely to be excluded from the normal distribution methods, whether based upon market forces or social/political processes.

The rule he suggested was that that people who had been excluded from these normal distribution methods had to be benefited in some way, however slight, but should never, under any circumstances, be harmed. This ethical principle, clearly applicable to all and understandable by all, can then be expressed as "Never take any action that harms the least among us, those with least income, education, wealth, competence, influence, or power."

The Principle of Contributive Liberty (Nozick, 1938–2002)

Robert Nozick agreed with John Rawls that society was an association of free individuals and that cooperation between those individuals was needed to generate social benefits in the form of marketable goods and services, but he argued that this cooperation came about as the result of the free exchanges of those goods and services to satisfy individual desires and that any exchange that was voluntary had to be just and regarded as proper.

The example he proposed of these free exchanges involved Wilt Chamberlain, a famous basketball player of the era. You could, he explained, set up whatever original set of holding of property and money you believed to be just and proper among all members of society, but if those same people were willing to pay to see Wilt Chamberlain play basketball, then, at the end of a given period of time, those holdings would be different, and it would be hard to argue that these new holdings were unjust and improper because all of the exchanges had been voluntary. If all voluntary exchanges were regarded as just and proper, then Rawls' rule from distributive justice that income inequalities had to work out for the benefit of everyone, and particularly for the benefit of those who were least able to look after their own self-interests due to a lack of education, income, or position, was clearly wrong.

Nozick proposed the dual rules that no one should interfere with the voluntary exchanges of other persons, and further that no one should interfere with the self-development efforts of those other persons, so that everyone could arrange their own voluntary exchanges to their own best advantage. Liberty, the right to develop skills, was more important than justice, the right to receive benefits, according to Nozick, because self-development led to greater personal abilities and consequently to greater social benefits. The ethical principle he proposed, once more applicable to all and understandable by all, was "Never take any action that interferes with the rights of others to develop and improve their skills and abilities because this interference would deny the rights of all of us, not just the least among us, to pursue our own self-interests through our own voluntary exchanges."

Conclusions on the Principles of Normative Philosophy

There are eight major ethical systems of belief, as summarized in Figure 4.2. They do not outwardly conflict with each other. An action such as lying that is considered wrong in one ethical system will generally be considered wrong in all others, but these ethical systems cannot be reconciled into a single, logically consistent whole.

FIGURE 4.2 Summary of the Principles and Problems in the Major Ethical Systems

	Statement of the Principle	Problem with the Principle
Self-Interests	Never take any decision or action that is not in the long-term, enlightened self-interests of yourself and of the organization to which you belong, due to the probability of retaliation by those who feel harmed.	Some people will go ahead with short-term actions that do harm to others in the belief that they can achieve a position of such wealth and power that they can ignore the possibility of future retaliation.
Personal Virtues	Never take any decision or action that is not open, honest, and truthful, and one that you would feel proud to see widely reported on the front pages of national newspapers and in the evening broadcasts of national news programs.	Some people can be open, honest, and truthful and even feel pride in decisions and actions that most of rest of us would view as exploitive, self-centered, and mean.
Religious Injunctions	Never take any decision or action that is not kind and compassionate toward others, and that does not build a sense of community, of everyone working jointly towards common goal.	Kindness, compassion, and a sense of community, with everyone working toward a common goal, would be ideal if everyone shared those traits. Everyone doesn't. We need something stronger to regulate behavior.
Government Requirements	Never take any decision or action that violates the law because the law represents the minimal moral standards of the full society.	The social and political processes that formulate the law tend to be slow to respond to new problems, and often fail to include the views of all groups and organizations.
Utilitarian Benefits	Never take any decision or action that does not generate greater benefits than harms for the society of which you are a part.	It is difficult to measure many of the harms, which often involve issues of life and health, and the distribution of the benefits and harms may be skewed, with the benefits going to one group, and the harms to another.
Universal Duties	Never take any decision or action that you would not be willing to see others, faced with the same or a closely similar situation, be free and even encouraged to take.	The principle, while truly universal, provides no means of comparison or relative ranking of alternatives. To make a reasoned choice, we need that ranking

(continued)

(concluded)

	Statement of the Principle	Problem with the Principle
Distributive Justice	Moral standards are based upon the primacy of a single value, which is *justice.* Everyone should act to ensure a more equitable distribution of benefits, because this promotes individual self-respect, which is essential for social cooperation.	The primacy of the value of justice is dependent upon acceptance of the proposition that an equitable distribution of benefits ensures social cooperation.
Contributive Liberty	Moral standards are based upon the primacy of a single value, which is *liberty.* Everyone should act to ensure greater freedom of choice, because this promotes market exchange, which is essential for social productivity.	The primacy of the value of liberty is dependent upon acceptance of the proposition that a market system of exchange ensures social productivity.

Each ethical system of belief, and its associated universal principle that is applicable to everyone and understandable by everyone, expresses a portion of the truth. Each system has adherents and opponents. And each, it is important to admit, is incomplete or inadequate as a means of judging the absolute primacy of the different moral solutions that may be proposed to a specific moral problem.

What do we do then, when we first encounter such a specific moral problem? The argument of this book is that we first define the problem in the familiar-by-now terms of who has been benefited, who has been harmed, whose rights have been recognized, and whose rights have been ignored; get some agreement on that definition as reasonably inclusive and accurate; and then apply the three evaluative methods in sequence:

1. *Economic outcomes.* Which alternative under discussion offers the best economic outcomes, given the presence of fully competitive input resource and output product markets, fully informed resources suppliers and product customers, and fully included external costs?
2. *Legal requirements.* Given that some markets are not totally competitive, many suppliers and customers are not totally informed, and most external costs are not totally included, which alternative most fully complies with the law regarding those conditions?
3. *Ethical duties.* Given that the laws regarding the degree or extent of market competition, supplier/customer information, and cost inclusion may not be totally clear or totally current, which alternative under discussion most fully meets the eight universal principles?

All moral solutions are a compromise. But the compromise has to be understood by all and accepted by most. If the group of moral philosophers who have been cited in this chapter are right that society consists of individuals in a free association, each of whom must cooperate with others to contribute to the well-being of all, then it is the conclusion of this chapter that you should decide if it is your function as a manager to provide a moral solution that continues that association, ensures that cooperation, and provides that contribution.

Case 4-1

Delays on the Tarmac

Continental Airlines flight 2816 left Houston, Texas at 9:23 P.M. on a Friday evening bound for Minneapolis/St. Paul. Due to thunderstorms in that area, the plane was diverted to the Rochester, Minnesota, airport, 90 miles southeast of the original destination. It landed there at 12:28 A.M. Saturday, and was kept on the ground, 50 yards from the terminal building, for nearly six hours before the passengers were allowed to get off the plane and go inside the terminal at 6:30 that morning (*USA Today,* August 11, 2009, p. 3A).

The aircraft was a small jet with 50 seats. It was crowded with 49 passengers and two babies who had to be held because there were not enough seats. As might be expected, conditions rapidly deteriorated. The babies and younger children cried, the toilet overflowed, the air became stagnant and smelly, and the adults grew first concerned, then frustrated and finally outraged—all without result. One passenger, a professor at a law school in St. Paul, described his reaction: "You're numb throughout the experience, and you almost don't know what's happening to you" (Ibid., p. 3A).

A spokeswoman for Express Jet, which operated the airplane under contract for Continental, later explained that due to the very late arrival, the airport did not have enough people on duty to allow the passengers to deplane safely and get to the nearby building. The airport manager, however, disputed that. He said that the personnel at Rochester were experienced at handling diverted flights and that an adequate staff was present to readily transfer the passengers.

The spokeswoman for Express Jet also said that the passengers were encouraged to get off the plane and go into the airport as soon as government security personnel reported for duty at 6:00 A.M. But the airport manager also disputed that statement. He explained that the government security officials had actually arrived at 4:30 A.M., but that their arrival time was irrelevant. The passengers, he continued, could have been kept within the protected area of the terminal, where restrooms, vending machines, and comfortable seats were readily available, so that further security processing would not have been needed.

A spokeswoman for Continental Airlines, which had contracted for the Express Jet flight, later explained that her airline had a policy to let passengers off flights after a three-hour delay, and that what had happened was unacceptable. Continental, she continued, would offer all passengers a refund for their tickets and a certificate for future flights.

Delays on airport tarmacs, with the passengers confined to their planes, are not all that unusual. The *USA Today* news story that serves as the basis for this case claimed that over the nine-month period from October 2008 to June 2009, there had been 686 delays of three to four hours, 156 of four to six hours, and 13 of more than six hours—for a total of 855 delays.

The *New York Times,* in a follow up story dated August 14, 2009, explained that legislation requiring airlines to return passengers to the gate after a three-hour tarmac delay had been considered but not passed by Congress following a 1999 blizzard in Detroit that kept multiple planes on the ground, trapping passengers for seven hours. This article continued that the "no more than three-hour delay" legislation had been reintroduced in 2006 after snow and ice at Kennedy International Airport in New York left large numbers of planes stalled and passengers confined for up to 11 hours, and was now—in August 2009—being recommended for bi-partisan reconsideration by Senators Boxer (D–CA) and Snowe (R–ME). This newspaper article concluded by explaining that the Air Transport Association, which represents the major air carriers in Washington, DC, strongly opposed any hard and fast timeline for returning to the gate, saying it could have unintended consequences for the passengers, including more cancellations and further delays.

Class Assignment

Would you recommend a "hard and fast timeline" for the period that passengers could be held on board a delayed airplane? If your answer is "no," how would you make that argument as a witness for the defense in a court case where passengers who had been on Continental Flight 2816 were suing that airline? If your answer is "yes," what would be that timeline in hours, and how would you make that argument in a letter supporting the legislation proposed by Senators Boxer and Snowe. Then, think about the following issues:

1. Why, in your opinion, do the airlines and the Air Transport Association object so strongly to a time limit for passengers to be held on delayed airplanes? Why has this issue dragged on for 10 years, since the 1999 blizzard in Detroit that kept passengers on board for seven hours? Is not a compromise possible?
2. Why, again in your opinion, did the senior pilot of the Express Jet, which operated the Continental flight from Houston to Minneapolis/St.Paul, not get off the plane, go into the airport, and reach an agreement with the airport manager to get the passengers off the plane and into the airport?
3. Lastly, and this should be interesting, it can be assumed that most members of a college or university class have flown on airlines. What is the best experience that you ever encountered? What is the worst? What changes in either government regulations or airline policies would encourage more of the former and fewer of the latter?

Case 4-2

Warren Buffett and the Need for Integrity

Warren Buffett, as doubtless most of the readers of this case already know, is the most successful investment manager in history. His company, Berkshire Hathaway, has generated immense returns for his stockholders and for himself—though he follows a simple and frugal lifestyle. He is also well known for brief but insightful comments about important topics ranging from the global economy to human character, often made in a self-effacing "someone once said" format. This later trait won him the title "Oracle of Omaha." One of those insightful comments about people is cited here:

> Somebody once said that in looking for people to hire you look for integrity, intelligence and energy. And, if they don't have the first, the other two will kill you. (John Woods, *The Quotable Executive,* McGraw-Hill, 2000, p. 136)

Class Assignment

What does the term "integrity" mean to you? Write out a definition that, if you were called upon in class, you would be proud to read aloud. And, how should you demonstrate integrity, as a manager, at work?

Case 4-3

CALPERS and the Recovery of Capital

The California Public Employees Retirement System (CALPERS) manages retirement benefits for approximately 1.6 million public employees, retirees, and their families within that state. These beneficiaries include state officials and workers; district school administrators and teachers; and members of local agencies such as city and town governments, police and fire departments, etc. The pension fund managed by CALPERS, and used to pay benefits to the retirees at the date of this case was large, holding $181 billion as of June 30, 2009.

But, there was a problem. The fund had lost nearly $60 billion during the financial downturn that started in late 2007, and the $181 billion left was no longer large enough to pay contracted benefits to all current and future retirees. CALPERS had what is termed a "defined benefit system"; that is, the annual amounts due to each retiree and his or her family were based upon that person's years of service, age at retirement, and final level of compensation. Employees were free to choose their own time of retirement, and if those choices remained the same in the future as they had in the past—and there was no reason to assume those choices would change—then there simply was not enough money in the existing pension fund to continue to meet pension obligations over the long term. At some point in the future—and that "point" had been subject to numerous different projections from 10 to 15 years—the payments would have to either stop or be severely reduced.

The state of California was operating at a deficit, and could not possibly "bail out" the pension fund and make up the losses. School districts and local governments were cutting staff and reducing budgets and said that they, too, could not make the contributions needed to shore up the plan. Appeals could be made to the federal government, but it would be forced to treat all states equally, and while there could be disputes about what was meant by "equally" within this context, it was felt that there was little chance that Washington would respond in any meaningful way. Lastly, it had been suggested that CALPERS could attempt to arbitrarily delay the retirement of state, district, and local workers to age 70, but for many of those employees—members of police and fire departments, school teachers, and the like, who frequently wear down under the physical and emotional pressures of their jobs and want to move on to something less stressful and more enjoyable—that would be an exceedingly unpopular option and would probably be strongly resisted.

The *New York Times,* on July 24, 2007, reported that the senior investment officer at CALPERS had strongly recommended that the pension fund make up for past losses by placing much larger amounts of money in higher-risk investments to gain greater financial returns. His argument was that global companies had been beaten down by the recession and that the eventual recovery would substantially increase the value of the riskier stocks, bonds, mortgages, and other investments that could be purchased now for sale later, when the pension obligation shortfall occurred.

Class Assignment

Are there other alternatives available to CALPERS beyond extending the retirement age of state and local employees covered by the fund, or increasing the risk level of the stocks, bonds, mortgages, and other investments held by the fund? What action would you recommend to the members of the board of directors at CALPERS? And lastly, is Warren Buffett's statement about integrity at all relevant in this very unfortunate situation?

The following two cases are real, though the names have been disguised. They were related to me after they graduated by students who had been in one of my classes either at the University of Michigan or at Stanford University, where I held a visiting appointment for a year. In each instance, the prior student objected strongly within the first few weeks of employment to what appeared to be an ingrained corporate practice and was either forced to resign (Sarah Goodwin) or promptly fired (Susan Shapiro). In your opinion, should these two new employees have been less aggressive and more thoughtful? Were those two situations, again in your opinion, worth taking a risk with their careers?

Case 4-4

Sarah Goodwin and Spoiled Food Products

Sarah Goodwin, a disguised name, had an MBA from Stanford University. She had majored in marketing, was interested in retailing, and had been delighted to receive a job offer from a large and prestigious department store chain in northern California. The first year of employment at this chain was considered to be a training program, but formal instruction was very limited. Instead, after a quick tour of the facilities and a welcoming speech by the president, each of the new trainees was assigned to work as an assistant to a buyer in one of the departments. The intent was that the trainees would work with five or six buyers during the year, rotating assignments every two months, and would make themselves "useful" enough during those assignments so at least one buyer would ask to have that person join his or her department on a permanent basis.

Buyers are critical in the management of a department store. They select the goods to be offered, negotiate purchase terms, set retail prices, arrange displays, organize promotions, and are generally responsible for the operations of the departments within the store. Each buyer acts as a profit center, and sales figures and profit margins are reported monthly to the senior executives. In this particular chain, the sales and profits were calculated on a "per square foot of floor space occupied by the department" basis, and the buyers contended, generally on a friendly basis, to outperform each other so that their square footage would be expanded. The buyers received substantial commissions based upon monthly profits.

Sarah's first assignment was to work for the buyer of the gourmet food department. This was a small unit at the main store that sold packaged food items such as jams and jellies, crackers and cookies, cheese and spreads, candies, and the like, most of which were imported from Europe. The department also offered preserved foods, such as smoked fish and meats, and some expensive delicacies, such as caviar, truffles, and estate-bottled wines. Many of the items were packaged as gifts, in boxes or baskets with decorate wrapping and ties.

Sarah was originally disappointed to have been sent to such a small and specialized department, rather than to a larger one that dealt with more general fashion goods, but she soon found that this assignment was considered to be a "plum." The buyer, Maria Castellani, again a disguised name, was a well-known personality throughout the store; witty, competent, and sarcastic, she served as a sounding board, consultant, and friend to the other buyers. She would evaluate fashions, forecast trends, chastise managers ("managers" in a department store are the people associated with finance, personnel, accounting, or planning—not merchandising), and discuss retailing events and changes in an amusing, informative way. Everybody in the store seemed to find a reason to stop by the gourmet food department at least once during each day to chat with Maria. Sarah was naturally included in these conversations, and consequently she found that she was getting to know all of the other buyers and could ask one of them to request her as an assistant at the next rotation of the assignment.

For the first five weeks of her employment, Sarah was exceptionally happy, pleased with her career and her life. She was living in a house, on one of the cable car lines, with three other professionally employed women. She felt that she was performing well on her first job and was making sensible arrangements for her next assignment. Then, an event occurred that threatened to destroy all of her contentment:

> We had received a shipment of thin little wafers from England that had a crème filling flavored with fruit: strawberries and raspberries. They were very good. They were packaged in foil-covered boxes, but somehow some of them had become infested with insects.
>
> We did not think that all of the boxes were infested, because not all of the customers brought them back. But, some people did, and obviously we could not continue to sell them. We couldn't inspect the package, and keep the ones that were not infested, because there were too many—about $9,000 worth—and because we would have had to tear the foil to open each box. Maria said that the manufacturer would not give us a refund because the infestation doubtless occurred during shipment, or even during storage at our own warehouse.
>
> Maria told me to get rid of them. I thought that she meant for me to arrange to have them taken to the dump, but she said, "Absolutely not. Call [name of an executive] at [name of a convenience store chain in southern California]. They operate down in the ghetto, and can sell anything. We've got to get our money back."
>
> I protested, but Maria told me, "Look, there is nothing wrong with this. The people down in the ghetto have never had luxury food items of this nature. These wafers will be sold very cheaply, and for most of the people who buy them it will be an opportunity to try something really good. Only a few people will get an infested box. They won't be very happy, but down in the ghetto they expect that when they see a low price on

an expensive product. They make the choice. We don't." (Verbal statement of Sarah Goodwin, to the case writer)

Class Assignment

What would you do in this situation? You can either ship the wafers or not. If you decide to ship the wafers, then be prepared to explain your action to the three housemates who probably will have the same initial reaction that Sarah had. If you decide not to ship the wafers, then be prepared to explain your action firstly to Maria and—if not successful there—to a senior executive in the department store chain to whom you might appeal. Remember, your career may be at stake.

Case 4-5

Susan Shapiro and Workplace Safety

Susan Shapiro, once again a disguised name, had an undergraduate degree in Chemistry from Smith College, a master's degree in Chemical Engineering from the Massachusetts Institute of Technology, three years' service as a sergeant in the Israeli army, and an MBA from the University of Michigan. The following is a nearly verbatim account of her experiences during the first month of employment with a large chemical company in New York:

> We spent about three weeks in New York City, being told about the structure of the company and the uses of the products, and then they took us down to Baton Rouge to look at a chemical plant. You realize that most of the MBAs who go to work for a chemical company have very little knowledge of chemistry. There were 28 of us who started in the training program that year, and the others generally had undergraduate degrees in engineering or economics. I don't know what you learn by looking at a chemical plant, but they flew us down South, put us up at a Holiday Inn, and took us on a tour of their plant the next day.
>
> As part of the tour, we were taken into a drying shed that had a roof but no walls, where an intermediate chemical product was being washed with benzene and then dried. The cake was dumped in a rotating screen and sprayed with benzene, which was then partially recovered by a vacuum box under the screen. However, the vacuum box technology is out of date now, and never did work very well. Much of the solvent evaporated inside the shed, and the atmosphere was heavy with the fumes, despite the "open air" type of construction.
>
> Benzene is a known carcinogen; there is a direct, statistically valid correlation between benzene and leukemia and birth defects. The federal standard is 10 parts per million, and a lab director would get upset if you let the concentration get near 100 parts for more than a few minutes, but in the drying shed it was over 1,000. The air was humid with the vapor, and the eyes of the men who were working in the area were watering. I was glad to get out, and we were only in the drying shed about three minutes.
>
> I told the foreman who was showing us around—he was a big, burly man with probably 30 years' experience—that the conditions in the shed were dangerous to the health of the men working there, but he told me, "Lady, don't worry about it. That is a sign-on-job (a job to which newly hired employees are assigned until they build up their seniority so that they can transfer to more desirable work). We've all done it, and it hasn't hurt any of us."
>
> That night, back at the motel, I went up to the director of personnel who was in charge of the training program and told him about the situation. He was more willing to listen than the foreman, but he said essentially the same thing: "Susan, you can't change the

company in the first month. Wait awhile; understand the problems, but don't be a troublemaker right at the start."

The next morning everybody else flew back to New York City. I stayed in Baton Rouge and went to see the plant manager. I got to his office by 8:00, and explained to his secretary why I wanted to see him. He was already there, at work, and he came out to say that he was "up against it that morning" and had no time to meet with me. I said, "Fine, I'll wait."

I did wait, until after lunchtime. Then he came up to me and said he didn't want to keep tripping over me every time he went in and came out of his office, and if I would just go away for awhile, he would promise to see me between 4:30 and 5:00.

It was 5:15 when he invited me to "come in and explain what has you so hot and bothered." I told him. He said that he certainly knew what I was talking about, and that every year he put a capital request into the budget to fix the problem, but that it always came back rejected—"probably by some MBA staff type" were his words—because the project could not now show an adequate return on investment, and because the present process was technically "open air" and therefore, not contrary to OSHA regulations.

I started to explain that OSHA never seemed to know what it was doing—which is true, in my opinion—but he stopped me. He said he was leaving to pick up his family because his daughter was playing in a Little League baseball game at 6:30, and then they would have supper at McDonald's. He said I could go along, if I didn't mind sitting next to his five-year-old son, "who held the world's record for the number of consecutive times he has spilled his milk in a restaurant." He was a very decent man, working for a very indecent company.

I told him I would go back to New York, and see what I could do. He did wish me "good luck," but he also asked me not to get him personally involved because he thought that "insisting upon funding for a project that won't meet targeted rates of return is a surefire way to be shown the door marked exit in large black letters." "The senior people up there are going to tell you that it's legal," he continued, "and you know, unfortunately, they're going to be right." (Verbal statement of Susan Shapiro, a disguised name, to the case writer)

Class Assignment

What would you do in this situation? You can either continue the campaign to change the benzene drying process or not. If you decide to continue, prepare a presentation that you would make to the people that the Baton Rouge plant manager called "the senior executives up there who are going to tell you that it's legal, and, unfortunately, they're right." If you decide to stop, be prepared to explain that decision to a close friend who believes strongly in environmental protection and workplace safety. Remember, your career in the company may be at stake. Can you make an effective presentation without being fired, or being placed in jobs where it is assumed you will eventually quit?

Case 4-6

HydroQuebec and the Generation of Electric Power

HydroQuebec is a public utility owned by the province of Quebec that provides electric service to the people of Quebec. Much of that power is now generated by a huge hydroelectric generating station in the remote wilderness of northern Canada. The term "huge" has been used advisedly. HydroQuebec constructed a dam 17 miles long across the valley of the La Grande Riviere, where it flowed into James Bay, the southern extension of Hudson's Bay. This dam, together with 10 smaller ones further inland on contributory rivers, created a reservoir that stretches nearly to the Newfoundland border to the east in the form of numerous interconnected lakes and streams. The entire reservoir system covers nearly 1,200 square miles and was constructed in the largely uninhabited open tundra (covered with small brush and thick moss) region of northern Quebec.

The tundra region of northern Quebec is a large area, more than 64,000 square miles, with heavy snowfall in the winter and ample rainfall in the summer. The surface is composed of layers of slate, with only a thin soil covering, and thus the water does not penetrate into the ground. Instead, it flows off in rivulets and streams. The land mass has a constant slope toward the west, and the rivulets and streams channel into larger waterways that eventually combine into four major rivers that eventually empty into either James Bay or Hudson's Bay. Together, they form a very large body of mixed fresh and sea water that separates northern Quebec from the rest of northern Canada to the west, and that joins with the Atlantic Ocean through the Hudson Straits to the northeast, at the tip of Newfoundland. The main James Bay dam was constructed at the mouth of the southernmost of the four major rivers that drain the tundra region. The complete reservoir system that it controls is capable of storing massive amounts of water.

Those massive amounts of water are then directed into an equally massive hydroelectric generating station that produces 14,000 megawatts of electric power, equivalent to the total output of 14 modern coal-fired or nuclear-based generating plants—but of course without the acid emissions or radioactive residues that are associated with those energy sources. The entire project, consisting of the dam, generators, and transmission lines, was completed in 1985. Originally, half of the power that was generated was used in southern Quebec, where it aided in the industrialization of that region. The balance of the power was sold to the six New England states and New York City, where it eliminated any need for the utilities in that area to build additional generating capacity for the next 10 years. Profits from the sale of this power—given that HydroQuebec is owned by the province of Quebec, not by private stockholders—were then used to fund improvements in education, health care, and infrastructure throughout Quebec, in both the northern and southern sections of that province.

The northern and southern sections of Quebec are very different. The northern section is primarily inhabited by indigenous peoples, the Cree Indians and Intuit Eskimos, who crossed the Bering Straits from Siberia 4,000 to 5,000 years ago. The current residents still, in large part, follow the nomadic lifestyle of their early forbearers: hunting and fishing on the land and whaling on Hudson's Bay. This native population at the time that the James Bay project was completed was not large. It consisted of approximately 6,000 Cree and 4,000 Inuit, both spread through the region in small settlements or family outposts.

The southern section of Quebec has a much larger population and a much more advanced economy. The area is populated in large measure by descendents of the European immigrants, primarily French, who began settling along the St. Lawrence River in 1620. The original settlers were fur traders, an occupation that required both the courage to explore unknown areas and the endurance to paddle canoes throughout those areas. They voyaged throughout the Great Lakes, reaching even the western portions of Lake Superior, on both sides of what eventually became the border between the United States and Canada. Fur trading was an extremely profitable endeavor at the time because the furs, particularly beaver hides, were badly needed for warm clothing in northern Europe.

The "easy riches" reputation of the traders soon attracted flocks of other immigrants, many of whom settled into the more fixed occupations of farming and lumbering. The population of the southern section grew rapidly and is now somewhat more than 7 million. French remains the official language and predominant culture, which sets Quebec distinctly apart from the other predominately English-speaking areas. Most of the southern Quebec inhabitants now live in the major urban centers of Montreal and Quebec City and in the smaller cities and towns that stretch along the St. Lawrence River from the Bay of St. Lawrence to the source at Lake Ontario, the easternmost of the Great Lakes. The capital is at Quebec City, and much of the heavy manufacturing has remained in that area. Montreal has become a center for finance, education, and advanced technology firms.

Profits from the sale of the electric power generated by the James Bay project are divided between the northern and southern regions according to an agreement reached between the leaders of the Cree and Inuit peoples and representatives of the Quebec government in 1975, before construction began on the project. This agreement essentially promised a $550 million compensation payment to the indigenous peoples of the north for the use of their land, though they also continue to receive a percentage of the annual profits.

The original funding for the north was spent on improved housing, health care, and education, as well as some economic and business development. The results have been impressive. Improved health care has greatly reduced infant mortality and increased the life span from 50 years to 70 years. Helped by those trends, the population of the Cree has risen from 6,000 to 11,000. The availability of better housing has brought many of the previously dispersed families into small towns and villages, and new schools, clinics, and even recreational facilities have been constructed to serve the inhabitants. Many of the residents of those towns and villages, however, still engage in hunting, trapping, and fishing on land and whaling at sea. The only notable difference is that snowmobiles have replaced the dog sleds and outboards motors the kayak and canoe paddles.

Payments to the southern region have been spent on educational improvement, particularly at the college and graduate school levels; infrastructure development; and business expansion. The results here have also been impressive. Southern Quebec, particularly the urban area along the St. Lawrence River, has become one of the most prosperous regions in Canada, rivaling Toronto, Ontario, and Vancouver, British Columbia. Much of this improvement is credited not only to the money dispersed from the profits of HydroQuebec but also to the availability of inexpensive hydroelectric power produced by that company for both homes and businesses. Most of the homes within Quebec have switched to electrical heating rather than continuing to use fuel oil, an important savings due to the harsh, wintry conditions of the province.

Why does a huge hydroelectric project that was completed in 1985, that generates carbon-neutral energy, and that has resulted in substantial benefits for two very diverse groups of people, belong in a 2010 book on business ethics? It is because only the southernmost river flowing into James Bay has been developed, and there is potential for three somewhat smaller projects at each of the major northern rivers that flow in Hudson's Bay. These "somewhat smaller" projects would not be minute. Each would produce another 3,000 to 4,000 megawatts of carbon-free power and create reservoirs covering 600 to 800 square miles.

There is demand in southern Quebec for the construction of these three new projects. That demand has arisen because almost all of the 14,000-megawatt output from the original James Bay project is now distributed at low rates throughout the province of Quebec, and there is little left over for what had been the far more profitable sales of electrical power to the six New England states and New York City. Those sales, if they could be renewed, would provide the funds for continued investments in health care, education and—particularly—economic development in both the northern and southern regions of the province.

The problem is that a majority of the Cree and Inuit Indians who live in the northern region, a total now of about 18,000 people, object strongly to the proposed expansion plan. They claim that when they agreed to the original James Bay project, they did not know much the reservoir that now stretches from the major dam near the coast back nearly 300 miles inland, with numerous branches following each prior river and stream bed in a complex pattern, would damage their daily lives. The impounded water, they say, covers much of the prime hunting and trapping land and makes it difficult to reach other time-honored spots.

An even more important problem than the difficult access to hunting and fishing lands, members of the two tribes explain, has been the transformation of fishing within the region. The tundra vegetation of small shrubs and moss that had covered the land for centuries decays when submerged and releases methyl mercury into the water. The amounts are small, but the mercury is absorbed by the smaller fish, which are then eaten by the larger fish, which are then caught and consumed by the local people, and this process of concentration has created harmful health effects. This problem will go away over time—as the submerged vegetation fully decays and the contaminated water flows from the reservoir lakes and inlets to the generating station and then out to Hudson's Bay and finally out to the sea—but the provincial government has felt forced to issue an edict forbidding the consumption of fish caught within the affected areas of the north. This edict has truly angered residents of those affected areas because fishing is a favorite occupation and fish a favorite food.

Albert Diamond, a Cree businessman who is also a member of the Grand Council of the Cree Nation, has tried to explain the attitudes of fellow tribal members towards both the environment and the future in amicable terms:

> When you see a figure that says we are going to flood 1,000 square kilometers, that does not sound like much, but when you actually see it and what once was a river now looks like a sea, that really hits you.
>
> There are quite a few Cree who want to have jobs but we want to make sure that people who want to live the traditional way can do so. We want to be able to give them that choice. (Albert Diamond, speaking on video titled "Hydro Power in Northern Quebec," produced by Managerial Responsibility, Inc., Ann Arbor, MI)

The Chief of the Cree Nation has refused to negotiate with Quebec government officials on the proposed expansion of hydroelectric generating capacity, saying that he will not sell the land—even though it had never been formally deeded to his people by treaty in earlier days, so he may not have that choice. He stressed the heritage and traditions of the Cree in much blunter language:

> It is hard to explain to white people what we mean when we say our land is part of our life. We are like rocks and trees, beaver and caribou. We belong here. We will not leave. (Mathew Coon-Come, speaking on video titled "Hydro Power in Northern Quebec," produced by Managerial Responsibility, Inc., Ann Arbor, MI)

Class Assignment

How would you decide if faced with this issue? Millions of people will benefit if the three new projects are completed. Only the members of the Cree and Inuit tribes who want to continue to live a traditional life will be harmed. Certainly you could pay all of the tribal members, majority and minority alike, a high price for their land. But, currently, most say they do not want to sell. You could take their land by eminent domain, and that might legally be fairly easy because the two tribes do not have formal deeds to the property. However, after 4,000 to 5,000 years living in the region, it would be hard to argue that they do not have a valid claim. There is no equivalent land in Canada that is not currently occupied either by native peoples or by recent emigrants, so you cannot simply ask the objecting majority of the Cree and Inuit to either move further east into northern Newfoundland or further west into northern Ontario. Both moves would disrupt the lives of other people already there. And, the majority of the Cree and the Inuit say that they do not want money. They want to stay right where they are—living their lives exactly as their ancestors have done for hundreds, if not thousands, of years; on land they consider to belong solely if not legally to them; and without interference from the provincial government that wants to build hydroelectric dams and generating plants in an environment that they consider to be the basis of their tribal character, culture, and lifestyle.

Chapter 5

Why Should a Business Manager Be Moral?

We have looked at economic outcomes (Chapter 2), legal requirements (Chapter 3), and ethical duties (Chapter 4) as means of resolving the moral problems of management, and we have found that none are completely satisfactory. None of those analytical methods can give us an answer that we can say with absolute certainty provides an equitable, fair-to-all balance between the financial outputs and the social impacts of a business firm. And none of those analytical methods can give us a means of truly convincing all of the other people who have been affected by those outputs and impacts, either positively or negatively, that our decision was indeed the best one possible.

But why is this important? Why should managers attempt to be moral in their decisions and actions? And, particularly, why should managers attempt to convince other people that they have reached the best balance of economic outcomes, legal requirements, and ethical duties that was possible, given the available alternatives? Perhaps we should all simply resolve not to lie, cheat, or steal, and then begin to look after the interests of the firm that has hired us to do exactly that to the very best of our abilities. Then, we could forget about any need to be moral beyond those elementary "don't lie, cheat, or steal" rules, and particularly, we could forget about any need to convince others of the logical nature of our morality. A totally amoral person—one who did not stop to think about the rightness or justness or fairness of his or her decisions, but instead concentrated upon profits for his or her employer and benefits for his or her self—might be expected to be far more successful in purely financial terms for both of those entities over any reasonable period of time. Why should all of us not do exactly that?

The answer on one level is that if we want others to worry about whether their treatment of us is right and just and fair, then we have to worry about our treatment of them. Reciprocity is the most logical reason for morality. But, the world is filled with people who are not logical in the sense of recognizing reciprocity and the need to be consistent. The world is filled with people who might well say, "We'll take our chances on your treatment of us later on, after we try to get what we want now, and if we do indeed get what we want now, then we won't have to worry about your treatment of us later on." How do we react to those people? Do we simply cede to them the first place in financial benefits and managerial positions, and hope that eventually they will learn that "what goes around comes around"? That is not a very satisfactory solution for most of the rest of us, who under that rationale would be forced to wait and hope for an eventual breakthrough in the attitudes or powers of those individuals.

Beyond reciprocity, however, as the reason for our moral actions toward others is—or perhaps ought to be—our concern for the quality of our own lives. If we are concerned about the sort of profession we have entered, the sort of organization we have joined, the sort of society we are constructing, and the sort of person we are becoming, then we have to start thinking about our duties and responsibilities to others. What do we really owe to our professions? What do we really owe to our employers? What do we really owe to our society? And what do we really owe to ourselves? But perhaps most important of all, how do we really reach a balance among all of those duties and responsibilities?

These are questions that people have worried about for centuries. In 399 BC, Socrates was put on trial in Athens for having "corrupted the youth of the city." He argued in his defense that all he had done was to ask the young people who attended his public forums to consider the goals and standards of their lives. There was nothing wrong with such teaching, he claimed, and ended with the closing statement that "The unexamined life is not worth living" (Plato, "Apology" in *The Dialogues* [of Socrates], B. Jowett, trans. New York: Random House, 1987). You can certainly interpret that expression following your own understanding, but perhaps he is saying that everyone should examine their duties and obligations to their professions, their organizations, their communities, and themselves. If so, it is necessary to get down to the absolute basics.

The most basic question in ethics is, "Do you have an obligation to leave the world a little better than you found it, or can you simply take what you want now, and let other people worry about making up for any shortfall later on?" Many people do recognize a personal obligation to other people to some extent, but they have never thought strongly about its nature and terms and have never sorted out that general duty into their specific responsibilities to their professions, their organizations, their communities, and their selves. And, it has to be recognized that there are some other people who choose to ignore this injunction to "leave the world a little better than they found it." The question once again is, Do we cede to those people the first place in financial rewards and managerial positions, and only hope that eventually they will become concerned with the quality of their lives and the nature and terms of their obligations to others? Perhaps we need something more than reciprocity of treatment and quality of life as the reason to be moral.

Trust, Commitment, and Effort

Beyond reciprocity of treatment and quality of life, the third argument in favor of moral action by managers is that of building trust, commitment, and effort among all people associated with their firm. Business firms are composed of individuals, groups, and other organizations that not only are passively willing to, but positively want to, make an effort to succeed. In business firms we call those individuals, groups, and other organizations "stakeholders."

The term "stakeholder" was clearly composed to contrast with the more familiar "stockholder." A stockholder is a person who owns a portion of a company. A stakeholder is a person who is associated with a company and, in a famous phrase, "can affect or is affected by the achievement of the organization's objectives" (Freeman, *Strategic Management: A Stakeholder Approach.* Pitman, Boston 1984, p. 46). The stakeholders in a business firm include the factory and office workers, functional and technical managers, senior executives, scientists and engineers, suppliers, distributors, customers, creditors, owners, and local residents. All, clearly, have an interest, a "stake," in the future of the firm. All, equally clearly, must contribute their efforts through cooperation and innovation if that future is to be successful and secure.

But why should these various individuals and groups contribute their best efforts, and be cooperative and innovative, for an organization that appears not to care about them? You are a worker on an assembly line in a factory. I am the manager of that factory. I recently downsized some of your friends who also worked on that assembly line. I have gradually made changes that increased the speed of that assembly line. I continually argue that your hourly wages are too high and your health care benefits too expensive. In short, I am the prototype, perhaps not of the typical manager, but of the frequently alleged manager. But perhaps you are about to give me my come-uppance.

Let us say that you have an idea for a simple change in the design of the product that you are manufacturing that would greatly facilitate the assembly and reduce the cost. After all, you work on that assembly day after day and hour after hour. You know far more about possible improvements in the manufacturing processes for that particular product than I ever will. Do you tell me about your idea?

The argument of this chapter is that, under current conditions, you probably will not tell me about your idea to greatly increase efficiency and reduce cost in the factory I manage allegedly for the benefit of the stockholders. Why? It would be fairly easy to assume that you would not tell me because you would not trust me. You would think that I would take credit for the idea, ask for and receive a large bonus from the owners for having invented it, and fire a few more of your friends because your idea saved so much time and effort that they were no longer needed. I might even fire you so that I would not have to worry about your telling others that the idea for which I have received so much credit and reward was, in reality, your own.

What should I, as a company manager, do in order to get you, as a company employee, to tell me about your new idea? Perhaps I can do nothing now, but perhaps earlier I should have established an expectation that everyone within the company would be treated in ways that had a convincing element of fairness. Perhaps I should have been far more attentive to the rights and well-being of others. Perhaps, in short, I should have been more moral.

Maybe the basic answer to the "Why be moral?" question is the need for managers to build trust, commitment, and effort among all of the individuals, groups, and organizations associated with their organization. Maybe trust is the essential first step, and perhaps we can't get commitment and effort without that trust. And, maybe trust is built upon our making and explaining our decisions and actions in a way that most people—probably, as was explained in earlier chapters, we'll never be able to fully convince everyone—can agree to be an equitable and fair-to-all solution to a generally recognized problem. This the first basic argument of this chapter, that trust of this nature requires, as was shown in Figure 5.1, a recognition of moral responsibility, an application of moral reasoning, and a possession of moral character or courage. These three characteristics are critical:

1. *Moral responsibility* is the recognition of moral problems. Perhaps this is the most essential managerial function of all: Before we can start to think seriously about a moral problem, we first have to comprehend that people are actually being hurt or harmed, or are having their rights denied or ignored, by our company's decisions

FIGURE 5.1 Building Trust, Commitment and Effort within an Extended Organization

Corporate Management in Extended Organizations	Recognition of Moral Responsibility What is "duty"? Application of Moral Reasoning What is "right"? Possession of Moral Character What is "integrity"?	Trust Commitment Effort

and actions. Many managers don't want to know that this is happening. If they don't know, the reasoning goes, they can't be held responsible. Perhaps, however, the most basic responsibility that managers can be said to have is to know what is happening to the wide range of the individuals, groups, and organizations—the stakeholders—associated with their company.

2. *Moral reasoning* is the process of examining and then resolving these recognized moral problems in a way that will be convincing to others. We can't just say, "Well, this will certainly benefit us as a company so I know you'll understand," or "We feel badly that this is happening to you, but as a company we have to continue to move forward." As you doubtless realize from having studied the first four chapters of this book, the major theme contained in those chapters is that managers, when faced with a difficult problem in which some people will be harmed or have their rights ignored, have to *logically* explain their decisions and actions in response to that problem, and *rationally* combine the economic outcomes, legal requirements, and ethical duties of the situation into a logical, equitable, and fair-to-all solution. Otherwise, they cannot build the trust, commitment, and effort among all the individuals, groups, and organizations associated with the firm that will enable everyone to *jointly* move forward.
3. *Moral character* is the possession of the courage to first recognize a moral problem and then propose a moral solution. Many mangers are not willing to face up to moral problems. They are not willing to say, "This is what is happening to some of the individuals, groups and organizations associated with our firm. These are the alternatives we have. And, this is what I recommend and why I recommend it." Managers with moral character know that their proposed actions will not be popular in some parts of their firm. They may fear reprisals from those parts. That is why courage is a part of character, and why integrity—the willingness to act on principle rather than preference—is essential to building trust, commitment, and effort among all of the stakeholders in an extended organization.

Extended Organizations

What is an "extended organization"? The term is used in Figure 5.1 on the development of trust, commitment, and effort, and is included in the subsequent discussion of those characteristics. It is an advancement of the stakeholder concept. Companies have become not only much larger, but also more dependent upon a wider range of other firms and institutions, beyond the formal boundaries and hierarchical controls of their own company. Material and component suppliers, for example, are clearly outside the formal boundaries and direct controls of a producing firm, yet they obviously influence the quality and cost of that company's goods and services. Many suppliers now participate in the original design of those goods and services, almost on a partnership basis, and most suppliers now promise "just-in-time" shipping deliveries, where failure to perform could shut down the product lines of their customers. The wide range of these dependencies is shown in Figure 5.2.

FIGURE 5.2 Components of an Extended Business Organization, with Multiple Stakeholders

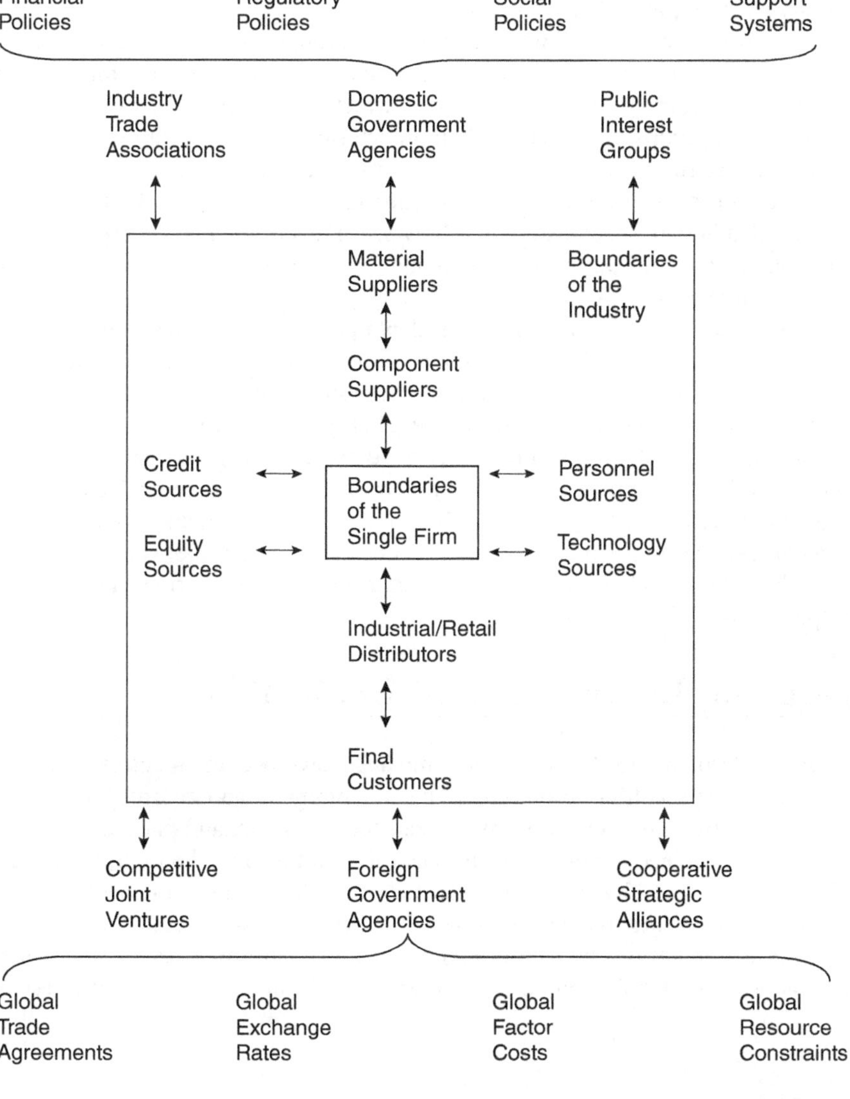

Wholesale and retail distributors, another example drawn from Figure 5.2, are also outside the formal boundaries and hierarchical controls of the central firm, yet here they can influence the price of the product, the level of service, and the degree of satisfaction received by the final customers. Many distributors are now relied upon not only for the prompt transmission of information about current sales trends, but also for the accurate anticipation of future customer needs. Both are obviously essential for the long-term success of the producing company.

Commercial banks, investment companies, research laboratories, and educational institutions are further examples of organizations that are outside the command and control hierarchy of a producing firm, yet they can influence the long-term success of that company. They provide personnel, technology, equity, and debt. Their cooperation is essential, given the changed conditions of corporate management. Companies that lack trained employees, modern methods, and adequate funds cannot possibly compete in our rapidly changing global environment.

Lastly, industry trade associations, public interest groups, and domestic and foreign political agencies are further examples of organizations that are outside the formal command and control hierarchy of the firm yet can affect the performance of companies. These associations, groups, and agencies help in determining (1) the national financial policies that set tax rules and interest rates; (2) the national regulatory policies that influence product/process designs and environmental requirements; (3) the national social policies that help to set educational achievement levels and health care costs; and (4) the national infrastructure systems, which include the communication networks and the transportation methods.

If you doubt that companies are now dependent upon the governmental policies and national systems just listed, think for a minute about the domestic automobile manufacturers who must meet mileage, safety, and emission standards in their cars, and provide educational training and health care benefits for their workers. It was recently claimed that health care benefits added $2,700 to the cost of each American car, a charge not included in the cost of automobiles produced in Europe or Japan, where the health care systems are financed by public, not private, revenues. Companies are starting to compete based upon their country's educational and health care systems, in addition to their own product designs, manufacturing costs, marketing methods, and quality reputations.

Cooperation, Innovation, and Unification

Let us say that you accept for now that companies have become much larger, more extended, and less susceptible to the hierarchical "command and control" of the formal management structure. What does that mean for managers, and particularly, what does that mean for the need to be moral, to recognize and resolve the mixtures of benefits and harms, and the balances of rights and wrongs, that occur in the decisions and actions of the firm? The argument of this chapter is that moral management is necessary to achieve the cooperation, innovation, and unification that are so essential for success in a competitive global economy. There are three basic steps in this progression

FIGURE 5.3 Relationship of Moral Management to Individual Attitudes, Organizational Behaviors and Competitive Success in a Rapidly Changing Global Economy

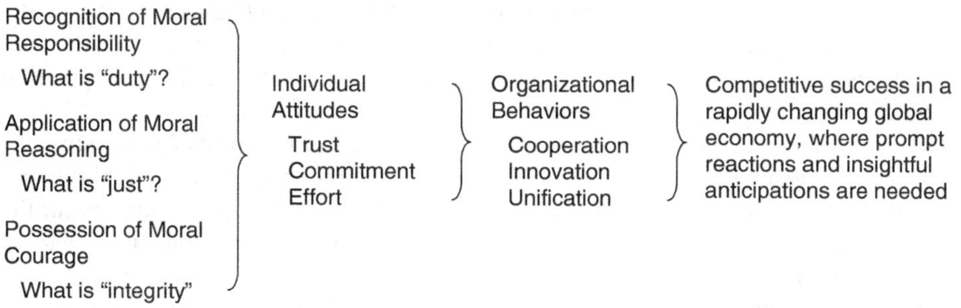

between moral management and competitive success. Each may be termed a "thesis" of this chapter. They are depicted in Figure 5.3, and described directly here:

1. *Moral management builds individual attitudes of trust, commitment and effort.* The first major thesis is the one that has been emphasized throughout this chapter: that treating individuals in the very diverse stakeholder groups in ways that those individuals can consider to be equitable and fair-to-all creates trust, that trust builds commitment, and that commitment ensures effort. Certainly there will be disagreements among those diverse groups of people—the stakeholders—on exactly what distribution of benefits and allocation of harms, and on precisely what recognition of rights and assignment of wrongs, can be considered to be equitable and fair to everyone in any given situation. Certainly some stakeholder groups will prefer one decision or action, while other stakeholder groups will prefer another. But the first thesis of this chapter is that as long as all of the groups together can agree that the decision process itself has been logically oriented toward an equitable balance—that is, that the decision process has considered the interests and rights of each of the groups according to known, consistent, and *communicated* principles—then there should be an increase in trust and commitment among all of the stakeholder groups, and that increase in trust and commitment should, in turn, lead to an increase in effort.
2. *Individual attitudes of trust, commitment, and effort lead to organizational behaviors of cooperation, innovation, and unification.* The second major thesis of this chapter is that the effort that results from stakeholder trust and commitment goes far beyond that which is based only upon financial incentives or commercial contracts. Stakeholder trust and commitment result in a willingness to contribute "something extra," a readiness to act with both energy and enthusiasm for the benefit of the firm. A story by Edward Carlson, then president of United Airlines, illustrates very succinctly this willingness to contribute something extra. Mr. Carlson is quoted as saying, "The president of a company has a constituency much like that of a politician. The employees may not actually go to the polls, but each one of them does elect to do his or her job in a better or worse fashion every day" (Peters and Waterman, *In Search of Excellence: Lessons from America's Best Run Companies*. New York, Harper & Row 1982, p. 289). Employees at all levels electing to their jobs in

better rather than worse fashion is exactly what is meant in this text by contributing something extra. That committed attitude among all of the stakeholders—not just the direct employees, but the essential suppliers, distributors, and customers; the needed credit, equity, personnel, and technology sources; and the influential industry associations, governmental agencies, and interest groups as well—leads to cooperation, innovation, and unification throughout the extended organization.

3. *Organizational cooperation, innovation and unification is essential for competitive success in a rapidly changing global economy.* The third major thesis of this chapter is that this committed attitude, this willingness to contribute something extra, this readiness to act with energy and enthusiasm for the benefit of the full organization on the part of all of the stakeholders is far more important now than in the past due to the changed conditions of global competition. Companies have become more aggressive. Technologies have become more advanced. Products have become more complex. Markets have become more diverse. Processes have become more oriented toward both quality and cost. Customers have become more insistent upon both value and choice. Changes in competitors, technologies, products, markets, processes, and customers have become more frequent. And, the thoughtfulness, speed, and cost of the firm's reactions to those changes—or, even better, in their anticipations of them—have become dependent upon the patterns of cooperation, innovation, and unification. Unification—the feeling that "we're all in this together"—has become critical to the success of the firm.

Unify and Guide

In summary, it is the argument of this chapter that it is no longer possible to manage organizations that must respond intelligently, quickly, and efficiently to technological, product, market, process, or customer changes on a "command and control" basis. Innovation is required, but corporate managers cannot command innovation. Cooperation is essential, but corporate managers cannot control cooperation. Something more is needed, and that something more is the "we're all in this together" feeling of unification.

Let us assume that you accept for now the proposal that this "we're all in this together" feeling of unification is essential for competitive success in our highly complex and rapidly changing global economy. Let us further assume that you also agree that the stakeholder groups—the people who are affected by and in turn can affect the performance of the organization—are now too diverse in their various activities for direct commands, and that they now extend too far beyond the hierarchical boundaries for effective controls. The question is, then, what takes the place of the outmoded "command and control" model? The answer of this chapter is "unify and guide."

This new method of management for extended organizations is dependent upon unification. Unification is the key. Unification means bringing all of the stakeholders of the firm—those within the company, those within the industry, and those within the society—together into an innovative and cooperative whole. Unification requires recognizing the impacts of company actions—both benefits and harms—upon the stakeholders of the firm, and then distributing the benefits and allocating the harms through a process that is acknowledged to be equitable and fair. Unification, or bringing everyone together into a cooperative and innovative whole, can be said to be the ultimate moral responsibility of management. But unification, the creation of this dominant sense that "we're all in this together," is not enough. The moral responsibilities of managers for unifying the stakeholders of an extended firm have to be combined with the practical responsibilities for guiding the actions of those stakeholders through the standard managerial methods of planning, investing, budgeting, measuring, and rewarding.

How can the moral responsibilities of management to create this culture of cooperation, innovation, and unification among the stakeholders be combined with the practical responsibilities of those same managers for the planning, investing, budgeting, measuring, and rewarding the actions of those stakeholders? This combination of attention to the stakeholders of the firm and of attention to the operations of the firm forms a managerial method that we call "unify and guide." It will be the topic of Chapter 6. It will also be introduced briefly here, at the end of this chapter, starting with Figure 5.4 that shows the components.

The first few steps in this process of combining the moral responsibilities of management with the practical responsibilities involves defining the organizational values, setting the corporate goals, and preparing a mission statement combining those values and goals in clearly understandable and truly believable terms.

The mission statement is the essential element. It should explain the reasons that a given company exists. If you accept that individual trust, commitment, and effort are essential to the success of the firm, because they lead to organizational cooperation, innovation, and unification, then the stated reasons for existence have to reflect the values and goals that are meaningful for each and relevant to all of the various stakeholder individuals, groups, and organizations. Otherwise, you won't get the essential "we're all in this together" outcome.

FIGURE 5.4 Proposed Means of Combining Moral Management and Practical Management to Unify and Guide a Business Organization Towards Competitive Success in a Rapidly Changing Global Economy

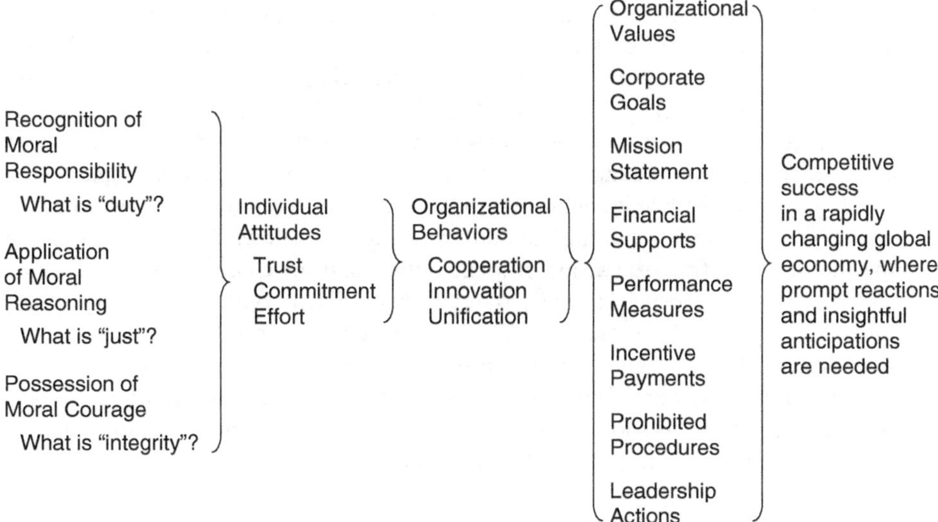

1. *Corporate values.* To avoid easy generalizations, think of corporate values as the duties the senior executives of the firm should—in your view—owe to the various individuals, groups, and organizations associated with that firm who can, in one way or another, affect the future performance and position of the company. These individuals, groups, and organizations would include owners of all types; employees at all levels; customers in all markets; the suppliers and distributors within the value chain; the sources of credit, equity, personnel, and technology within the industry; and the trade associations, government agencies, and interest groups within the society. What—again in your view—is important to each of these individuals, groups, and organizations? How—once more in your view—should the company attempt to reach a balance of economic outcomes, legal requirements, and ethical duties that may not be preferred but will be understood if not accepted by all of those stakeholders? In short, how can the company begin to think about unification based upon similarities rather than separation based upon differences?
2. *Organizational goals.* To avoid easy generalizations, once again think of company goals as the end points the senior executives of the firm should—in your view—set for the various dimensions of performance that are possible. What—again in your view—should the senior executives want to accomplish along such dimensions as financial performance, technological achievement, industry position, market share, customer satisfaction, manufacturing efficiency, employee loyalty, environmental protection, public reputation, and social contribution? What—once more in your view—should the various groups associated with the firm want to accomplish on each of these dimensions? Remember that scientists and engineers would doubtless like greater technological efforts, while the owners and creditors probably would prefer higher financial returns, but there is a clear connection between the two. In short, all of the individuals, groups and organizations associated with a firm may not be as dissimilar in their objectives as they at first appear, and it is possible to build upon the similarities that are all based upon the *long-term* competitive success of the firm.
3. *Mission statement.* Think of the mission statement as the means of combining the duties that the firm holds toward others with the goals that it has set for itself. What role, as a result of this combination, should the firm attempt to play within the market, the industry, the economy, and the society? It is frequently difficult to express managerial values and organizational goals in explicit numerical terms. Consequently, it is suggested that you compromise with a mission statement that speaks only generally about the duties you believe that the firm owes to others and the end points you want the firm to achieve *over time,* but much more specifically about the means you want to use and the standards you want to follow. The intent is to define the future of the firm, the scope of its activities, and the character of its operations so clearly that everyone will understand, "This is where we're going to go, this is what we're going to do, and this is how we're going to act." Think in terms of a document that will create a challenge for every individual, group, or organization associated with the firm. Think also in terms of a document you would be *proud* to hand to employees, to show to customers, to send to suppliers and distributors, and to distribute to all of the stakeholders associated with the firm.

One of the most insightful statements I have ever encountered about the responsibilities of management is that you need a business mission for the heart and a corporate strategy for the mind. I agree totally. Think about this in the context of the following cases:

Case 5-1

Procter & Gamble and the Focus on Stakeholders

Procter & Gamble is a very large consumer products company. It makes and markets laundry detergents, cleaning supplies, soaps and cosmetics, razors and blades, toothbrushes and toothpaste, infant diapers, paper towels, toilet paper, pet food, and a few snacks and beverages. Brands include Tide, Cascade, Dash, Cheer, Bounce, Mr. Clean, Swifter, Pantene, Olay, Head & Shoulders, Secret, Sure, Gillette, Pampers, Luvs, Always, Tampax, Charmin, Bounty, Iams, Pringles, and Folgers. The company is headquartered in Cincinnati, Ohio, and operates globally. Procter & Gamble, in short, is a very dominant consumer products firm.

Procter & Gamble is also a very profitable consumer products firm. For years it has recorded steady increases in revenues, profits, and stock prices. Revenues in 1995 were $12.17 per share; in 2008—despite the start of a very severe recession—they had grown to $27.53 per share. Annual profits in 1995 were $0.93 per share; in 2008 they had grown—again despite the severe recession—to $3.64 per share. Stock prices at the end of 1995 were at $19.95 per share; at the end of 2008 they were at $60.40 per share. No one could say that this did not constitute excellent financial performance. Procter & Gamble, however, does not focus on creating profits for *shareholders;* instead they concentrate on establishing relationships with *stakeholders.*

Stakeholders, as described in the text, are people who are associated in some way with the company, and—in the famous phrase—can affect or are affected by the achievement of the company's objectives. These people include factory and office workers, functional and technical managers, senior executives, scientists and engineers, suppliers, distributors, customers, creditors, owners, and local residents. All, clearly, have an interest, a "stake" in the future of the firm. And all, equally clearly, must contribute their best efforts for Procter & Gamble to continue to be so successful.

The chairman and CEO of Procter & Gamble, A. G. Lafley, believes that this broader focus on stakeholders rather than shareholders is needed because of the broader range of demands, requirements, and responsibilities that are encountered in a global economy. He spoke of this broader range in an interview with a reporter from the *Wall Street Journal* that was published in 2006, and is reproduced here:

> A. G. Lafley, Procter & Gamble's chief executive, doesn't talk much about shareholders. Instead, he talks about stakeholders.
>
> Who are those stakeholders? Well, add together the company's employees; the retailers and distributors and wholesalers the company sells to; its suppliers; the employees of those retailers, wholesalers, distributors and suppliers; the 2-1/2 billion people who

consume P&G products; the communities all these people live in; and—oh yes—the people who happen to own Procter & Gamble common stock, and pretty soon the real question becomes:

Who on earth isn't a Procter & Gamble stakeholder?

Mr. Lafley makes no apologies for this expansive definition of his responsibilities. And he isn't particularly bothered when I suggest that it makes the CEO job sound like a global political role. "I've concluded I'm in it [the global political role] anyway, and I might as well deal with it."

A conversation with Mr. Lafley is a lesson in how dramatically CEO's like Mr. Lafley think it [the global political role] has changed.

It's not that shareholders don't matter. In fact, shareholders are more demanding than ever. Mr. Lafley recalls that in the 1980s and early 1990s, his predecessors John Smale and Ed Artzt would meet with analysts and investors "only once a year in Cincinnati, give a formal, tightly prepared presentation, and then take very few questions." In contrast, Mr. Lafley has frequent contacts with investors and analysts.

But the outside demands don't stop with the investors. Consumers, he says, are also more demanding. "We used to think we were just taking care of the consumer buying Tide," he says. But "this consumer is also a citizen, is also a member of the community." He or she may care about how P&G treats the animals it uses in tests, for instance, or the company's policies regarding global warming . . .

The problem with all this, as some critics see it, is that it distracts the CEO from his main job. "The shareholders hired the guy to be CEO and not Procter & Gamble's representative to the world," gripes Steven Milloy.

Mr. Milloy helps run a new group called the Free Enterprise Action Fund, a modest-sized mutual fund whose mission is to force CEOs to get back to basics and stop bowing to the agendas of activist groups.

On Friday, Mr. Milloy plans to be at the annual meeting of Goldman Sachs Group Inc., to complain about CEO Hank Paulson's conflict of interest in chairing the board of the Nature Conservancy, an environmental activist group. A few weeks later, he'll be on hand for General Electric Co.'s annual meeting, pushing a shareholder resolution that calls on the conglomerate to show the science behind its decision to embrace anti-global-warming measures.

"The role of these companies is to increase society's wealth by generating shareholder wealth," he [Mr. Milloy] says.

Mr. Lafley agrees that P&G's first job is to make money. Under his leadership, the company has done a good job of that. "If we aren't successful," he says, "we don't have a right to do the other stuff."

He says his definition of his job has evolved over time. "I came into this job in June of 2000, and my head was down for at least a year, year and a half, because the company was not performing well," he says. "Then when my head came up, all hell was breaking loose. We had Enron, WorldCom, Adelphia, Tyco."

That led him into a much broader "dialogue among stakeholders," he says. As he sees it, this is not an exercise of choice; it's a requirement of the job.

"Like it or not, we are in a global economy and a global political world," he says . . . "The responsibility is huge." (*Wall Street Journal,* March 29, 2006, p. A2)[1]

Class Assignment

Where do you stand on the question of the proper focus of a business firm: stakeholders or shareholders? Should the senior executives of a large and prosperous consumer products firm be concerned about the rights and well-being of the wide range of the individuals, groups, and organizations associated in some way with the operations of the company, or should they worry far more about increasing value and generating profits for the owners of the firm? You can obviously pick either side of the argument, but what reasons would you give to convincingly support your stand?

Let us set up a non-classroom stage for this debate. Assume that it is about three years in the future and that you have worked for a given company for about two years, ever since you graduated from your college or MBA program. Assume that you are returning from a business meeting in San Francisco; assume you find when you get to the airport that the plane is very full in the regular or tourist section, though a few seats remain in first class; and lastly assume that the clerk at the check-in counter notes that you are well dressed and very presentable in appearance—you came to the airport directly from your business meeting—and he or she says that they are going to move you into the first class cabin at no additional charge. This actually does happen upon occasion; you are pleased—as are most other travelers—and do not object. When you get onto the plane, and find your assigned place, you recognize the individual who will be sitting next to you on the trip back to your home city. He or she is a senior vice president of your own company, leading the division for which you work. You introduce yourself, explain how you happen to be occupying a first class seat, and then open a book or magazine and start to read—or, even better, open your computer and start to work—as an indication that you are not going to disturb your seat row companion during the flight.

About 30 minutes into the flight, after coffee has been served and the seat belt sign turned off, your companion hands you his or her copy of the *Wall Street Journal,* points to the article quoted extensively in this case, and says, "Read it and tell me what you think." You read it at breakfast, at the hotel, that morning, so you are generally familiar with the content, but you go over it once again to make certain you understand that content. Now you have to respond to the senior vice president. You can't just agree with that person, you can't just be a "yes man" (or "yes woman") because you don't know what he or she thinks. You've got to give your own opinion, but clearly that opinion has got to be thoughtful; you are going to have to offer a rationale that supports your opinion.

A major theme of this text is that it is necessary for managers at all levels to be able to support their opinions, to be able to logically convince others of what they believe to be "right" in any given context. It is suggested that you structure your response to the senior vice president by saying, "I like (or dislike) what Mr. Lafley has to say, and here are the three (or four or five) reasons I agree (or disagree) with him." Clearly you are going to be evaluated by the senior vice president of your division. If you want to try for a home run, or chance the risk of a strike-out, you could add "I think that it would work (or not work) in our company because . . ."

It is suggested *strongly* that you write out an outline of your response for this make-believe exercise before your class. You will find that opportunities to be favorably noticed by senior executives come along very seldom during your career; practice here so that you will be ready when—and if—this happens to you in real life.

Case 5-2

Johnson & Johnson and the Worldwide Recall of Tylenol

Johnson & Johnson is a long-established manufacturer of health care products and pharmaceutical drugs. The company is best known by consumers for products such Band-Aids and Tylenol tablets, but it is better known by physicians for minimally invasive surgical instruments and highly sophisticated diagnostic systems. It is a firm that has grown consistently over time, with a stock price that went from $12.00 per share in 1989 to—adjusted for stock splits—$124 per share in 2009.

The company has a very unusual Mission Statement, or affirmation of the purpose of the firm, which focuses on corporate duties rather than financial profits. This statement has been widely distributed among active employees, and is *not* considered to be "window dressing," or a hypocritical desire to appear socially concerned while everyone really focuses on the "bottom line." This was proven a number of years ago when a person in Chicago, for reasons that have never been discovered, put tablets containing arsenic in unsold bottles of Tylenol on store shelves through that city and the suburbs. Six people died. It could not quickly be proven that this had occurred purposely at the retail stores in Chicago and not accidentally at the manufacturing plant in New Jersey. Consequently, Johnson & Johnson removed, in a matter of days, every package of Tylenol from every store in America and abroad, at a cost of more than $100 million, to protect its customers. Those packages were later replaced, free of charge to all retailers and to any customers who had returned unused portions of purchased packages, with new drugs in "tamper-proof" containers. The senior executives at the time explained that this prompt and complete response was required by the Credo or Mission of the firm:

> We believe that our first responsibility is for the doctors, nurses, and patients, to mothers and all others who use our products and services.
>
> - In meeting their needs everything we do must be of high quality.
> - We must constantly strive to reduce our costs in order to maintain reasonable prices.
> - Customer orders must be serviced promptly and accurately.
> - Our suppliers and distributors must have an opportunity to make a fair profit.
>
> We are responsible to our employees, the men and women who work with us throughout the world.
>
> - Everyone must be considered as an individual. We must respect their dignity and recognize their worth.
> - They must have a sense of security in their jobs. Compensation must be fair and adequate and working conditions clean, orderly and safe.

- Employees must feel free to make suggestions and complaints.
- There must be equal treatment for employment, development and advancement for those qualified.
- We must provide competent management and their actions must be just and ethical.

We are responsible to the communities in which we live and work, and to the world community as well.

- We must be good citizens—support good works and charities and bear our fair share of taxes.
- We must encourage civic improvements and better health and education.
- We must maintain in good order the property we are privileged to use, protecting the environment and natural resources.

Our final responsibility is to our stockholders. Business must make a sound profit.

- We must experiment with new ideas. Research must be carried on, innovative programs developed, and mistakes paid for.
- New equipment must be purchased, new facilities provided, and new products launched.
- Reserves must be created to provide for adverse times.
- When we operate according to these principles, the stockholders should realize a fair return.

Class Assignment

The prompt and complete action by Johnson & Johnson was exceedingly well received by consumer advocates and physician groups within the United States, but there was considerable grumbling among financial analysts and fund managers. The general feeling among most of the professionals on Wall Street was that $100 million was too large an amount to spend for all stores in all parts of the world. "They should have just taken the product off the shelves in Chicago where the deaths actually occurred, at maybe a cost of $1 million" was a common comment.

1. What is your opinion on the recall? Should Johnson & Johnson have taken Tylenol off the shelves just in the Chicago area, and waited to see if that solved the problem, or were they correct in removing the product from all stores everywhere in the world? Be ready to convincingly support your position.
2. What is your opinion of the Credo or Mission of Johnson & Johnson? Would you like to work for a company that apparently takes its duties to customers, employees, suppliers, distributors, local communities, and the world population seriously? Why don't other companies operate on the same list of priorities, with stockholders at the bottom?

Case 5-3

Nucor Corporation and the Treatment of Employees

Nucor Corporation is a new and different type of steel company. Traditional steel companies smelt iron ore, coal, and limestone in blast furnaces to produce cast iron, which is then refined while still in molten form through the use of Bessemer converters to generate steel ingots, which in turn are rolled into steel sheets, plates, bars, and beams for eventual sale to industrial customers. Nucor avoids the blast furnace and Bessemer converter processes; instead, this company melts scrap steel in electric arc furnaces and then directly rolls the output into the needed sheets, plates, bars, and beams. It is a business model that is termed "mini-mill" because the plants are much smaller, with far lower capital investments, and are dispersed throughout the country, with far lower transportation costs for the incoming raw materials and the outgoing finished products. It is also a business model that has been exceedingly successful in the globally competitive steel business.

Steel was one of the first of the basic industries to become competitive on a global scale. The raw materials—ore, coal, and limestone—are easily available. The needed technologies—blast furnaces and Bessemer converters—are widely known. The output products—sheets, plates, bars, and beams—are readily shipped. Originally, most developing countries lacked the capital to build the expensive plants, but given that their labor costs and environment restrictions were far lower, the needed capital was soon provided by foreign investors. The resulting competition drove many of the traditional American and European steel producers into retrenchment, bankruptcy, or both. Nucor Corporation, however, seems untroubled:

> Nucor continues to rocket ahead, with earnings records being easily set in the first and second quarters of 2006. What's more, current healthy backlogs suggest the recent double-digit percentage growth in steel sales and the moderate increases in the range of steel products from welded joists to cold finished bars [both high value-added products] will continue during the 3rd and 4th quarters. Assuming that energy and steel scrap costs remain fairly stable, this quality steel and steel products giant should enjoy a third consecutive year of eye-catching earnings growth. (*Value Line Investment Survey,* September 22, 2006, p. 581)

Financial analysts cited the simpler production processes, the smaller investments needs and the lower transportation costs (due to the dispersed plant locations) as the reasons for Nucor's continued success, but there was something else. That "something else" was discussed in an article recently published in *BusinessWeek:*

> It was about 2:00 P.M. on March 9 when three Nucor Corp. electricians [at different company mills, across the country] got the call from their colleagues at the Hickman (Ark.) plant. It was bad news: Hickman's electric grid had failed. For a mini-mill steelmaker like Nucor, which melts scrap steel in an electric arc furnace to make new steel, there's little that could be worse. The trio immediately dropped what they were doing and headed [for Hickman]. Malcolm McDonald, an electrician from the Decatur (Ala) mill, was in Indiana visiting another facility. He drove down, arriving at 9 o'clock that night. Les Hart and Bryson Trumble, from Nucor's facility in Hertford County, N.C., boarded a plane that landed in Memphis at 11 P.M. Then they drove two hours to the troubled plant.
>
> No supervisor had asked them to make the trip, and no one had to. They went on their own. Camping out in the electrical substation with the Hickman staff, the team worked 20-hour shifts to get the plant up and running again in three days instead of the anticipated full week. There wasn't any direct financial incentive for them to blow their weekends, no extra money in the next paycheck, but for the company their

> contribution was huge. Hickman went on to post a first quarter record for tons of steel shipped.
>
> What's more amazing about this story is that at Nucor it's not considered particularly remarkable. "It could have easily been a Hickman operator going to help the Crawfordsville (Ind.) mill," says Executive Vice President John J. Ferriola, who oversees the Hickman plant and seven others. "It happens daily."
>
> In an industry as Rust Belt as they come, Nucor has nurtured one of the most dynamic and engaged workforces around. The 11,300 nonunion employees at the Charlotte (N.C.) company don't see themselves as worker bees waiting for instructions from above. Nucor's flattened hierarchy and emphasis on pushing power to the front line lead its employees to adopt the mindset of owner-operators. It's a profitable formula: Nucor's 387 percent return to shareholders over the past five years handily beats almost all other companies in the Standard & Poor's 500 stock index, including New Economy icons Amazon.com, Starbucks and eBay. And the company has become more profitable as it has grown. Margins, which were 7 percent in 2000, reached 10 percent last year. (*BusinessWeek,* May 1, 2006, p. 56f)[2]

Nucor employees are known widely for their close-knit attitudes and cooperative behaviors. These come partially from the company's underdog identity at its beginning—the firm was derided then as an underfunded and unstable start-up by executives at the industry giants that since have failed—but primarily from an insistence by Kenneth Iverson, the founder, that people will make exceptional efforts if you reward them richly, treat them with respect, and give them real power.

There is no question but that employees at Nucor can be rewarded richly. The pay rate for a front-line worker at that company is just $10.00 per hour, less than half the rate of experienced steel makers at other companies, but there is a bonus, paid weekly, that is tied to the production of defect-free steel by an employee's entire shift. That bonus can triple the typical take-home checks. And, there is an annual distribution based upon reported profit. Combined, these policies on basic pay, weekly bonus, and annual distribution result in production workers who frequently earn somewhat more than $100,000 per year.

But, there are penalties that go with the rewards. If a given shift makes a bad batch of steel that is shipped to a customer and results in problems for and complaints from that customer, then the pay of all members of the shift is docked three times what the bonus would have been. Shift managers and department managers at each mill are also compensated on this reward-penalty policy. Their basic pay rates are about 75 percent of the industry average for their positions, but they receive annual distributions based upon the return on assets of their shift or their plant. In a good year, that annual distribution can equal their basic pay for the full year. The payment policy based upon shift or mill results is said to ensure a team approach to problems:

> This high stakes teamwork can be the hardest thing for a newly acquired plant [Nucor now buys many failed steel plants from large steel companies] to get used to. David Hutchings, a shift supervisor or "lead man" in the rolling mill at Nucor's first big acquisition, its Auburn (N.Y.) plant, describes the old way of thinking. The job of a rolling mill is to thin out the steel made in the hot mill furnace, preparing it to be cut into sheets.

[2] Reprinted from May 1st, 2006 issue of Bloomberg BusinessWeek by special permission, copyright © 2006 by Bloomberg L.P.

> In the days before the Nucor acquisition, if the cutting backed up, Hutchins would just take a break. "We'd sit back, have a cup of coffee, and complain: 'Those guys stink.'" he says. "At Nucor, we're not 'you guys' and 'us guys'; all of us are 'us guys'. Wherever the bottleneck is, we go there and everyone works on it." (*BusinessWeek,* May 1, 2006, p. 56f)[3]

Executive pay is also geared toward team building. The annual distributions for plant managers at each production site, or for departmental managers at the headquarters office, depend upon the corporate return on equity, not on the performance of the plant or department.

> [The plant manager at] Nucor's Vulcraft plant in Grapeland (Tex.) remembers that he wasn't on the job two days before he received calls from every other manager in the Vulcraft division offering to help however they could. Vulcraft manufactures the steel joists and decks that hold up the ceilings of shopping centers and other buildings. "It wasn't just idle politeness. I took them up on it." And, they want him to, he notes. "My performance influenced their paychecks." (*BusinessWeek,* May 1, 2006, p. 56f)

Even the pay of the Chief Executive Officer at Nucor is tied tightly to performance, and limited to a set percentage of the pay of front-line steel makers. The pay of a typical CEO at an American company averages 400 times that of the typical workers within his or her firm; at Nucor it never goes above 14 times. Given that the average steel maker at Nucor makes more than $100,000 in a good year, the Chief Executive Officer at that company obviously does not suffer as long as company performance remains high:

> "In average to bad years, we earn less than our peers in other companies. That's supposed to teach us that we don't want to be average or bad. We want to be good." (Statement by Nucor's V.P. for Human Resources, quoted in *BusinessWeek,* May 1, 2006, p. 56f)

The *BusinessWeek* article stressed the payment amounts and methods at Nucor, but there are other factors that help to create the distinctive attitudes and behaviors. The hierarchy at Nucor is compressed. There are only three levels between the Chief Executive Officer and the front-line workers: vice president, plant manager, and shift leader. Responsibility at Nucor is delegated. Given the narrow hierarchy at the company, workers are expected to solve operating problems on their own, with just the approval of the shift leader. Stability at Nucor is emphasized. Newly hired members of the firm are told that they will have jobs as long as they remain cooperative and productive. Innovation at Nucor is stressed. Employees at all levels are expected to continually recommend improvements in the company's processes through their experiences at work, and in the company's products through their contacts with customers. And lastly, respect at Nucor is guaranteed; there is said to be only one cause for dismissal at Nucor, and that is treating a fellow employee with a lack of consideration and courtesy.

Class Assignment

The treatment of employees at Nucor is obviously very different from the treatment of employees at other "old-line" industries such as steel, cars, car parts, textiles, clothing, and basic chemicals. List the treatment goals that you would like if you were

[3] Reprinted from May 1st, 2006 issue of Bloomberg BusinessWeek by special permission,

employed at Nucor, and then add the underlying policies on which those goals are based, and the resulting attitude and behavior changes. For example:

Treatment Goals	Underlying Policies	Attitude and Behavior Changes
High compensation ($100,000) for front-line workers	Low ($10/hr) hourly rate	Worry about output quantity
	Substantial weekly bonus	Worry about output quality
	Large annual distribution	Work cooperatively, as teams

Remember, not all of the treatment aspects and underlying policies that you might like at Nucor are compensation based, or even employee focused. Make certain that you include the full range. Then, consider the following questions:

1. In your opinion, why don't other companies in other industries adopt these policies? There is nothing that is "rocket science" about them.
2. It is easy to say that those other companies did not adopt these different policies because they did not know of them. Nucor came along later. But, why did these ideas not originate with those other companies? Once again, there is nothing "rocket science" about them.

Case 5-4

Student Tuition Increases at the University of California

The University of California was founded in 1869, with one campus, 10 faculty members, 38 students, and an assigned mission to provide superior educational programs for the residents of the state so that they could contribute to the advancement and governance of California. In 2009, 140 years later, there were 10 campuses, 220,000 students, 170,000 faculty and staff, and a worldwide reputation for excellence.

This record of steady growth and outstanding success, however, came to a halt just shortly before the anniversary year of 2009. The problem stemmed from a major reduction in state funding. The University of California system, which comprises all 10 campuses, is a public institution and was dependent upon obtaining a major share of its funding from the state. But, California had simply run out of money.

For years, there had been absolutely no problem with money. California was one of the most prosperous states in the country. Motion pictures and television programs were produced very profitably for global distribution in Hollywood, to the south. Computing and communication start-up ventures dominated technological advancements in Silicon Valley to the north, and were even more profitable. Enough fruits and vegetables to feed most of the rest of the country were grown on the rich farm lands south of Sacramento, in the center of the state, and provided steady if not excessive incomes. The population increased steadily, as people were attracted from other states and other nations by the ready availability of jobs and the pleasant conditions of life. Homes were built to accommodate the new arrivals in fast-growing suburbs around each of the major urban centers. Times were good, wages were high, and state budgets expanded to provide a broader range of social services, while state taxes were reduced to offer larger incentives for investment and growth.

But the financial costs of those social services had been underestimated, and the expected growth of the supportive economy had been overemphasized. The tech bubble burst in 2001. Income levels went down, capital gains nearly vanished, high-tech ventures closed, and California faced rapidly declining tax revenues. It was then discovered that the state employees' pension fund had made a series of poor investments in some of the more adventuresome financial derivatives that were so popular during this period, and the state was forced to make up those losses (see Case 4-3, "CALPERS and the Recovery of Capital"). The housing boom came to an abrupt and absolute halt in 2007, and the recession of 2008 quickly followed, with investment losses and home foreclosures spread throughout the population. The state of California faced a huge budget deficit at the start of 2009:

> Governor Schwarzenegger and lawmakers worked to close a record $60 billion gap from February through July [of 2009] with $32 billion in spending cuts, $12.5 of temporary tax increases, $8 billion of federal stimulus money and; more than $6 billion in other one-time fixes. (*BusinessWeek,* December 24, 2009; online edition)

Those emergency actions did not solve the underlying fiscal problem, however. Tax revenues continued to decline. Despite the emergency efforts listed in the excerpt that were enacted during the spring of 2009, it was still expected that the state would face a $6.3 billion budget gap in the 2010 fiscal year and an estimated $14.4 billion gap for the 2011 fiscal year. The easy solutions had all been tried, and the harder ones had gain little popular support:

Governor Schwarzenegger had called for a special election on May 19, 2009, to approve increases in both personal and corporate income taxes and extensions of existing sales taxes to many currently uncovered goods and services. Those tax increases and coverage extensions would have brought the state budget gap down to manageable proportions, but the voters rejected both proposals. The California Constitution requires that all new taxes be approved by either a simple majority in a statewide referendum or by a two-thirds vote in the state senate. The state senate had already rejected all permanent tax increases, so expense reductions within the state budget were the only alternative left.

The University of California system was particularly vulnerable to expense reductions dictated by the state. Many of the expense levels of the other social services were set by law. The reimbursement amounts for Medicare and Medicaid were set by the federal government, though paid by the state. Pension payments for retired state employees were established as written contracts at the time of each recipient's retirement, and given the shortfalls in the pension reserves, much of those amounts now had to be paid by the state. Support for higher education, however, was more a matter of tradition than of law. Legislators and voters alike had been proud of the University of California system and felt that it contributed greatly to both the well-being and the reputation of the state, and while the good times rolled, budget requests submitted from the president's office of that system were seldom rejected. But in 2008 the good times no longer rolled, and budget request denials became common:

> The [2009 calendar year] was only a few days old when the financial bad news started. Governor Arnold Schwarzenegger's proposed 2009 budget [the fiscal year runs from July 1 to June 30] appropriation for UC fell millions short of what the university had requested. In a May 19 special election, voters had nixed several propositions that would have generated new states revenue. As a result the university's total budget gap grew to a projected $531 million. By the time of the [special] election, UC already had frozen senior managers' salaries, cut bonuses and incentive pay, downsized the Office of the President, reduced freshman enrollment for 2009–10 and raised student fees by 9.3 percent. By summer, it became clear that the funding shortfall was far worse: $831 million. In July, the Regents approved a plan to enact system wide furloughs, ranging from 11 to 26 days, depending upon the pay bracket—amounting to a pay reduction of 4 to 10 percent—over a 12 month period beginning Sept. 1, 2009. Cost-cutting efforts at campuses included layoffs and reducing faculty recruitment. (University of California News Release, dated December 21, 2009, online version)[4]

The president of the University of California, Dr. Mark Yudoff, decided that drastic actions to increase revenues were needed to close that $831 million budget gap explained earlier. He proposed, and the governing board of that system agreed, that a substantial tuition increase was the only solution. Student tuition payments (called "fees" in the California terminology) had traditionally been kept low in order to fulfill the original mission of a superior education for all residents of the state. Undergraduate fee payments were only $7,125 per year prior to the 9.3 percent increase that had been enacted during the spring of 2009. That brought the total to $7,788. Now Dr Yudoff proposed and the Board of Regents approved a much larger 32.0 percent increase that was to take place in two stages: from $7,788 to $8,373 in 2010 and then to $10,302 for 2011.

Student reactions were immediate and negative, and took two forms. The first consisted of protest rallies. Students gathered outside administrative buildings and blocked access, or occupied instructional offices and refused to leave, but the numbers were not as large nor the actions as compelling as the organizers doubtless had hoped, and the turmoil declined as the days went past. A more common reaction was student concern over the impact of the earlier budget cuts on the quality of their education and on their ability to pay the new fee increases: One student, Maria Isabel Rocha, said she was particularly frustrated over shorter library hours and fewer teaching assistants.

Ms. Rocha, 19, said she already worked two jobs and higher fees would mean taking on another or even taking a quarter off to make money to afford tuition. (*New York Times,* November 20, 2009, online edition)

It can be assumed, though none of the public newspaper accounts or university news releases mentioned this, that poorer students, such as Ms. Rocha, who were currently on scholarships would receive a percentage increase in their scholarships to match the percentage increase in their fees. That is, if Ms. Rocha had received $2,000 in student aid before the planned increase she would receive $2,640 after the 32 percent tuition increase had been fully implemented.

It can also be assumed, though none of the newspaper accounts or university statements provided detail here either, that the planned tuition increase would result in substantial additional university revenues to make up for the sharply reduced state allocations. The University of California at all campuses had 220,000 students. Let us suppose that 70 percent of that number (156,000) were on some form of scholarship aid, and 30 percent were not (64,000). Let us further suppose that this scholarship aid averaged about 50 percent of the tuition payments before the planned increases, and therefore it would average about that for the planned increases themselves which, once again, were to go from $7,788 in 2009 to $10,302 in 2011 (an increase of about $2,500). If 50 percent of that amount were to be refunded to students in the form of higher scholarships, that would leave 50 percent, or $1,250, for the university. Overall, then, the planned tuition increase would result in higher revenues for the university system of 156,000 students × $1,250 increased tuition less scholarship amount + 64,000 students × $2,500 increased tuition, for a total revenue gain of $355 million.

Obviously, $355 million would certainly help, but it was less than half of the $831 million shortfall expected in 2010. Many administrators and faculty members were dissatisfied. They did not immediately call for additional tuition increases, beyond the 32 percent plan already approved, but it was clear that they felt more money from some source was badly needed, and they could no longer count upon state allocations:

> "Dismantling this institution; which is a huge economic driver for the state, is a stupendously stupid thing to do, but that's the path the Legislature has embarked on," said Richard A. Mathies, dean of the College of Chemistry here at Berkeley, long the system's premier campus. "When you pull resources from an institution like this, faculty leave, the best grad students don't come, and the discoveries go down.
>
> As the litany of cuts continues, there is a growing worry that senior faculty members may begin to defect. In fact, some colleges around the nation have begun identifying funds to use to recruit University California professors.
>
> Mr. Yudof [president of the University of California system] rejects suggestions to retrench, like adopting a two-tiered system in which the Santa Cruz, Riverdale and Merced campuses would be teaching institutions and no longer focus on research.
>
> "My mission is to defend, protect, enhance and grow the University of California," Mr. Yudof said. He added that he hoped that the current measures would be enough to get the system back on track. (*New York Times,* November 20, 2009, online edition)[5]

There were, however, a number of faculty members, primarily from outside the University of California system, who publicly advocated the use of much larger tuition charges to replace the vanishing state support allocations. Many of these advocates cited the tuition charges at equally prestigious public universities such as those in the Big Ten (averaging just under $13,000 per year for in-state students and somewhat over $30,000 for out-of-state and foreign students) or at high-demand private institutions such as those in the Ivy League (averaging considerably more than $30,000 for all students), and defended similar amounts for the University of California:

> It might seem that raising state college tuition is plainly a bad thing. High tuitions mean students will find it harder to finance college—and may not even attend, or may drop out due to costs. And for the students who attend state colleges, many of whom are of modest means, the tuition crunch may be especially painful.
>
> The truth is that increasing public college tuitions are not a problem at all. Indeed, the biggest problem in pricing tuition at public universities is not that the poor pay too much, but that the rich pay too little. (Op-Ed article published in the *New York Times,* November 23, 2009, online edition)[6]

> The student body at the University of California is composed of students from all walks of life. Every socioeconomic group is represented. That is as it should be. Brains not bucks needs to be the north star of admissions.
>
> That does not mean that every student should pay the same admission. Robin Hood is our teacher. He says take from the rich and give to the poor. Charge each student what they can afford. Some will pay list price. Some will pay nothing . . . Tuition should be scaled to the economic capacity of the individual undergraduate. (A "Room for Debate" article published in the *New York Times,* November 22, 2009, online edition)[7]

> Since most of the financial benefits of college go to the student, he or she should pay a large portion of college costs. Even with the large tuition increase, University of California fees are well below those of many other prestigious flagship public universities.
>
> Many attendees come from moderately to very prosperous families that can shoulder this extra burden. Lower income students are largely protected by UC financial aid policies and by an increasingly generous federal student assistance program. (Another "Room for Debate" article published in the *New York Times,* November 22, 2009, online edition)[8]

Class Assignment

1. Assume that you were one of three students who have been selected in a competitive contest to address the Board of Regents of the University of California during a meeting at which they plan to consider raising the tuition once again, from the recently approved $10,302 in 2011 to something closer to what is understood will soon be the Big Ten level, $15,000 for in-state undergraduates and $35,000 for out-of-state and foreign undergraduates, in 2013. Graduate tuition rates were to be left to the graduate schools themselves, but it was assumed that most of them would go beyond those amounts, perhaps $20,000 for in-state students and $40,000 for out-of-staters. Obviously, you can offer support or opposition to this new tuition plan that will be under discussion or put forward a totally different alternative. You have been told that you and the other students will be limited to five minutes, with a two-minute grace period. What position will you take, *and how will you word your argument to*

be convincing within the time limits imposed? Please bear with me if I make the suggestion that after graduation, when you have an opportunity to make recommendations to a group of senior people who think that they know far more about the topic than you do, that you have to be explicit, exact, and brief.

2. Chapter 5 emphasized the need for unification in both business firms and non-profit organizations. Do you believe, from what you have read in this case, that the students, parents, faculty, staff and administrators, and parents in the University of California system truly think of the funding issue in the unified terms of "we're all in this together"? Do you assume that there is considerable cooperation among those groups and across departments? Do you expect that there is much innovation? If not, do you think that the recommendation and argument you plan to make to the Board of Regents, if adopted, would help to pull everybody together?
3. Lastly, you are at a college or university, or you would not be reading this textbook. Are the students, faculty, staff and administrators at your college or university truly unified in the sense of believing that "we're all in this together," or do they remain, in the classic phrase, "in separate silos"? Is there cooperation among those different groups? Is there innovation among their programs? Do you believe that, if there were greater cooperation and innovation across disciplines, it would improve the quality of your education? If so, what one action or policy change would you recommend to the Board of Regents at your college or university to gain that cooperation and innovation and thus improve the quality of your education?

Case 5-5

Expanding Waistlines and Shrinking Profits

Expanding waistlines have become a major health care problem in the United States. Today nearly 66 percent of all American adults are considered to be either obese or overweight, up from 50 percent in 1980, and the percentage of adults in the worst, or obese, category has grown to 34 percent, from just 16 percent in 1980. The reasons, of course, are changes in diet, with more fast foods and fewer home cooked meals; changes in occupation, with more desk and service assignments and fewer factory or farming jobs; and changes in lifestyle, with more hurried "got to get this done right now" tasks and far less time for active outdoor recreation or energetic garden, lawn, or home maintenance activities.

Obesity and overweight are defined and measured using a metric termed the body mass index (BMI). The BMI was developed in Europe about 1840, but it is still used today as a simple yet surprisingly accurate indication of the amount of excess fat within a human body. "Excess fat" is defined as the amount above the minimum needed for the maintenance of life and reproductive functions. This minimum amount is termed "essential fat," and varies between men (2 percent to 5 percent) and women (10 percent to 13 percent). Very few people get down to these essential levels, except for dedicated athletes in endurance sports and passionate weight lifters with "six-pack abs."

Note: Darren Morris, University of Michigan, MD, 2010, and MBA, 2010, served as co-author of this case.

The BMI is calculated by dividing a person's weight in kilograms by the square of that person's height in meters. The metric scale is used because of the European origin. If you would like to calculate your own BMI, and if you happen to live in a country that uses pounds and inches for measurement, it can still be done fairly easily. Divide your weight in pounds by 2.2 and your height in inches by 39.37, and put those figures into the formula given here. You can then evaluate your resulting BMI and your risk of disease in the table that follows:

$$\text{BMI} = \frac{\text{Weight (kg, given 1 kg} = 2.2\ \text{lb)}}{\text{Height (m}^2\text{, given 1 m} = 39.37\ \text{in.)}}$$

Group	BMI	Disease Risk Relative to Normal Weight
Underweight	Below 18.5	—
Normal weight	18.5–24.9	—
Overweight	25.0–29.9	Increased
Obese, Class I	30.0–34.9	High
Obese, Class II	35.0–39.9	Very high
Obese, Class III	Above 40.0	Extremely high

Researchers have found a close correlation between the BMI index and actual body fat content. Although this weight/height relationship to body fat does vary slightly with age and gender (as explained previously, women naturally have higher levels of essential fat), these small variations are not considered to be clinically significant. The BMI and body fat content relationship does vary meaningfully, however, for such people as construction workers, farm laborers, and football players, where physical strength is a requirement; more technically advanced measuring methods are used in those cases to account for the muscular tissue.

These more technically advanced methods to measure body fat content start with simple skin-fold thickness tests using calipers, but then move on to three others that are listed here in the order of increasing complexity and cost:

- Total immersion testing, in which an individual is submerged in a vat of water and the displacement measured to get the size of the body in cubic inches, which can then be divided into the weight in pounds to obtain a ratio to adjust the BMI.
- Bioelectrical impendence testing, in which low-voltage electrodes are attached to the body at multiple points to get the average level of resistance (muscular tissues are better conductors than fatty deposits) to get the actual percentage of fat, which can be translated into the BMI.
- X-ray absorptiometry testing, which is the gold standard for body composition measurement; here, an individual is exposed to X-rays that reflect differently from the different types of body tissues, and again the results in actual fat percentage can be translated into the BMI.

Overall, however, the BMI is fast, inexpensive, and reasonably accurate and is the measure most frequently used for routine clinical evaluations of body fat content.

Why is there a need for "routine clinical evaluations of body fat content"? The reason is that major health problems are associated with excess body fat. The substantial rise in the number of obese individuals, and particularly of those in the higher Class II and III categories, has brought equally substantial increases in such severe medical conditions as hypertension, type 2 diabetes, coronary heart disease, high LDL cholesterol (the bad kind), stroke (clogged arteries in the brain), osteoarthritis (deteriorated joints in the body), and some forms of cancer (endometrial, breast, and colon). These problems are serious enough that it is thought that the lifespan of today's children will be shortened by two to five years, and thus bring about the first reversal in average life expectancy for U.S. citizens since the government first started keeping records in 1900.

These dramatic increases in serious medical conditions among persons who are classified as obese have, of course, brought equally dramatic increases in the health care costs that are borne by individuals, employers, insurers, and the government. A 2009 study (Finkelstein et al., *Health Affairs,* July 2009, pp. 822–831) estimated that obesity is responsible for additional medical spending of $147 billion per year. On average, the annual cost of health care for an obese individual is $1,429 higher than that for an otherwise similar but normal weight individual, an increase of 42 percent. This extra cost is not segregated out or billed separately to those persons; instead, it is paid by the normal health care reimbursement methods, with individuals charged out-of-pocket for an average of 16 percent of the spending and private insurers (primarily employer provided) and public agencies (primarily taxpayer funded) covering the remaining 84 percent. In short, most of the additional medical cost caused by those who are overweight or obese is borne by everyone else within the society.

The continual growth in the obese population is felt to be a major cause of the equally continual growth in the cost of employer-provided health care insurance, which rose 78 percent in the years from 2001 to 2006. And, the twin conditions of obesity and overweight are also said to be responsible for an estimated 39 million lost workdays each year, which of course both decreases office and workplace productivity and increases replacement and/or overtime expense for the employers. Obese and—to a lesser extent—overweight individuals have created a very major problem for both employers and insurers.

Employers and insurer agencies have jointly tried a number of different approaches in an effort to effectively address these increasing costs and lost workday problems. Wellness programs have been started at workplaces of all types and sizes, as companies have attempted to help their employees pursue healthier lifestyles. Onsite fitness centers, subsidized gym memberships, sponsored athletic teams, and freely provided nutrition counseling have all been tried—and in most instances found wanting. Only the high-tech and bio-tech firms on the East and West coasts have reported successful outcomes, and that is frequently explained by the presence of a much younger workforce at those firms and the existence of a far more participatory and easy-going culture. "Techies" seem to be attracted to the company gym if they know that the company president may well be on one of the adjacent treadmills, indicating that it truly is considered not only OK but fully approved to work out during business hours.

Some employers have even tried small financial incentives ($10 to $15 per month) for employees who go to the fitness centers, use the gym memberships, participate on the athletic teams, or meet with nutritional counselors a given number of times per month. But, these have not been overly successful. And, forced menu changes in company cafeterias, with grilled chicken breasts and fruit salads replacing fried hamburgers and potato chips, have turned out to be absolute "no-no's."

Positive financial incentives have not worked. There is now growing interest in trying negative financial incentives. It is currently illegal under federal law for group health plans (such as employer-provided insurance policies) to deny coverage or to charge higher premiums based upon the general health status of the employee, including his or her excess weight. But, it would be legally permissible if there were a provision that allowed overweight or obese individuals to obtain waivers from their physicians if it was felt that achieving a healthy weight would be unreasonably difficult due to an existing medical condition. It is assumed, however, that most physicians are so aware of the severe illnesses that result from overweight and obese conditions among their patients that they would be extremely hesitant to sign such a waiver. In short, negative financial incentives probably could be legally applied.

It is felt, though, that the negative financial incentives would have to be reasonably substantial to be effective. Advocates of these incentives are in general agreement that a charge of $10 to $20 per month for an obese employee will not be large enough to alter his or her behavior, nor the behavior of his or her family. Obese conditions tend to extend throughout an entire family whose members generally share the same lifestyle, with similar eating and exercising habits. It would be almost impossible, most advocates for negative incentives explain, for an employee to sit at the dinner table eating whole grains, fruits, and vegetables while everyone else was enjoying grilled hot dogs or barbecued ribs, or for that employee to go for lengthy walks in the evening while everyone else was sitting on the couch, watching television and nibbling snacks.

The spouse should be encouraged to participate in the weight loss program, these advocates continue, partially as a show of support for his or her mate and partially as a means of reducing the total health care costs for the full family. Spouses and children are normally covered by employer-provided health insurance policies, and while children do not generally incur immediate overweight- or obesity-related health care costs (these come later in life), spouses do, and their cooperation is badly needed. Lastly, it has been proposed that there should be a sliding scale of charges for the different obese and overweight classifications of the employees in order to push those who most need to act to do so quickly, before the expected medical problems do occur.

At the time that this case was being prepared (late fall 2009, in the midst of the debate on health care reform), we were unaware of any formal proposal that would include both substantial penalties to alter behavior and a sliding scale to place the emphasis where it was most needed. Perhaps the advocates were hesitant to propose concrete policies because of the furor that other major changes had encountered. Consequently, we have prepared one that would *recoup approximately half of the total extra costs* now recorded nationally for obese and overweight employees, both for those who were covered separately and for those who were covered with their families, and that would place the desired emphasis upon those employees who were in the most costly categories:

	Employee Only per Month	Employee and Family per Month	Employee Only per Year	Employee and Family per Year
Class III	$100	$200	$1,200	$2,400
Class II	50	100	600	1,200
Class I	20	40	240	480
Overweight	10	20	120	240

If the proposed charge of $2,400 for a Class III employee and family seems high, it should be understood that a 6-foot-tall employee or spouse would have to weigh 295 pounds just to reach the threshold of this classification, and that some members of the group are well over 400 pounds, with waist sizes of 60 inches and beyond. The average *extra medical costs for all obese individuals and spouses* (that is, the average for Classes I, II, and III combined) is $2,860; it can be readily understood that the individuals and families in the two higher classification—such as the one just described—incur costs that go far above that average additional expense.

It should also be understood that these charges would be waived for all employees and spouses who were making “adequate progress” in weight loss. This adequate progress might be defined as a loss of two or more pounds per month, which is achievable. Quarterly screenings by medical personnel would be required, but those screenings would include tests for such asymptomatic (not yet obvious) conditions as early diabetes, rising blood pressure, and increasing cholesterol. In short, true preventive care could be extended to those most in need of prevention, and this too would decrease costs.

It is generally felt by the advocates for negative financial incentives that if an employer were, in cooperation with their health care insurer, to adopt a sliding scale of forceful monthly penalties combined with personal progress exemptions and preventive care opportunities, there would be three major advantages:

- A sharp reduction in the company costs for coverage. Costs would go down, either as obese employees and spouses, driven by the negative incentives, lost some weight and improved their health, or as those unwilling to make the effort and sacrifice required did not lose weight but were then forced to pay approximately half of the additional charges.
- A just allocation of the overall costs for coverage. Employees in the underweight and normal weight categories would no longer be forced to fully subsidize those in the Class I, II, and III obese categories. In short, the costs would be placed upon those whose behaviors incurred them.
- A longer and more enjoyable life for the obese employees and their spouses who did meet the monthly targets for weight loss. There is absolutely no question but that the health conditions of the successful participants in such a program would greatly improve, as would their life span, personal appearance, and self-esteem.

Opponents, however, have been quick to point out that substantial weight loss is not an easy and pleasant task. Anyone who has successfully lost weight and kept it off can tell you that it is necessary to get used to feeling hungry much of the time. For dieters who do not work in strenuous calorie-consuming occupations, breakfast becomes a glass of orange juice and two slices of dry toast. Lunch a salad, with bland fat-free dressing. And dinner tends to be fish or chicken, with rice or noodles, and a mix of vegetables, all without butter or those tasty cheese toppings. It is also hard to enjoy being convivial with friends when you are limited to a single glass of wine or bottle of beer, and you absolutely cannot snack on the attractive offerings that are so frequently spread out before you. Still, many people have worked through those difficulties, but there are three possible roadblocks:

- Family or cultural traditions. It is generally understood that there are no inherited causes of overweight or obese conditions, but overconsumption of high-calorie meals can be a learned behavior. The family may always have enjoyed large servings of meat-based dishes, or the region may have emphasized the appeal of high-fat-content items such as barbecued ribs.
- Economic and geographic restrictions. Healthy foods such as fresh fruits and vegetables and whole grain breads and pasta products are more expensive than mass-produced items, and in many depressed neighborhoods, the more perishable items are often not available. Within those neighborhoods, fast foods seem to always be promoted: not-too-costly and tempting.
- Social concerns. Eating tends to be a group activity. Children sit together in school cafeterias and criticize their friend's food choices. Employees go out together to local restaurants and may comment on their colleagues' menu selections: "Why are you eating rabbit food?" In eating, as in so many other group activities, there is a tendency to "go with the crowd."

Another important issue that has to be addressed is what happens to the obese and overweight employees and spouses who make a sincere effort to lose weight and improve health but, due to their family and cultural traditions, their economic and area restrictions, or their very real social concerns, fail to make measurable progress. Some of them would simply give up. They might say, "We can't seem to lose weight and we can't afford to pay the fines or fees," and just surrender their insurance. They would then join the growing numbers of uninsured, and rely upon impromptu visits to the emergency room at a local hospital for the health care they need for themselves and their children, where their costs will be paid by the hospital; an area charity; or the city, state, or federal government. These costs, of course, eventually come back upon the rest of society.

There are, as there are to so many of the critical issues in health care reform, two sides to the weight loss proposals of the type described earlier in this case. Advocates claim that it is essential that individuals begin to take responsibility for their own well-being and that the negative incentives provide an equitable means to accomplish that, and get closer to the desirable goal of "more health at less cost." Opponents have lambasted the program as an unfair "fat tax" imposed upon employees and spouses who, from early family influences and current social and economic limitations, may have had little choice in their eating habits and lifestyles.

Class Assignment

In December 2009, when this case was being readied for publication, the U.S. Senate was debating a proposed health care plan. Proponents of that plan were pleased that it was reasonably inclusive; many more Americans were to receive coverage. Opponents of the plan were concerned that it was overly expensive; it would add to the deficit during a period of economic recession. People in the middle were disappointed that more direct actions to control costs had not been included. There were no limits on legal claims for medical malpractice, which allegedly caused physicians to order large numbers of unneeded tests and procedures. There were no provisions for negotiating costs for the bulk purchases of pharmaceutical drugs and medical supplies, which apparently brought far higher unit prices in the United States than in foreign countries. And lastly, there were no methods for putting the primary responsibility for health care upon the individual; people who smoked heavily, were grossly overweight, or lacked any exercise were to receive exactly the same benefits as everyone else under the proposed insurance plans.

Assume that you are the president of a medium-sized service firm, with branches in the three major cities within your state. Assume that you have approximately 2,000 employees. Assume that you are greatly troubled by the rising costs of health care insurance; those costs have more than doubled for your company since 2001. And, also assume you are greatly concerned by the effects of the economic recession; your company no longer has the income it needs to keep pace with those rising costs. You soon will have to start cutting costs wherever you can.

Now, assume that the faculty from your major state university have teamed up with the managers of your existing health care insurer and have come to you with the proposal that you adopt the negative financial incentives exactly as described earlier in this case. The dean of the medical school at your state university, who led the delegation along with the CEO of your insurance company, said, "We think that the cost savings that will come from bringing down the diagnostic and treatment costs associated with overweight and obese conditions will be far greater than have been estimated. But, we have no way of demonstrating that until we can try it." The CEO of the insurance company added, "We agree with that. But, if we do this we want to do it right, with force and energy and leadership." Both the dean of the medical school and the CEO of the insurance company asked you, after you agreed to consider their proposal, not to take a vote among your employees. "We've been down that road, and the outcome will be 'No' because so many people are overweight now, and fearful of the remedy, though that remedy is not as bad as they expect."

The group who came to visit with you left some summary figures about your workforce, derived from the insurance company's payment of claims for various medical conditions over the past five years. Similar to the national population, about 35 percent of your employees are obese, and another 30 percent overweight, for a total of 65 percent. You know you could confirm that by wandering about the offices in your headquarters building. There you would find good people sitting at their desks, working hard on computers or conversing with others, who smile or nod as you pass, but many of their rear ends bulge out more than just a little bit past the edges of their chairs. And you know that you could confirm the illnesses associated with those fat bulges by looking at the monthly totals for missed workdays and the consequent need for overtime and replacement costs.

You further know that one of the reasons the faculty from the university and the executives from the insurer decided to come to you is that you are in excellent physical condition. You have never run a marathon, but you do compete in 15-kilometer races and occasionally participate in shortened triathlons (mixed swimming, biking, and running).

Lastly, you understand that you are being asked to do something that you have never done before. You are being asked to interfere with the personal lives of your employees and—even worse—of their families. Your standard has always been that once they leave the company's parking structure, your employees' lives are their own, to develop and enjoy as they see fit. But, you're being asked to change that.

You know that those who succeed in losing weight will have longer lives, and probably better lives, with more development and more enjoyment as they engage in a common effort within the firm, and have more energy for activities outside the company. You also know that the common effort and increased energy will help your company to get through the economic downturn, which you fear will be more extensive than is currently expected. And you know that this cost-control effort, if successful and then documented and published by the university, will greatly increase the reputation of your firm and bring additional contacts and sales. Lastly, you know that this would help your society, by showing that there are ways to control health care costs and by demonstrating that business firms can and should take a leading role in that effort.

What would you do? If you decide to go ahead, how would you justify that action to those employees and family members? If you decide not to implement the program, how would you explain that decision to the university faculty and insurance executives?

Chapter 6

How Can a Business Organization Be Made Moral?

Up to this point, both the text and cases of this book have assumed that there was time to decide what was the equitable or "fair-to-all" thing to do when faced with a situation in which some individuals, groups, or organizations associated with the firm were being harmed or having their rights ignored in ways outside their own control, while others were being substantially benefited. Both the text and cases emphasized the need to analyze this situation by combining the economic outcomes, legal requirements, and ethical duties to reach a balance that was logically convincing, before acting. That, both the text and cases then explained, was the way to build individual attitudes of trust, commitment, and effort and organizational behaviors of cooperation, innovation, and cohesion. Finally, both the text and cases of this book concluded that those moral aspects of management, when combined with the practical aspects of management—preparing a mission statement to reflect the values and goals of the firm and then designing the financial supports, the performance measures, incentive payments, and the "don't do" lists to reinforce those values and goals—would lead to competitive success in the rapidly changing global economy.

But, suppose that there just isn't time to do all this. Suppose that a judge within a courtroom has issued a verdict demanding change, or that a majority of the board of directors is insisting upon change, or that national newspapers and television news programs are reporting, in very graphic terms, the need for change. In short, what do you when a major problem or managerial crisis occurs? This is the topic of this last chapter. How can this be done? Figure 6.1 shows the steps.

Rather than working through this graphic with definitions in very exact terms of each of the steps in responding promptly and forcefully to a managerial crisis, I should like to lead off with an example of the need for that combination of immediate and forceful action. The example is the wreck of the *Exxon Valdez.* This wreck created the largest oil spill—11,000,000 gallons—that had ever occurred in the United States, up until the British Petroleum well blowout in the spring of 2010. It caused severe environment damage along large stretches of the Alaska coastline, killing seabirds, ruining fishing grounds, and resulting in massive financial losses for both company stockholders and local residents alike. This was a managerial disaster that did not have to happen,

FIGURE 6.1 Responding Promptly and Forcefully to a Major Problem or Crisis in the Operations of a Business Firm

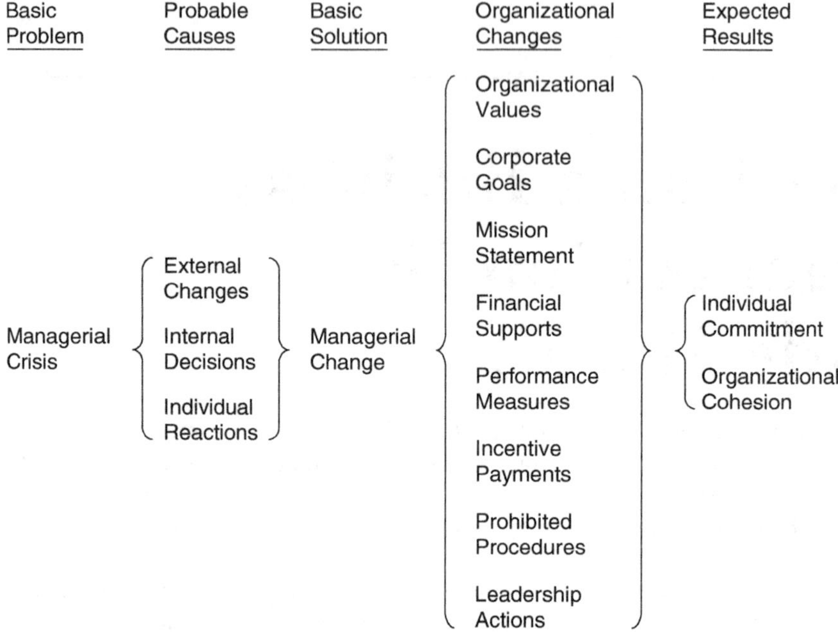

and the cause was a lack of trust, commitment, and effort on the individual level, and of cooperation, innovation, and unification at the organizational level, throughout the corporation. No one did his or her job properly. Instead, everyone at the upper level was trying to reduce investments and cut expenses; everyone at the middle level was trying to get by as best they could, with no money for improvements or incentives; and everyone at the lower level had simply given up caring. The result was an almost total failure of managerial responsibility throughout the firm.

The Failure of Managerial Responsibility throughout Exxon

At 9:30 P.M. on Thursday, March 22, 1989, the oil tanker *Exxon Valdez* left the oil terminal at Valdez, Alaska, loaded with 1.26 million barrels of oil. The *Valdez* was the largest tanker owned by Exxon. It was nearly 1,000 feet long and weighed 280,000 tons (fully loaded).

When the ship left port, it was under the command of Captain William Murphy, the harbor pilot. Harbor pilots are responsible for steering both incoming and outgoing tankers through the Valdez Narrows, a 0.5-mile wide approach to the port of Valdez. After exiting the Narrows and achieving the sea lanes in Prince William Sound, Captain Murphy turned over command to Captain Joseph Hazelwood and left the ship. Captain Murphy testified later that he had smelled alcohol on the breath of Captain Hazelwood, but that he made no comment and took no action. He knew that it was common practice for both the officers and crew of oil tankers to drink while in port.

Captain Hazelwood, immediately after assuming command, radioed the Coast Guard and requested permission to alter course to avoid large chunks of ice that had broken loose from the Columbia Glacier and were floating in the outbound shipping lane. Permission was granted. Captain Hazelwood then turned over command of the vessel to Third Mate Gregory Cousins and went below to his cabin. Mr. Cousins was not licensed to pilot a ship in the sea channels approaching Valdez. Mr. Cousins and others later testified that it was common practice to turn over command of oil tankers to non-licensed officers.

Captain Hazelwood had set the automatic pilot to steer the ship southward into the inbound shipping lane, and he had instructed Mr. Cousins to maintain the course until after the ice chunks from the glacier were passed, and then to return northward to the outbound lane. No inbound traffic was expected, and permission for this course change had been granted by the Coast Guard, so no danger was anticipated. At 11:55 P.M. Mr. Cousins ordered a course change of 10 degrees right rudder to bring the tanker back to the proper lane within the channel. There was no response. At 12:04 A.M. the lookout, who was on the bridge rather than at the normal station on the bow of the tanker, sighted the lighted buoy marketing Bligh Reef, a rock outcropping only 30 to 40 feet beneath the surface. Mr. Cousins ordered emergency hard right rudder. Again there was no response. In the hearing that followed the accident, it was determined that either Captain Hazelwood had not informed Mr. Cousins that the had placed the ship on automatic pilot, or that Mr. Cousins and the helmsman had not remembered to disconnect the automatic pilot, which prevented manual steering of the vessel.

At 12:05 A.M. the *Exxon Valdez* ran aground on Bligh Reef. The hull was punctured in numerous places, and 260,000 barrels, approximately 11,000,000 gallons, of crude oil spilled from the badly ruptured tanks. At that time it was the largest oil spill in the history of the North American petroleum industry.

At 12:28 A.M. one of the officers on the ship radioed to the Coast Guard that it was aground on Bligh Reef. "Are you leaking oil?" a Coast Guard operator asked. "I think so" was the reply.

At 3:28 A.M. crew members of the responding Coast Guard boarded the *Exxon Valdez,* and reported that oil was gushing from the tanker. "We've got a serious problem," radioed the Coast Guard officer on board the tanker. "There's nobody here . . . Where's Alyeska?"

"Alyeska" was the Alyeska Pipeline Service Company that both managed the oil pipeline, which brought crude oil 800 miles from the oil fields at Prudhoe Bay to Valdez, and ran the oil terminal at Valdez. It was responsible, through a formal agreement with the state of Alaska, for the containment and recovery of all oil spills within the harbor and sea lanes. That agreement was expressed in a detailed written plan, 250 pages long, that listed the equipment and personnel that were to be kept available by Alyeska, and the actions that were to be taken by Alyeska, to react promptly to oil spills.

The stated goal of the written plan was to encircle any serious oil spill with floating containment booms within five hours of the first report of the occurrence, and to recover 50 percent of the spill within 48 hours. The stated goal was well known within the area, and accounted for the perplexity of the Coast Guard officer. When he reported, "There's nobody here," he was referring not to the captain and crew of the tanker, but to the oil spill recovery team and equipment from Alyeska.

The Coast Guard officer also noted the smell of alcohol on the breath of Captain Hazelwood, and reported to his base in very blunt terms that he suspected that the captain was drunk. He was unable to establish the degree of intoxication, due to the lack of a testing kit, but he did request the assistance of the Alaska State Police to conduct the tests as soon as possible. Those tests were conducted the following morning, and did establish that the level of alcohol in Captain Hazelwood's bloodstream at the time was twice the legal limit.

At 6:00 A.M. on Friday, March 23 (six hours after the accident), officials from Exxon flew over the grounded tanker for the first time, and reported a massive oil slick streaming away from the tanker. They contacted the Alyeska oil terminal and ordered a quicker response and greater effort. The problem, the manager at that terminal reported, was that the single barge capable of handling the long containment booms had been out of service for two weeks and had been unloaded for repairs. Workers were preparing to reload the barge, he said, but the only employee who was capable of operating the crane needed for reloading had not yet reported for work. Later that morning the loading was completed and the barge was taken in tow by a harbor tug. At 2:30 P.M. the barge arrived at the wreck site, carrying all of the containment booms that were available at the terminal, and a number of centrifugal pumps to help in removing the remaining oil from the *Valdez.*

At 7:36 A.M. on Saturday, March 24 (31.5 hours after the accident), Exxon began pumping oil from the *Valdez* to a second tanker moored alongside, the *Baton Rouge.* At about the same time, seven Alyeska "skimmers," or barges with vacuum equipment designed to siphon oil off the surface of the water, arrived at the site. The skimmers, however, were designed to recover oil that had been bunched in a compact mass by containment booms. Those booms were still not in place, due to a shortage of tugs and to some degree of confusion in the means of unloading the booms and placing them in the sea. By nightfall, only 1,200 barrels of oil had been recovered.

By 11:00 A.M. on Sunday, March 25 (59 hours after the accident), the *Exxon Valdez* was finally encircled by containment booms. It had taken 2.5 days to get the booms in place, despite the original plan, which called for full containment of any spill within five hours. Most of the oil was now outside the booms in a slick that covered 12 square miles, and the wave action had begun to convert the crude oil to an emulsified "mousse" mixture of oil and water that quadrupled the volume. This emulsified mixture now lay 5 to 9 inches thick upon the surface of the sea. The specific gravity of the emulsified mixture was very different from the specific gravity of either water or oil, and the skimmers were no longer effective except when working on fresh seepages close to the grounded tanker, within the booms.

At 6:00 A.M. on Monday, March 26 (78 hours after the accident), the Coast Guard admitted that the situation was out of control. The first two days had been calm, but Sunday night winds as high as 73 miles per hour had arisen and driven the emulsified oil and water mixture 37 miles from the wreck site. It was swathing the islands and beaches throughout Prince William Sound with solid bands of black petroleum "gunk," the accepted term for the residue that is left after the more volatile elements in crude oil have evaporated. The skimmer barges and boom-tending boats had been forced to retreat to sheltered water. Flights into the Valdez airport, bringing additional supplies and people, had been halted. Most of the oil that had remained in the unruptured tanks of the *Exxon Valdez* had been pumped out, but it was now thought to be impossible to recover any further substantial amount of the spill. Eventually, marks of this spill stretched 700 miles along the coast, spoiling fishery resources, wildlife refuges, and national parks in one of the most scenic regions of the country and killing sea birds, fish, and mammals in one of the prime marine habitats of the world.

> Nearly two months after the biggest oil spill in American history, Alaskan officials say not a single mile of beach has been completely cleaned and that the death tolls of birds, fish and mammals continues to mount.
>
> Large patches of oil, untended in rough and remote seas, are still washing up on pristine Alaska beaches more than 500 miles from the reef in Prince William Sound where the *Exxon Valdez* went aground March 24.
>
> The oil from the spill of 11 million gallons hit 730 miles of coastline, Alaskan state officials said today. Of that, only four miles have been declared cleaned.
>
> *****
>
> The ecological toll of the spill thus far includes more than 11,000 birds of 300 different species, 700 Pacific seal otters, and 200 bald eagles, according to a tally by the State Department of Environmental Conservation.
>
> Biologists say that the actual number of dead wildlife could be three to five times higher than those found because many of the animals have been washed out to sea or taken by predators.
>
> *****
>
> On some beaches in Prince William Sound the oil is more than three feet thick, lodged in the rocks and providing a reservoir of fresh contamination at every high tide. (*New York Times,* May 19, 1989, p. 1)[1]

The causes of the accident, while obviously related to the intoxication of the captain and the subsequent command of the ship by an unlicensed third mate, were thought to be more complex than that simple explanation. Two additional factors were mentioned in the early hearings of the Federal Transportation Safety Board that investigated the oil spill.

- *Tired crew members.* The crew members on the tanker were said to have been exhausted from working long hours, and not fully alert. The *Exxon Valdez* normally carried a crew of 20 persons. This crew size was considered to be typical for crude oil tankers, but it was substantially smaller than that required by Coast Guard regulations and union requirements on merchant cargo ships. The oil companies had argued that the new technologies automated the operations of their tankers and eliminated the need for a larger crew. The modern equipment, however, had to be manned and maintained, and consequently the automation did not keep the officers and crew from working extensive amounts of overtime and frequently going long stretches with little or no sleep. Crew members on the *Exxon Valdez* testified that they had worked an average of 140 hours of overtime per month per person for the six months prior to the accident. One hundred and forty hours of overtime per month and 20 days at sea per month plus the regular 8-hour watches works out to be 15 hours per day.

  > Many of the crew members were exhausted, a routine feeling on Exxon ships, they testified. (*New York Times,* May 22, 1989, p. 10)

- *Ignored sailing rules.* There were definite violations of sailing rules. Captain Hazelwood advised the Coast Guard that he was taking the ship on a southwesterly course, into the inbound shipping channel, to avoid floating ice chunks. That was considered to be perfectly proper, and normal under the circumstances, though permission was never granted for this maneuver except when the inbound lanes were completely free of other shipping. Captain Hazelwood, however, did not advise the Coast Guard that he then altered course ever further to the south, out of the inbound shipping lanes and into waters close to Bligh Reef, nor that he had engaged the autopilot. Permission for the further course change would almost certainly have been refused, had the Coast Guard been informed, and Coast Guard rules are very definite that autopilots should never be used except in the open sea. Both improper actions certainly contributed to the final grounding of the ship.

> Your children could have driven a tanker up through that channel. (Statement of Paul Yost, commandant of the U.S. Coast Guard, quoted in the *Wall Street Journal,* March 31, 1989, p. 1)

Within Alaska, public reactions to the accident and to the lackadaisical practices that apparently led to the accident centered on the potential damage to the fishing resources and consequently on the harm to the livelihood of a substantial portion of the state's population. The Alaska coast from Prince William Sound northward is known as the richest salmon and crab fishing ground in the world. Exxon assured the fishing boat operators that they would be compensated for any losses they suffered as a result of the oil spill, and explained that the company had insurance that would protect it against claims for negligence up to $500 million.

Outside of Alaska, public reactions to the accident and to the lackadaisical practices revealed in the hearings focused on the fouling of the environment and the destruction of the wildlife:

> Already thousands of birds have died, and biologists fear that a significant portion of the Sound's 12,000 sea otters—which lose buoyancy when just 10 percent of their body is covered in oil—may be in jeopardy.
>
> Those who know these bejeweled waters—rich in fish, fowl and fauna like few other places on earth—believe the damage will be monumental and long lasting. (*Wall Street Journal,* March 31, 1989, p. 1)[2]

Public reactions to the accident also were not mollified when the chairman of Exxon, Mr. Lawrence Rawl, decided not to go to Alaska and supervise the cleanup operations directly. Instead, he remained in New York City, and made no direct comment upon the oil spill or cleanup operations for seven days. Other officials within Exxon also refused to comment. The first statement by the president of Exxon U.S.A., the holding company for Exxon Shipping which owned the grounded tanker, was made on May 9:

> We do not know what caused this accident . . . Exxon's response was prompt and consistent with the previously approved contingency plan. (Mr. Bill Stevens, quoted in the *Detroit Free Press,* May 9, 1989, p. 7A)[3]

In fairness to Exxon, it should be explained that company officials felt that public reactions to the oil spill were extreme and did not take into account several mitigating factors. First, they thought that the public did not really understand that the company could not be held responsible for the intoxication of Captain Hazelwood. Secondly, they thought that the public did not fully realize that the company had been prevented from using chemical dispersants on the oil.

Chemical dispersants, it should be understood, do not destroy the oil. Instead, the effect of the dispersant is to lower the surface tension of the oil to the point where it will break up and disperse in the water in the form of tiny droplets. The problem is that these tiny droplets are in a size range that is easily ingested by marine organisms on the lower end of the marine food chain, and therefore gradually impact marine creatures on the higher end of that chain. The extent of that impact has never been studied under all climatic conditions. It is known that dispersants make an oil spill much less visible; there is no certainty that they make it any less toxic.

Despite the lack of certainty about the effect of the dispersants, company officials thought that chemicals should have been used as soon as it was apparent that the containment and recovery efforts had failed, and before the beaches were fouled and the wildlife killed. Mr. Rawl, the chairman of Exxon, in an interview with *Fortune* magazine, said environmentalist acting with the state of Alaska had prevented the company from applying the dispersants promptly (the *New York Times,* May 22, 1989, p. 10).

Mr. Lee Kelso, director of the Alaskan Department of Environmental Conservation, disagreed strongly that his department was responsible for any delay in the use of the chemical dispersants:

> Exxon was free to use dispersants on the vast majority of the oil slick, and did not do so. (Statement by Lee Kelso, quoted in the *Wall Street Journal,* April 3, 1989, p. 1)

Mr. Lee Raymond, president of the Exxon Corporation, said that he blamed "ultimately the Coast Guard" (*Wall Street Journal,* April 3, 1989, p. 12) for the delay in the use of dispersants, explaining that it had required a test before granting permission.

Coast Guard officials denied that they had required testing, saying that it was only common sense to gauge the effectiveness of the treatment under the wind, wave, and water temperature conditions that existed at the time.

Government reactions to the oil spill centered not on the causes of the accident, and not on the consequences of the oil spill or the disputes about testing, but focused on the slowness and ineffectual nature of the clean-up. The federal attitude seemed to be that accidents do occur, that seamen have been known to consume excessive amounts of alcohol in the past, and that under conditions of stress people may forget about test conditions and requirements. But, in the view of the government in Washington, there was no excuse for the inability firstly of Alyeska and then of Exxon to deal promptly and effectively with the spill itself.

The contingency plan that had been developed by Alyeska and approved by the state of Alaska envisaged containment within five hours and recovery of a minimum of 50 percent of the oil by skimmers within 48 hours. Containment, as stated previously, took 59 hours and estimates of the amount of oil actually recovered ranged from 0.4 to 2.5 percent. A number of reasons for the ineffectiveness of the response by Alyeska and Exxon were given in hearings held by the National Transportation Safety Board.

It should be explained, before discussing the results of these hearings before the National Transportation Safety Board, that the Alyeska Pipelines Service Company is not a subsidiary of the Exxon Corporation. It is a consortium owned by the seven oil companies who have drilling rights on the North Slope of Alaska and thus transport crude oil from the North Slope to Valdez Bay by a massive pipeline. Representatives of all seven companies serve on the board of directors of Alyeska. Exxon is the second largest owner, and is said to participate actively in the management of the company.

The first reason given for the slowness of response was a shortage of equipment. The oil spill contingency plan required Alyeska to maintain two barges, loaded with containment booms, and ready for use. At the time of the spill, only one barge was available. The other had been scrapped as old and obsolete, but its replacement was still in Seattle. There was a requirement in the contingency plan that Alyeska notify the state Department of Environmental Conservation if any equipment was out of service for any period of time. Alyeska now concedes that it failed to provide this notification.

The barge that was available had been damaged by a storm in January. It was still considered to be seaworthy, but the containment booms had been unloaded to facilitate repair. Repairs had been delayed, according to testimony by Alyeska officials, because the company had been unable to locate a licensed marine welder. Environmentalists at the hearing displayed the Valdez telephone book that listed four companies that claimed to provide licensed marine welding services.

Seven thousand one hundred feet of containment booms were stored at the oil terminal. The contingency plan did not specify an exact lineal footage that was to be kept in stock, but it can be understood that 7,100 feet would be enough to contain a spill around a 1,000-foot tanker only if the booms could be placed quickly, before the oil spread out upon the surface of the water. Three thousand feet would be required just to encircle the hull.

Ten skimmers, which are large suction units that can be mounted on barges and used in essence to vacuum oil from the surface of the sea, were available as promised in the contingency plan. However, replacement parts were not kept in stock, and equipment breakdowns were common because the machines were not designed to work on the emulsified mixture of oil and water that was formed rapidly through wave actions on the non-contained spill.

Other equipment that was needed either was missing or could not be found quickly. Heavy ship fenders, essential for the second tanker to come alongside the *Exxon Valdez* and pump out its remaining oil, couldn't be located for hours because they were buried under 14 feet of snow. Half of the required 6-inch hose, needed for the pumping, never was found and replacements had to be flown in from Seattle. The emergency lighting system, to illuminate the boom-laying and oil pumping work at night, was finally discovered off base, being readied for use in the Valdez winter carnival.

As a final example of the shortage of equipment, it was determined after the accident that there never had been enough chemical dispersant stored in Valdez to treat the oil spill, even had there been no disagreement or misunderstanding about permission to use this material.[4]

[4] "Elements of Tanker Disaster: Drinking, Fatigue, Complacency," by Timothy Egan, *The New York Times*, May 22, 1989, p. B7.

In addition to the shortage of equipment, there was also a shortage of personnel. The oil spill contingency plan required Alyeska to have a crew of 15 persons on duty at all times. These were not oil spill experts. These were hourly paid workers responsible for the normal operations of the terminal, but according to the plan that should have included all of the skills and trades necessary to respond to emergencies, whether oil spills at sea, oil leaks on land, or oil fires at the terminal.

At the time of the spill, only 11 workers were on duty. Unfortunately, none of those people knew how to operate the crane, which was needed to load the barge with the long and heavy containment booms. A crane operator was finally located, but he was also the only one who knew how to drive the forklift, and he spent the morning after the accident, when speed in response was essential, running back and forth between the forklift and the loading crane.

Lastly, there was a lack of training. Alyeska had dismissed its oil spill response team in 1981. This was a group of 12 persons originally set up to contain and then clean up spills throughout Valdez Harbor and Prince William Sound. The duties of the spill response team were assigned to regular employees at the plant. At the time of dismissal, Alyeska had claimed that this arrangement would be superior as they would have "120 people trained in oil spill response rather than 12":

> Some of the cited 120 scoff at this. One senior employee says he has had "zero oil spill training, none." He recalls being summoned to two spills over the years. "I didn't know what the hell I was supposed to do, and when I found the guy I was supposed to report to, he did not know what the hell we were supposed to do either. We just stood there watching."(*Wall Street Journal,* July 6, 1989, p. 1)[5]

Some of the operating managers within the oil industry have been greatly concerned by this tendency to replace specialized teams with personnel from the general workforce:

> You either have a team of people who are dedicated to a specific task, and trained to perform that task under any and all conditions, or you have nothing. The Valdez terminal didn't have that trained team, and it showed.
>
> We run into this same problem continually with fire drills. Previously, every refinery had a fire department, with fire engines, a fire chief, and a fire crew. Now, they just have the engines and, if they are lucky, they still have a chief who knows what he is doing and can teach the others. We are not lucky, and we don't still have a chief. It is company policy to run a drill once every six months. The bell rings, and all of the 9:00 to 5:00 desk jockeys jump on the truck, and away they go. When they get there, they don't know how to turn on the hydrant, they don't know how to work the pump, they don't know how to lay the hose and fight the fire, and they don't know what is safe and what isn't. We have not had a fire since the department was disbanded, but when we do it is going to get very bad very fast.
>
> I can understand exactly what happened at Valdez. They had not had a major spill in 18 years, but when they did it got very bad very fast. (Statement of oil industry executive made in confidence to the case writer)

The shortage of equipment, the shortage of personnel, and the lack of training were caused, it now appears, by deliberate policy decisions reached by the senior management of Exxon Corporation, who pushed strongly for cost reductions at Alyeska during the mid-1980s. These policy decisions were not taken arbitrarily. They were in response to a change in the basic economic conditions of the oil industry.

Oil prices fell from $32/barrel in 1981, at the height of the power of OPEC (Organization of Petroleum Exporting Countries) to $12/barrel in 1987, and then rose slightly to stabilize in the range of $15 to $20/barrel. The major oil companies are all vertically integrated, with divisions for the exploration, production, and refining of crude oil, and for the distribution and marketing of oil products. The lower price for crude oil brought exploration nearly to a halt, and severely reduced the profits that came from production.

The large vertically integrated oil companies reacted slowly to the changed economic conditions, but the reaction—when it came—was dramatic and harsh. Costs were reduced. Employees were discharged. The changes at Exxon were particularly dramatic because the company for years had prided itself on a generous, almost paternal attitude toward its employees. In January 1986 Mr. Clifton Garvin, chairman of Exxon Corporation since 1975, commented to *Fortune* magazine about personnel polices at the time that his company's selection as one of the 10 "most admired" firms with the United States.

Six months later, Exxon Corporation was in the midst of an extensive restructuring effort that would eventually change the company from one of the "most admired" to one of the most disliked:

> Exxon is giving workers until May 30 to decide whether to resign. If it doesn't get enough volunteers, it will resort to involuntary terminations. Based on Exxon's earlier announcement of a 26 percent budget cut, guesses on the final body count range from 15 percent to more than a third of all its employees. Analysts figure that the restructuring will provide Exxon with gains in efficiency and profitability, and that by conserving cash the company will be better able to buy oil properties if prices stay low. (*BusinessWeek,* May 5, 1987, p. 32)[6]

The generous, almost paternal attitude of the company toward Exxon employees had disappeared. Nearly one-third of all of the company's workers, almost all of those over 50 years of age, were told they had to retire early or be fired:

> With oil companies cutting production in the face of falling crude oil prices and a hard-noised head chopper named Lawrence Rawl in the president's chair, at least part of Exxon's worldwide workforce of 145,000 seemed destined for the block. In late April, the world's largest oil company offered 40,500 employees the option to retire early or quit with compensation. (*Fortune,* May 16, 1986, p. 11)

The new chairman of Exxon, Mr. Lawrence Rawl, who replaced Mr. Clifton Garvin in the spring of 1986, apparently believed that he had been selected by the board of directors to reduce costs and increase earnings, despite the probable impact upon employee morale. Rawl made it clear that his main concern was the bottom line and his responsibility to shareholders. He didn't shy away from looking at waste and taking steps to eliminate it if it would improve profitability.[7]

The cutbacks in staff extended throughout Exxon to the Exxon Shipping Company—the 20-person crews on that company's oil tankers reportedly were to have been reduced to 15 persons had the accident not intervened—and to the Alyeska Pipeline Company:

> When oil prices began falling in 1981, the owners of Alyeska ordered it to save even more on costs. In late 1982, Alyeska managers prepared what they thought was a lean budget and presented it to a meeting of the owner's committee in San Francisco. According to former Alyeska officials who were briefed on the meeting at the time, committee members cited a figure, roughly $220 million, and asked if the budget was under that; told that it wasn't, they rejected it out of hand.
>
> "There was an overall attitude of petty cheapness that severely affect our ability to operate safely," recalls Mr. Woodle who came over from the Coast Guard to run the terminal's marine operations just in time to see their budget slashed by about a third. "I was shocked at the shabbiness of the operations." (*Wall Street Journal,* July 6, 1989, p. 1)[8]

Management of a Moral Company

The oil spill from the *Exxon Valdez* coated 750 miles of Alaska coastline. It severely impacted the livelihood of commercial fishermen, almost destroyed the food sources of native Indians, and resulted in the death of 40 percent of the bald eagles in Alaska, killed 80 percent of the sea otters in Prince William Sound, and eliminated 200,000 various species of birds along the coast. It also resulted in a $2.4 billion fine by the federal government, a $2.8 billion verdict in a civil trial, an additional claim of equal size by the indigenous peoples of the region, and a ruined reputation for the Exxon Corporation among the general public.

But, the Exxon Corporation did not change its pattern of operations. It appealed both the fine by the federal government and the penalty in the civil trial, contested the additional claim by the native Indians, and continued on its existing strategy of cost reductions and investment restrictions. The argument that the attorneys for Exxon made in their courtroom appearances, and the explanation that the spokespeople for Exxon expressed in their public announcements, was that Exxon should not be held responsible for the actions of company employees who so clearly violated company policies. That is, both Exxon groups admitted that Captain Hazelwood was intoxicated at the time of the accident, but claimed that company executives did not know that he tended to drink heavily while on shore and would have fired him had they known. This argument—that a company should not be held responsible for employee actions that violated company policies—did not gain much traction among those persons affected by the oil spill, but it

[7] Fortune, April 14, 1986.

[8] WALL STREET JOURNAL. CENTRAL EDITION by WALL STREET JOURNAL.

did within the legal system. It took many years after the clean-up of the oil spill had been completed before a final settlement of the federal fines and civil claims was reached.

Suppose, however, a settlement had been achieved, and a court had ordered Exxon to take prompt action to ensure that such an accident could not occur in the future and, if by some unforeseen set of circumstances it did occur, that there had to be trained employees, proper equipment, and adequate supplies on hand to deal with the situation promptly. Or, suppose that there was a stockholder revolt. The wreck, and the damage to the wildlife and the coastline, had occurred before there was a strong environmental movement, except for isolated groups such as the Sierra Club. But, there was outrage expressed by many individuals and groups. Suppose that the stockholders, in reaction to that public outrage, had banded together and forced the board of directors to act. And, suppose you were one of the "good guys" within Exxon who had earlier warned about the possibility of a major oil spill and were now expected to participate actively in the restructuring of the firm. What would you do?

The argument of this chapter is that you would not have the time to build the individual attitudes of trust, commitment, and effort nor the organizational behaviors of cooperation, innovation, and the particularly important "we're all in this together" unification that probably would have prevented the wreck of the *Exxon Valdez* in the first place. You are going to have to rely, at the start, on the practical techniques rather than the moral methods of management. You are going to have to follow the pattern of activities that were shown in Figure 6.1 at the opening of this chapter, and that is repeated here, in Figure 6.2 for easy reference as we work through the shown steps or stages.

FIGURE 6.2 Responding Promptly and Forcefully to a Major Problem or Crisis in the Operations of a Business Firm

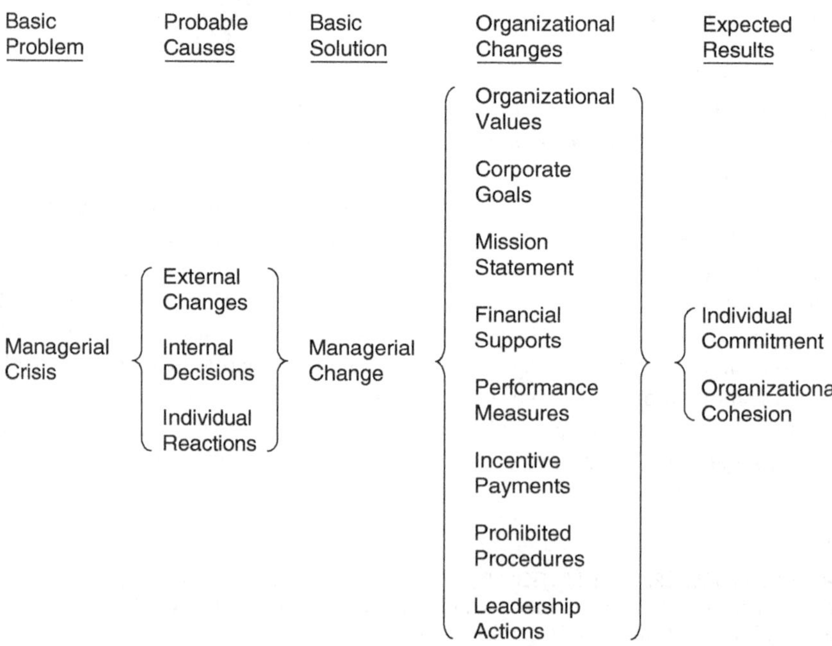

The basic problem is clear. I have asked you to assume that you were a member of a managerial group ordered by a court, or instructed by the board, to take such actions as will ensure that a harmful oil spill and delayed clean-up will not occur again. I don't believe that it is an overstatement to call this a managerial crisis because major organizational changes in values, goals, policies, and systems will be needed.

The probable causes of this managerial crisis have been described earlier in the chapter. They started with the external change of a decline in the price of crude oil from $32/barrel in 1982 to a range of $15 to $20/barrel in 1987. That sharp drop in revenues led to the internal decisions to cut costs and reduce investments, which in turn brought about obvious shortages of equipment and supplies and clear lacks of personnel and training. Employees felt overworked and underappreciated. It was as if they said to themselves, "If you—the managers—don't care what happens then we—the workers—won't care either." The result was that the largest tanker in the Exxon fleet ran aground on the most clearly marked reef in the Valdez harbor, and the company was totally unable to deal with the resultant oil spill in a timely, effective, and legally prescribed manner. This sequence of causes, and their consequences, are summarized in Figure 6.3.

FIGURE 6.3 Actions which Led to the Wreck of the *Exxon Valdez* and the Slow Clean-up of the Resulting Oil Spill

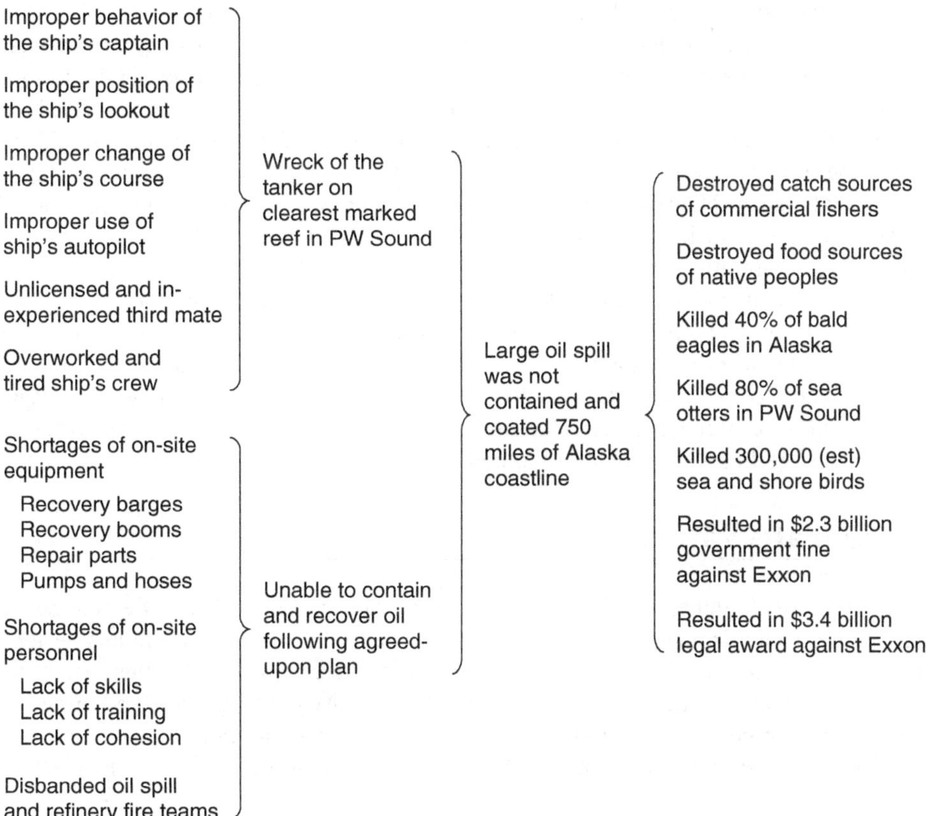

Now, back to the series of steps that would be needed to comply with the court order or board directive that I have asked you to assume that you had received, and that were part of a group responsible for its implementation. That implementation would start with a very basic managerial change in outlook and emphasis.

Managerial Change

If the total focus of corporate management is placed upon financial benefits for the stockholders, with little or no attention paid to the well-being and rights of other stakeholders, the result—according to this text—will be a lack of trust, commitment, and effort among those other stakeholders at the individual level and of cooperation, innovation, and unification at the organizational level.

That is exactly what happened at Exxon Corporation. At the time of the wreck, Exxon was being managed with sole attention to the financial well-being of the stockholders and—given the large bonuses that could be expected from reporting profit increases during a financial downturn—the senior executives as well. Lawrence Rawl had boasted that he was "bottom-line" oriented, that he planned to fire employees and cut expenses to increase profits—with no concern for those to be fired within the extended company or for those to be harmed throughout the Alaskan community. Under economic outcomes, the company did not recognize the external costs that were imposed upon the commercial fishers, the native Indians, and the active environmentalists. Under government requirements, the company did not obey the law, in the form of the spill response contract that had been signed with the state of Alaska. Under ethical duties, the company was not open, honest, and truthful about their actions, did not select the greatest net benefits for society, nor act in ways they would be willing to have all others act. The result was a clear lack of committed effort by employees on the tanker: No one was willing to report the frequent drunken behavior by the captain or to object to the continual violations of sailing rules that jointly led to the tragic accident. The result was also a complete lack of committed effort by employees at the terminal: no one made any attempt to correct the shortage of equipment and the absence of training that led to the slow response. That lack of trust, commitment, and effort brought about, eventually, a huge cost to the company and a heavy charge to the society. What else should have been done? Here are the next steps in the sequence of organizational changes that earlier were shown in Figure 6.2.

Corporate Values

To avoid easy generalizations, think of corporate values as the duties the senior executives of the firm should—in your view—owe to the various individuals, groups, and organizations associated with the firm who can, in one way or another, affect the future performance and position of the firm. These individuals, groups, and organizations would include owners of all types (both institutional and individual); employees at all levels; customers in all markets; and the full range of suppliers, distributors, creditors, local residents, national citizens, and global inhabitants. Think about what issues are probably important to each of those individuals and groups. Then, think about the extent to which the senior executives of the firm should recognize these factors that are important to each of those individuals, groups, and organizations. In short, think about how the company should begin to plan for unification based upon similarities rather than separation based upon differences.

Clearly, Exxon owed profitable operations to the owners, but they also owed them the duty of avoiding large fines and penalties. Perhaps they could not have owed continued employment to all of the workers, given the changed conditions of the oil industry, but they could have attempted to balance the harms imposed upon employees by salary and wage reductions at all levels of the firm rather than relying upon "head chopping" at the lower levels. They also could have provided the workers who remained with better conditions, such as less forced overtime on the oil tankers, and improved training, such as better instruction for the response teams at the oil terminals. It would be hard to argue that they did not owe an unharmed environment to the local residents and forthright information on the level of preparation to the state officials. None of these duties, beyond profits owed to the shareholders, apparently were recognized by Lawrence Rawl and the other senior executives at Exxon.

Organizational Goals

To avoid easy generalizations here, think of company goals as the end points the senior executives of the firm should—in your view—set for the various dimensions of performance that are possible. What—again in your view—should the senior executives want to accomplish along such dimensions as financial performance, technological achievement, industry position, market share, customer satisfaction, productive efficiency, employee loyalty, environmental protection, public reputation, and social contribution? What—once more in your view—should the various groups associated with the firm want to accomplish on each of these dimensions? As with the corporate values, there will be differences among these groups. Scientists and engineers doubtless would like to emphasize technological advances, while the owners and creditors probably would prefer to focus on financial outcomes. The two may not be as dissimilar as they at first appear; if Exxon had been positioned within the industry to take advantage of their perceived strengths and weaknesses and their expected opportunities and threats, there would have been an obvious connection between those two. Again, think about how the company should begin to plan for unification based upon similarities rather than separation based upon differences.

Exxon placed total emphasis upon financial performance and set very explicit goals along that dimension. The accident, and the total of $5.2 billion in fines and penalties, could have been avoided with greater emphasis upon technological achievement (better methods of tanker control and spill clean-up), employee morale (less drinking by tanker officers and more training for terminal employees), environmental protection, and public reputation. The basic question in proposing goals for a corporation is whether it is possible to plan for profits, or whether instead it is better to plan for the actions and outcomes that lead to profits. Exxon, it is very clear, planned for profits, and paid the price.

Mission Statement

The mission statement is the means of combining the duties that the firm owes to others with the goals that it has set for itself. What role, as a result of this combination, should the firm attempt to play within the market, the industry, the economy, and the society? It is difficult if not impossible to express meaningful corporate values and valid organizational goals in explicit numerical terms. Consequently, managers should think about the possibility of forging a compromise with a mission statement that speaks only generally about the duties they want to observe and the goals they want to achieve, but much more specifically about the means they want to use and the standards they want to follow. The intent is to define the future of the firm, the scope of its activities, and the character of its operations so that everyone will clearly understand, "This is where we're going to go, this is what we're going to do, and this is how we're going to do it." Put yourself in their place, and think in terms of a document that will create a challenge for everyone associated with the firm. Think also in terms of a document you would be *proud* to hand to employees, to show to customers, to send to suppliers and distributors, to mail to shareholders, and to publish for local residents and national citizens.

Exxon, at the time of the wreck of the *Exxon Valdez,* did not have a mission statement. Instead, it had a Code of Conduct, which is reproduced here:

> Our company policy is one of strict observance of all laws applicable to its business:
>
> A reputation for scrupulous dealing is itself a priceless company asset.
> We do care how we get results.
> We expect candor at all levels and compliance with accounting rules and controls.
>
> It is the established policy of the company to conduct its business in compliance with all state and federal antitrust laws:
>
> Individual employees are responsible for seeing that they comply with the law.
> Employees must avoid even the appearance of violation.
>
> Competing or conducting business with the company is not permitted, except with the knowledge and consent of management:
>
> Accepting and providing gifts, entertainment, and services must comply with specific requirements.
> An employee may not use company personnel, information, or other assets for personal benefit.
> Participating in certain outside activities requires the prior approval of management.

What would have happened had Exxon Corporation had a mission statement similar to the one adopted by Johnson & Johnson that was previously printed in Case 5-2? Here the order of priorities was very clear: customers, suppliers, distributors, employees, and local residents come first, with company owners at the very end. Just having a different mission statement that emphasized duties and goals in set rankings rather than policies and prohibitions without priorities probably would not have avoided the wreck or improved the clean-up. But, it is the argument of this text that having such a mission statement bolstered by proper financial supports, performance measures, incentive payments, prohibited procedures, and leadership actions would have made a substantial difference.

Financial Supports

Within every firm, in very simple terms, someone has to sell the products (marketing), manufacture the goods (production), and supervise the cash flows (finance). In slightly more complex terms, someone also has to gather the data (information systems), develop the people (human resources), and apply the technologies (research and development). In very much more complex terms, someone has to select the strategy (strategic planning), define the tasks (activity planning), and design the structure (organizational planning). People at all of these levels, from the least to the most complex, need money, or more properly the authority to spend money, in order to observe the values and achieve the goals set in the mission statement.

Financial supports provide that authority to spend money to observe values and achieve goals. This money comes in two forms: capital and cost. Capital represents the long-term investments needed for buildings, equipment, and inventory; those amounts are "capitalized" or recorded as an asset on the balance sheet. Cost represents the short-term expenditures required for employee salaries and outside services; these amounts are "expensed" or deducted from revenues on the income statement. The issue in financial supports is whether the capital is allocated and the costs are budgeted to maximize the profits for the company or to fulfill the duties and meet the goals listed in the mission statement.

It is very clear that Exxon had not made the long-term capital investments that were needed for equipment and inventory to be able to contain and then recover the oil spill. Only one of the two barges specified in the contract with the state of Alaska to transport the containment booms to the site of a spill was available, and that had been damaged and not repaired. An adequate number of containment booms were not available. Spare parts for the skimmers were not in stock. Only 69 barrels of chemical dispersants were on hand; not the 10,000 barrels that were required. Obviously, the emphasis here had been on profits, not duties and goals.

It is also very clear that Exxon had not budgeted the short-term cost amounts that were needed for personnel and training to be able to contain and then recover the oil spill. The specialized oil spill recovery teams had been disbanded. Only 11 general purpose workers were on duty at the time of the wreck, not the 16 specified in the contract with the state of Alaska, and none of those employees had been specifically trained to respond to oil spill emergencies. There was a lack of cohesion in the containment and recovery efforts caused, in the view of the marine managers of the Valdez terminal, by "an overall attitude of petty cheapness that severely affected out ability to operate safely" (*Wall Street Journal,* July 6, 1989, p. 1). Obviously, here also the emphasis had been on profits, not duties and goals.

Performance Measures

Performance measures are the means of evaluating the performance of the persons assigned to the various critical tasks designed to implement the strategy and achieve the mission of the firm within capital investment and expense budget constraints. Many of these performance measures are financial in nature—simple restatements of the capital allocations and revenue/expense budgets. Others are numerical, and are related to such aspects of job performance as unit output, customer satisfaction, product performance; workplace safety, employee morale, and environmental preservation. Setting these performance targets for people assigned to critical tasks is felt to be an important aspect of corporate management; it is frequently said that, "If you can't measure 'em, you can't manage 'em." The issue in performance measures, as in financial supports, is whether the measures are set to maximize the profits for the company or to fulfill the duties and meet the goals of the mission statement.

None of the published accounts of the hearings and trials that followed the wreck of the *Exxon Valdez* spoke specifically of the performance measures that were is use by the Exxon Corporation. It can be assumed, however, given the restrictions on capital allocations and limitations on budgeted expenses, that all of them focused on profits. It would appear that none of the managers at Valdez were measured on the availability of response equipment and inventory, or on the training and capability of recovery employees.

Incentive Payments

Incentive payments are the means of rewarding the performance of the persons assigned to the various critical tasks designed to implement the strategy and achieve the mission of the firm. They are the method by which the people supervising the programs and managing the divisions are rewarded for meeting the performance targets that they have been assigned. These rewards can be financial (bonuses or commissions), positional (promotions and raises), or reputational (recognition and praise). They are usually tied very closely to the performance measures; if an individual meets the target that was set on—for example—divisional profit, customer satisfaction, or workplace safety, then the incentive payments reward that achievement. These rewards for meeting performance targets often have an impact upon the occurrence of moral problems that can charm others, particularly if the size or the importance of the incentives for the manager can overcome that person's judgment as to what is best for the firm. Bonuses and commissions that form a very high percentage of an employee's total compensation package often lead toward "cutting corners" and "taking risks."

Again, none of the published accounts of the hearings and trials that followed the wreck of the *Exxon Valdez* spoke specifically of the incentive payments. It can be assumed here also, however, that most if not all of them focused on rewarding the managers who met their profit, revenue, and cost objectives. Had those managers received a bonus, or a promotion, or even just recognition and praise for having response equipment and inventory on hand, or for having trained employees ready to react, the spill probably would not have been left uncontained for 59 hours rather than the 5 hours specified in the contract with the state of Alaska.

Prohibited Procedures

Prohibited procedures are a published listing of procedures and/or actions that simply will not be tolerated by the company. This listing of behavioral standards, often termed a "Code of Conduct," generally differs in two important ways from the mission statement. The mission statement usually is very idealistic; the conduct code frequently is very realistic. The mission statement is very general; the code is very specific. Examples of prohibited acts that are often included in a Code of Conduct are "Employees of this company may accept no gifts, lunches, dinners, or other forms of entertainment with a value over $25.00," or "Employees of this firm must never falsify accounting records or expense accounts." There often is an emphasis upon financial limits, not mission priorities, in these prohibited procedures.

The Code of Conduct of the Exxon Corporation was reproduced earlier in this chapter. Essentially, it says that laws should never be broken, bribes should never be paid, and benefits should never be accepted. It does not, however, say that ship's officers should never be intoxicated, safety equipment should never be unavailable, or safety training should never be neglected.

Leadership Actions

Often it is possible for the senior executive of an organization to take a dramatic action, or issue a memorable statement, that will indicate to members of the organization the relative weight to be given to profitable outcomes versus social or environmental impacts. It is easy, in many business organizations, to forget the values, goals, and priorities of the mission statement if those differ from an everyday focus on financial performance. It is hard, in most business organizations, to get people, even diligent employees, to carefully read memos or attentively listen at meetings about social or environmental performance. This is particularly true in large organizations in which there are hundreds of memos and numerous meetings. Senior executives, however, simply by the way they publicly choose to spend their time or voice their concerns, can clearly indicate their priorities.

Apparently no senior executive at Exxon had been at the Valdez terminal to publicly inspect spill response capability, or had attended environmental meetings to energetically endorse spill prevention technology, since Lawrence Rawl had become chairman. Mr. Rawl did not go to Prince William Sound after the grounding of the tanker, which seems to indicate his position on the financial performance versus social and environmental performance question. Prior to the wreck, there were many things senior executives could have done, had the company included environmental protection in the mission statement, to convey the importance of that protection. Inspection of sites, interviews with employees, and presentations of awards would all have been possible. These were not done at Exxon, and the result was not only severe damages to the society but huge charges against the company.

Conclusion

This has been a long and complex chapter that covered what may appear to be a wide range of topics—from a review of the content of Chapter 5 to a description of the wreck of the *Exxon Valdez* to a listing of the steps needed to form and then follow a mission statement. But the important element, and what I hope that you gained from reading it, is the need to pull together the moral aspects of management and the practical aspects of management. That, in my view, is the true meaning of leadership.

Case 6-1

Exxon Corporation and the Lack of a True Mission Statement

In Chapter 6, immediately after the Code of Conduct of Exxon Corporation that existed at the time of the oil spill had been shown, readers were asked: "What would have happened had Exxon had a Mission Statement similar to the one adopted by Johnson & Johnson?" That Johnson & Johnson statement was previously printed in Case 5-2, and is reproduced here:

> We believe that our first responsibility is for the doctors, nurses, and patients, to mothers and all others who use our products and services.
>
> - In meeting their needs everything we do must be of high quality.
> - We must constantly strive to reduce our costs in order to maintain reasonable prices.
> - Customer orders must be serviced promptly and accurately.
> - Our suppliers and distributors must have an opportunity to make a fair profit.
>
> We are responsible to our employees, the men and women who work with us throughout the world.
>
> - Everyone must be considered as an individual. We must respect their dignity and recognize their worth.
> - They must have a sense of security in their jobs. Compensation must be fair and adequate and working conditions clean, orderly and safe.
> - Employees must feel free to make suggestions and complaints.
> - There must be equal treatment for employment, development and advancement for those qualified.
> - We must provide competent management and their actions must be just and ethical.
>
> We are responsible to the communities in which we live and work, and to the world community as well.
>
> - We must be good citizens—support good works and charities and bear our fair share of taxes.
> - We must encourage civic improvements and better health and education.
> - We must maintain in good order the property we are privileged to use, protecting the environment and natural resources.

Our final responsibility is to our stockholders. Business must make a sound profit.

- We must experiment with new ideas. Research must be carried on, innovative programs developed, and mistakes paid for.
- New equipment must be purchased, new facilities provided, and new products launched.
- Reserves must be created to provide for adverse times.
- When we operate according to these principles, the stockholders should realize a fair return.

Class Assignment

The order of priorities within the Johnson & Johnson Mission Statement are very clear: customers, suppliers, distributors, employees, and local residents come first, with company stockholders at the very end.

1. In your opinion, would this type of "company stockholders at the very end" Mission Statement have helped Exxon to avoid the very destructive oil spill and delayed clean-up that occurred? Or, is that type of Mission Statement applicable only to high-profit pharmaceutical and consumer product firms, not to "down and dirty" oil companies?
2. One argument that people make about the Johnson & Johnson Mission Statement is that it is necessary to make people want to follow it, that it is necessary to implement it with the measurement and incentive systems. If that type of statement were adopted by Exxon, what changes in performance measures and incentive payments would you recommend?

Case 6-2

Sarah Goodwin and the Need for Corporate Change

Sarah Goodwin, as described in Case 4-4, accepted a job at a department store chain soon after graduation. During the training program, while working for one of the store's most popular buyers, she was asked to ship defective food products to a convenience store chain that served many of the poorer sections of Los Angeles. She refused, but was then fired for not going along, for not being a "team player." She appealed to the president of the department store chain, but was treated brusquely at their meeting and even taunted by the corporate attorney who was also present. He said, "You have no proof."

Sarah, however, was not without resources. Her father was the senior partner in a San Francisco law firm. Sarah asked him for help. He hired an investigative firm to find the needed proof in the form of some of the infected food products—small boxes of imported crème wafers that had become infested with insects—and shipping papers or payable invoices from the department store chain to the convenience store office listing those products. When Sarah's father had that proof, he insisted upon a meeting with the full board of directors of the department store. At that meeting, which Sarah also attended, he opened one of the boxes, insects scrambled over the boardroom table and directors jumped back, out of their seats. After order was restored and some clean-up was attempted, he then passed around copies of the shipping papers and invoices for the infested products and issued his dictum: "Fire the president and attorney today, or my firm will a file suit against your department store chain in a downtown Los Angeles courtroom for civil damages tomorrow." The board did fire the president and attorney that day.

Assume that a new president and attorney were quickly hired. Assume that both were adamant that this type of action that had deliberately harmed poorer people would not happen again. Assume that they hired the consulting firm for which you have worked since graduation to help in restructuring the company, and that you were one of the employees of that firm assigned to this task.

What you and the other members of the assigned task force soon found was that the department store chain, under the management of the recently discharged and replaced president, had embarked upon a cost-cutting effort that demoralized many of its employees. The reasons they had done so can be summarized very briefly. High-end department stores such as Saks Fifth Avenue, Neiman Marcus, and Lord & Taylor (those that focused on style merchandise, served an exclusive clientele, and had a downtown location) had dominated retailing for many years, until about 1975 when the industry underwent extensive change. Small specialty shops began to offer similarly styled goods with more personalized service in the suburbs, and European clothing designers decided to offer lines of their branded products for sale through mid-level chains and even—eventually—discount stores. The high-end department stores expanded to the malls, but somehow were never able to recreate the ambience and prestige of their large and elegant downtown locations. The senior executives attempted to respond to these external changes by merging with equivalent stores in different cities to gain economies of scale and of scope, but this did not work out well either. There are few economies of scale or of scope in stylish merchandise sold to upper-income customers in different locations.

Finally, the senior executives decided that if they were unable to increase sales and maintain prices, they would reduce expenses, the other half of the profit equation. They began to put pressure on both store managers and department buyers to cut costs and reduce inventories. Buyers, who for years had enjoyed going to Europe to view styles and make purchases directly from the famous designers at their spring and fall showings, were now told to stay home, look at samples, and buy over the telephone from Asian manufacturers. "Stretch" budgets were introduced (budgets that were based on aggressive estimates of desired revenues and costs rather than historical projections of actual figures), and buyers were now measured and rewarded on a "profits per square foot of selling space" basis. This forced the buyers for each department to compete with the buyers for all the other departments for both selling space and personal income, and it destroyed the easy "us against the managers" camaraderie that previously had marked the interactions of buyers in most of the high-end department stores.

Some of the buyers just gave up. They felt that they had lost their prestige and authority and decided to do whatever they needed to do to just get by until retirement, or until they could find a new job in one of the smaller specialty stores that were prospering in the suburbs. They cut corners and took chances. They didn't worry about what might happen to the company, which, they felt, had treated them badly. The decision described in Case 4-4 to transfer a shipment of imported wafers that had somehow become infested with insects down to a convenience store chain in a poor section of inner city Los Angeles in order to "get our money back" probably came from that lack of regard for the well-being of the company.

How do thoughtful managers re-introduce this "regard for the well-being of the company" feeling? Assume that by the time you joined the consulting firm team assigned to the department store chain, members of that team working with the recently appointed senior executives had designed a new strategy for the department store chain: to position it in a distinct and growing market segment and to operate it with a proven management process.

The new market segment was to consist of upper-middle-income families in the 35- to 65-year-old age group who wanted current styles, quality selections, less than "high-end" prices, and excellent personal service. This was a market segment with an income level above that of the large national chains such as Sears, Target, or T.J Maxx but below that of the small specialty shops. The proven management process was to be modeled on that used by Walmart; it was to feature accurate sales information and knowledgeable demand projections by store location that would be shared with both designers and suppliers so that together—the store, the designer, and the supplier—they could select the lowest cost means of maintaining proper level stocks of the best-selling goods. Assume that by the time you joined this team, the department store senior executives and consulting company team leaders had already defined the organizational values, proposed the corporate goals, and created the mission statement to convey the new direction of the chain:

Organizational values (duties owed to those associated with the firm):

- Customers—attractive styles, good quality, reasonable prices, and *excellent* service.
- Employees—continual opportunities to participate in selecting the goods and styles, negotiating the prices, setting the order volumes, and advising on marketing and advertising.
- Designers—continual treatment as an integral part of the company, with full information.
- Suppliers—continual treatment as an integral part of the company, with full information.
- Owners—if we collectively can tie together customers, employees, designers, and suppliers, company profits will follow.

Corporate goals (endpoints to be reached by the firm):

- Industry position—we want to dominate the current style, good-quality, reasonable price, and excellent service market segment in our geographic region.
- Market share—we want to have 50 percent of sales in our market segment and our geographic region.
- Technological achievement—we must have the most advanced information system in our market segment so that we can accurately forecast sales.

- Employee skill—we must have the most customer-friendly employees in our market segment so that we can insightfully anticipate styles.

Mission statement (combined organizational values and corporate goals):

- Our company will dominate the high-style, good-quality, reasonable price, and personal service retail market for consumer goods. We will achieve this position through (1) high levels of employee training to provide that personal "know your customer" service so that we can anticipate our clients' wants; (2) high levels of capital investment to provide that "know your market" information so that we can forecast our own sales trends; and (3) working closely with our exclusive designers and suppliers to respond quickly, accurately, and well to those wants and trends. Anticipating needs, forecasting trends, and cooperating with designers and suppliers will result in both lower costs and higher quality. Lower costs and higher quality will generate better profits.

Class Assignment

The financial supports, both capital allocations and revenue/cost budgets, will be based upon decisions by senior management: how much to spend each quarter on computer programming, consumer advertising, and employee training, etc. There are no difficult-to-evaluate workplace safety and environmental protection issues that need to be included here, as there are for most manufacturing firms. Therefore, you should focus on the following two questions:

1. What performance measures and incentive awards would you recommend for (a) senior-level executives at the corporate offices; (b) mid-level managers in the major functional and technical areas such as product advertising and information processing; (c) product-level buyers for each of the major lines such as women's clothing, men's clothing, home furnishings, etc.; and (d) store-level personnel at each of the branches who are in direct personal contact with the chain's customers and need to be involved in selecting styles and forecasting sales.
2. What prohibited procedures and leadership actions would you recommend to begin to pull people together, to get cooperation and innovation from individuals and groups throughout the organization? First, list five procedures that you would totally prohibit. Go beyond the obvious "Don't ship infested wafers to economically distressed sections of major cities". Think about the future, not the past, and focus on the upper levels of management, not the staff and operating people throughout the firm. Second, list five innovative actions that you would recommend to the CEO. What can he or she do, beyond sending memos and giving speeches, to convey what is important in the new strategy. This is "management by walking around". Where should he or she go outside of corporate headquarters, and what should he or she do while there?

Case 6-3

Susan Shapiro and the Need for Corporate Change

Susan Shapiro, as described in Case 4-5, accepted a job at a large chemical company soon after graduation. During the training program, on a visit to one of the company's plants, she encountered a chemical process that was harmful to the health of the workers. She complained to senior management, but her warnings were ignored and eventually she was fired.

You'll have to assume for this case that instead of being ignored and fired, Susan's warnings had been heeded. Assume that the president of the company had met with her and asked her to be part of a task force assigned to recommend changes to put greater emphasis upon the company's responsibilities to employees, customers, and local residents. What should be done?

Before you start work on those changes it is important for you to understand that chemical companies within the United States at the time of this case had begun to encounter strong price competition from developing countries. The process technologies had become widely known. The raw materials were easily available. The needed funds were readily raised. Suddenly companies in third world countries could produce most of the so-called intermediate products and were beginning to move into the more advanced outputs. They had the advantages of lower labor costs, fewer safety requirements, and almost no environmental constraints so that their cost structures were very advantageous. The American producers soon recognized that they had to improve their product offerings and automate their process methods, and do this quickly.

Assume that the president of the chemical company, during their meeting, told Susan that he or she had been greatly concerned that safety and/or environmental issues were going to be neglected during this period of research and development (R&D) focus. "All of our money," the president continued, "is going into technological development. We keep warning the finance people that they have to find the funds needed for essential plant maintenance and worker safety projects, but it is so easy to say 'no' when the money is in New York and the problem is in Louisiana. They think that they're helping our company but in reality they're harming our workers. Fixing that is one of the assignments of the integration task force that you are to join tomorrow morning."

Lastly, assume that Susan spent all of her time between that meeting with the president of the chemical company and her introduction to the other members of the task force studying the reports of that group. She found that they had already defined the organizational values, proposed the corporate goals, and created an organizational mission statement, as shown here:

Organizational values (duties owed to those associated with the firm):

- Customers—highest quality products and absolute on-time deliveries from our automated processing units.
- Workers—continual training for the skilled, not manual, jobs required by the automated processing units.
- Managers—money and people needed to continually improve and maintain the automated processing units.
- Engineers—money and people needed to continually explore the relevant technologies and develop new products and design better processes.
- Owners—if we can develop new products and design better processes and then operate our automated processing unit efficiently we will be able to fully satisfy our ultimate customers, and if we can achieve all three of those objectives we be able to offer outstanding returns to our stockholders.

Corporate goals (endpoints desired by those associated with the firm):

- Product design—be an industry leader.
- Process innovation—be an industry leader.
- Processing efficiency—be #1 in the industry.
- Customer satisfaction—aim for 100 percent.
- Workplace safety—aim for 100 percent.
- Employee loyalty—aim for 100 percent.
- Environmental protection—aim for 100 percent.
- Public reputation—be the industry leader.

Mission statement (combined organizational values and corporate goals):

- Our company will be #1 in the basic petrochemical industry in manufacturing efficiency. This will enable us to provide our customers with unexcelled product quality and absolute on-time delivery. We will achieve this position by investing the capital and spending the money to be an industry leader in product design, process innovation, and employee skill. If we are among the industry leaders in all of those factors, and achieve our #1 ranking in processing efficiency, we will have built a lasting company of which we can all be tremendously proud.

Class Assignment

Focus on the design of the financial supports, the performance measures, and the incentive awards that you believe will be needed to observe the duties and achieve the goals of the mission statement, and be prepared to explain why your recommendations should lead to higher levels of individual commitment and organizational cohesion throughout the firm.

Case 6-4

Enron Corporation and the Highway to Failure

Enron Corporation was formed in 1985 through the merger of two natural gas pipeline companies. The result was the largest gas distribution network in the United States, with 38,000 miles of pipeline stretching from the production sites in the southwestern and mountain states to the industrial users and residential customers in the northeastern and midwestern regions.

Originally, the natural gas industry had been regulated by the federal government. Pipeline companies purchased gas at federally approved costs from the producers and then sold that gas at federally approved prices to the users. The demand was steady and the margins were set. It was hard for a pipeline company not to make money:

Note: This case is based upon three books published soon after the bankruptcy: (1) Brian Cruver, *Anatomy of Greed: The Unshredded Truth from an Enron Insider,* New York: Carroll & Graf Publishers, 2003; (2) Loren Fox, *Enron: The Rise and Fall,* Hoboken, NJ: John Wiley & Sons, 2003; and (3) Mini Schwartz with Sherron Watkins, *Power Failure: The Inside Story of the Collapse of Enron,* New York: Doubleday, 2003.

> In the beginning, the gas business operated just like any regulated public utility. Producers sold their natural gas at just and reasonable rates to interstate pipeline companies that, in turn, transported that gas for sale to local distribution companies at just and reasonable rates . . . It was a steady, lucrative monopoly for the pipelines. Everyone knew, year in and year out, how much money they'd be taking in. (Schwartz with Watkins, 2003, p. 25)[9]

All this steadiness and certainty changed soon after the merger. The natural gas industry was deregulated, and purchase costs at the wellhead and sales prices at the distribution point began to swing wildly, back and forth, with daily changes in supply and demand. Kenneth Lay, the newly appointed president of Enron, saw this as an opportunity, not as a problem:

> Enter Ken Lay who believed that the opportunity to let the market set the price of gas, instead of the government, promised enormous benefits to everyone. In the coming years, the fight to deregulate would become his mission . . . Rules were made to be broken, and success went to the business man who was ready to embrace change—someone who was a "visionary." (Schwartz with Watkins, 2003, p. 25)

Kenneth Lay's vision was to use complex financial instruments called derivatives and hedges to absorb the risks of the cost and price swings. Derivatives are essentially contracts to either buy or sell a set amount of a given commodity—in this case, natural gas—at a set cost or price at a set time in the future. The risks of these futures contracts could be reduced in part by having a huge data base that contained all costs and prices for the past purchases and sales of natural gas, and records of all economic situations and weather conditions that might have affected the past supply and demand of that natural gas. Computer-based models could then be developed to forecast future supply and demand levels, and the expected cost and price changes over time. The risks of these future or derivative contracts could be further reduced by the use of hedges. Hedges essentially are offsetting derivative contracts where the price of one commodity is expected to move in opposite directions to the price of another, given a certain event. For example, the price of natural gas could be expected to increase in the event of severe winter weather in the Northeast or Midwest; the price of lumber and other building materials could be expected to decline as that same harsh winter weather reduced construction activity throughout the region.

Both derivatives and hedges sound simple when described briefly; in reality, they are statistically very complex and require people who are technically trained to develop the derivative models and imaginatively minded to envisage the hedge relationships. Kenneth Lay believed that it was the people who would set Enron apart, and enable his company to succeed in a very competitive environment:

> My goal when I first came into this business was to try to get a superstar in every key position. You must have the very best talent, and then let them develop a good strategy." That was the gospel of Key Lay. A company staffed with the best and the brightest, who were allowed to develop to their fullest potential, could not be beat. (Schwartz with Watkins, p. 35)

[9] From Power Failure: The Inside Story of the Collapse of Enron by Mimi Swartz and Sherron Watkins, copyright © 2003 by Mimi Swartz. Used by permission of Doubleday, a division of Random House, Inc.

Industry deregulation, quantitative finance, and entrepreneurial talent all came together at Enron during the 1990s, and the company grew very rapidly. College graduates with high grades but no experience were hired as analysts and put through a two-year training program. Those that succeeded were very well paid; those that failed were let go with very short notice. MBAs were hired only if they had three to five years of experience in investment banking or corporate consulting. The MBAs were not put through a training program; instead, they were expected to contribute right from the start. Again, those who succeeded were very well paid; those who did not were told to look for other opportunities. Enron became known for their aggressive, innovative, entrepreneurial culture:

> Throughout the 1990s, the company increasingly developed a name as a center for smart, ambitious, young professionals. The gleaming 50-story office tower in downtown Houston buzzed with activity from early in the morning until late at night. It was more than just an office. It was the place to be. For those interested in the latest trends in the energy business—or in business, period—Enron was the place either to learn the ropes or to land when a person was ready to succeed. (Fox, p. 77)[10]

These aggressive, innovative, determined-to-succeed employees became very good at what they did, and what they did was to analyze huge amounts of data, develop derivative contracts based upon that analysis, and then market hedge trades to offset the risks. The earlier "winter weather affects the price of both natural gas and construction lumber" example may have made the process of creating and selling futures options seem straightforward and routine; in reality, it frequently was intricate and complex, as illustrated by the following anecdote:

> Enron also had the usual football and basketball pools, but the traders added so many complicated financial instruments on top of the standard bets—swaps, derivatives, costless collars, and other semi-comprehensible financial structures—that only the shrewdest people really knew what they were betting on (a game or a series of games) and how much they were actually in for ($10, $500, or much, much more). Many knew how to maneuver themselves into a winning position no matter what. As one trader described his bets on the January 1996 Super Bowl, "If Pittsburgh wins I make $1,500, but if Dallas wins I make $1,500." (Swartz with Watkins, p. 80)[11]

Enron, during the period from 1996 to 2000, grew very rapidly. It had become a large, integrated energy company, trading futures contracts for both gas and electricity, with a number of newly formed divisions assigned to apply what was felt to be a proven business model to other commodities (drinking water, scrap metal, bandwidth capacity, etc.) throughout the world. It was staffed with innovative, intelligent and self-confident employees at the senior executive, middle management, and commodity trading levels alike. Kenneth Lay, as CEO, attempted to hold these diverse products, distant locations, and aggressive workers together through stated values, assigned goals, performance reviews, and incentive payments:

[10] Reprinted with permission from John Wiley & Sons, Inc.

[11] From Power Failure: The Inside Story of the Collapse of Enron by Mimi Swartz and Sherron Watkins, copyright © 2003 by Mimi Swartz. Used by permission of Doubleday, a division of Random House, Inc.

1. *Stated values.* The core values of the company were described simply, but emphasized continually with posters on walls throughout the building and pamphlets handed out in every training program. There were four of these basic values:
   - Respect. We treat others as we would like to be treated ourselves. We do not tolerate abusive or disrespectful treatment. Ruthlessness, callousness and arrogance do not belong here.
   - Integrity. We work with customers and prospects openly, honestly and sincerely. When we say we will do something, we will do it; when we say we cannot or will not do something, then we won't do it.
   - Communication. We have an obligation to communicate. Here, we take the time to talk with one another . . . and to listen. We believe the information is meant to move, and that information moves people.
   - Excellence. We are satisfied with nothing less than the very best in everything we do. We will continue to raise the bar for everyone. The great fun here will be for all of us to discover just how good we can really be. (Cruver, 2003, pp. 42–43)[12]
2. *Assigned goals.* The goals of the company were also stated simply and emphasized frequently. There were two types: companywide and division-only. Companywide goals focused on the stated need for Enron to be the leader, originally in the natural gas industry, then in the energy industry, and finally in the global economy. Brian Cruver, who worked as a trader at Enron and is the author of one of the books upon which this case is based, described his reception as he entered the lobby of the building on his first day at work in 1999:

   > I looked up and saw a banner the size of a mobile home. "From the World's Leading Energy Company To the World's Leading Company." The banner hadn't been there a week earlier [when he had interviewed for the job]. (Cruver, 2002, p. 3)

   Divisional goals were designed to forward that leadership ambition. They concentrated on "meeting the numbers," which meant growing the business and attaining steady increases in revenues and returns. New product divisions were given time to get established, but once established they were expected to contribute to the overall sales, profits, and success of the firm.
3. *Performance reviews.* There were few excuses for failure. Success was simply expected, and ensured by a semi-annual weeding-out process that was formally termed the Peer Review Committee, but that most employees simply referred to as "rank and yank." A committee consisting of senior executives asked "peers"—all workers within a given group or division—to fill out forms evaluating other members of the group or division on such qualities as innovation, effort, and imagination. Those forms were combined with accounting records that detailed the financial performance of the group or division, and then each member was ranked on a forced curve from 1 to 5: 1's were considered to be excellent; they were termed "water walkers," but there could be only 10 percent of them. There could be 15 percent

[12] From the book Anatomy of Greed: The Unshredded Truth from an Enron Inside by Brian Cruver. Copyright © 2002 by Brian Cruver. Appears by permission of the publisher, Carroll & Graf Publishers, A Division of Avalon Publishing Group, Inc.

of the 2's, 35 percent of the 3's, 25 percent of the 4's, and there had to be at least 15 percent of the 5's. The 5's were considered to be failures. They might be great performers, but that performance mattered only relative to the other employees within the group or division, and the past performance of that group or division relative to other groups and divisions.

People who got 5's were "redeployed," which meant that they were given a desk, a computer, a telephone, and two weeks to find another job in or out of Enron. The section of the building that contained those desks, computers, and telephones was called "the departure lounge"; going there "meant that you got fired, only in a really slow and painful way." (Quotations from Cruver, 2003, p. 63)

4. *Incentive payments.* Employees at Enron who received 1's and 2's in a steady series on their semi-annual evaluations could expect substantial rewards, with position promotions, salary increases, year-end bonuses, and—best of all, in the view of the large numbers of financially oriented people who had been attracted to Enron—big stock options:

> The Enron millionaire factory was in full force through the '90s, and into the new millennium. Shiny new MBAs from the top schools, former consultants from McKinsey and Andersen, and military geniuses making the transition to private industry—they all came to Enron seeking a fortune. If they could survive the culture, the PRC, and the demands of meeting growth targets from quarter to quarter, then they believed that they had won something much more valuable than a lottery ticket.
>
> * * * * *
>
> It wasn't the salary, though many executives took home a few million a year. It was the bonuses and the stock options. The bonus was the reward for meeting targets, from quarter to quarter. It was paid at the beginning of the new year based on the prior year's performance. The size of the bonus often dwarfed the employee's salary. There was literally no cap on the bonus . . .
>
> The stock options were a long-term incentive, although it didn't take Enron stock very long to leave the option price in the rearview mirror. A typical executive would accumulate options by the tens or hundreds of thousands. By the time the options were vested and could be cashed out, they would be worth millions. (Cruver, 2003, p. 67–68)[13]

It was not just the money that brought people to Enron. It was also the opportunity to be a part of something that was totally new and different. The company put together a recruiting video in 1998 that talked about the wisdom of open markets and the need for individual innovation, and that wound up with an unrehearsed conversation between Kenneth Lay and Jeffrey Skilling:

> "A lot of organizations like to stamp out the non-conformist, the non-convention thinker," Lay said, "but a lot of times they're the people who really are the future because they're thinking about things differently, they're coming up with new ideas." "Yes," Skilling replied, "you know when you work for Enron you're going to see the newest things, the newest products, the newest services, the newest ways of thinking about things."

[13] From the book Anatomy of Greed: The Unshredded Truth from an Enron Inside by Brian Cruver.

> As they spoke, the video cut to scenes of bright young Enron employees hammering out their differences on whiteboards, and weathered men inspecting pipelines at dusty, remote locales. A smiling Asian woman draped a lei over a beaming Ken Lay, while her countrymen in business suits nodded and bowed gracefully. "If there's one thing I hope we can achieve," Lay said, "it's to create an environment where our employees can come in here, and realize their potential."
>
> Skilling waited just a beat before agreeing. "It's a wild ride," he said, and then both men laughed. They laughed the way people do when they've pulled off something they never thought they could. (Swartz with Watkins, p. 105)[14]

The challenging divisional goals and the rigid performance reviews meant that high reported profits were important for each group or division; the members were evaluated on whether they "met their numbers" relative to all other groups and divisions. The generous stock options meant that high reported profits were important for the company as a whole; the stock market responded quickly to increased earnings and thus hastened the day when senior executives, middle managers, and option traders alike could "take their money and run"—and retire with a substantial fortune.

This dual focus on reported profits at the divisional and organizational levels brought about accounting and banking methods that—everyone admitted—were on the edge of legality and that—no one confessed—would eventually lead to the bankruptcy of the firm. These accounting and banking methods were termed "mark-to-market" accounting and "special purpose entity" financing.

Mark-to-market accounting essentially is a way to recognize the profits associated with long-term futures contracts. Kenneth Skilling, the president of Enron, had made his reputation early in the transformation of the company when, as a trader, he arranged a huge futures contract to sell natural gas to an electrical utility in New York State over a 20-year period at a high but set price, and then hedged all of the supply contracts so that substantial profits were assured.

Standard accounting treatment of those profits would force the company to wait for the completion of the first fiscal year following the signing of the contract; add up all of the revenues received from the sale of the gas associated with the contract; deduct all of the variable costs for the purchase of the gas and the operation of the pipeline system to deliver the gas; and finally, subtract all of the overhead expenses that came from making the offer, negotiating the contract and arranging the hedges. Standard treatment would require that this same process (accrual accounting) be followed for each subsequent year over the length of the contract. The problem was that the overhead expenses, almost all of which came in the first year of the contract, were very large and would exceed the revenues of that year. Enron would be forced to report a substantial loss for a contract that every other natural gas supplier and/or pipeline company in the country wished that they had had the skill, the resources, and the nerve to arrange.

There was an alternative accounting treatment, termed "mark-to-market." Enron, due its huge trading volume, had been able to build up price and cost curves that showed the gradually increasing selling prices and purchase costs for natural gas that

[14] From Power Failure: The Inside Story of the Collapse of Enron by Mimi Swartz and Sherron Watkins, copyright © 2003 by Mimi Swartz. Used by permission of Doubleday, a division of Random House, Inc.

were expected, over time. That is, the cost of gas to be purchased for delivery tomorrow on the "futures" market was expected to differ only slightly from the cost of gas to be purchased for delivery today on the "spot" market because there is very limited risk of change in the supply/demand ratios over that very short time period. The cost of gas to be purchased for delivery in five years, however, was expected to differ very markedly from the cost of gas to be purchased for delivery today because there is so much more that can go drastically wrong (or dramatically right) in those supply/demand ratios. Hundreds of thousands of futures trades recorded by Enron over lengthy periods of time generated hundreds of thousands of data points on price and cost charts, and those data points formed gradually increasing price and cost curves that could be claimed to represent *market* valuations of the increasing risks.

These price and cost curves could then be applied to the "book" for the original contract that listed all of the futures contracts and hedge swaps for the full 20-year period associated with the original sale, and then the profit could be estimated, based upon these *market* valuations. The term "market" has been italicized in both sentences because it is important to recognize that these valuations are not random estimates, but are based upon economic exchanges between assumedly intelligent and experienced traders, each allegedly acting in his or her own self-interests and/or in the self-interests of his or her firm. If the expected profits for the full contract were reported, then the "front-loading" of the overhead costs would not matter and, it was felt, a much more accurate picture of the financial performance of the firm could be recorded. It would be necessary, of course, to redo these market-based computations at the start of each subsequently fiscal year, using the then current—and doubtless somewhat different—price and cost curves, but this did not appear to create any particular difficulties given the availability of high-speed computer equipment.

At this time (mid-1990s) "mark-to-market" accounting had been formally approved by the Financial Accounting Standards Board (FASB) and was part of the published 30,000-page listing of those approved standards. It was not approved for and could not be used by manufacturing companies who were forced to record sales revenues, variable costs, and the allocated portions of fixed expenses at the time of shipment of their physical products, but it was extensively used by financial institutions, consulting firms, and service providers. It could easily be argued that Enron was essentially operating as a combined financial institution, consulting firm, and service provider in the natural gas industry, and thus was entitled to use mark-to-market accounting despite their delivery of a physical product. The use of this new accounting method was quickly approved by the company's auditor (Arthur Andersen), the company's legal advisor (Vinson and Elkins), and the company's Board of Directors.

> Enron's board went along with its risky accounting strategies. In one presentation to the board's audit committee, in February 1999, David Duncan—Andersen's lead partner on the Enron account—included a handwritten note that read: "Obviously, we are on board with all of these, but many push limits and have a high 'others could have a different view' risk profile." In the discussion that followed that meeting, Andersen didn't recommend changing any accounting practices, and board members didn't advocate a more prudent approach or even request a second opinion. Board members

> didn't characterize Enron's accounting structure as high-risk, but as "leading edge" or innovative—the sort of innovation they expected given the big fees they paid. Andersen (Fox, p. 158)[15]

"Special purpose entity" financing—the second of the accounting and banking edge of legality methods that eventually brought about the bankruptcy of the firm—essentially is a way to provide additional capital for a high-growth firm without that added capital appearing either as debt or equity on the liability side of the balance sheet. Large amounts of additional debt on the liability side of the balance sheet would reduce the creditworthiness of the firm and raise its interest cost. Large amounts of additional equity would reduce the rate of increase in earnings per share and lower its stock price.

Andy Fastow, the chief financial officer of Enron, thought that he had found a way to get the additional capital that Enron needed without affecting either the interest cost or the stock price of the firm. He called this new method "special purpose entity" financing, or SPE. All that was required was to form a subsidiary that was partially owned by a different firm or individual and nominally controlled by that different firm or individual; as such, according once again to the 30,000-page book of Federal Accounting Board Standards, the subsidiary could report its profit and loss figures separately from those for Enron, and its assets, liabilities, and equity did not have to appear on the Enron balance sheet. Assets could be transferred from Enron operations to a newly formed subsidiary, bonds could be sold by Enron bankers to fund those recently transferred assets, but then the money (which was considered payment for the Enron assets) could be used by Enron managers for general corporate purposes without either the assets or the bonds of the subsidiary having to be consolidated on the Enron balance sheet. These conditions fully met the requirements of the Financial Accounting Board and the Securities and Exchange Commission, were quickly approved by Arthur Andersen, solidly endorsed by Vincent and Elkins, and enthusiastically affirmed by the Enron board of directors.

At the end of 1998, Enron had $7.8 billion in long-term debt on the balance sheet, and another $7.6 billion in debt that had been recorded off the balance sheet, in special purpose entities. Andy Fastow felt that he had been given clear authority to continue these processes of what he felt to be financial sophistication, not financial manipulation:

> To effectively juggle Enron's capital needs, Fastow transformed the finance department much the way Skilling had transformed Enron's sales department. He more than doubled the finance staff, loading it with experts in investment banking, commercial banking, and corporate finance. Rather than just raise debt or issue stock, Fastow's finance department became a manager of risk; it sold securitizations, parceled out the company's risk into other vehicles, took on investing partners, and marketed debt as a way to participate in the sure growth of everything that Enron touched. "Essentially, we would buy and sell risk positions," Fastow explained. (Fox, pp. 156–157)[16]

[15] Reprinted with permission from John Wiley & Sons, Inc.

[16] From the book Anatomy of Greed: The Unshredded Truth from an Enron Inside by Brian Cruver. Copyright © 2002 by Brian Cruver. Appears by permission of the publisher, Carroll & Graf Publishers, A Division of Avalon Publishing Group, Inc.

The "mark-to-market" accounting methods greatly improved the income statements of Enron, and the "special purpose entity" financing methods greatly improved the balance sheets. Now the company was ready to grow, and the booming stock market of the late1990s was ready to reward in very substantial terms all public firms that could post consistent gains in earnings per share, and to severely penalize all those that failed. This was the New Economy. All limits were thought to be off. Recessions were felt to be a relic of the past. People throughout the financial community believed that a threshold had been passed, and that continuous growth in the order of 10 percent to 15 percent per year was not only possible, but that it was the duty of senior corporate executives to generate steady increases in shareholder value within that exalted range:

> The stock price became the indicator of corporate health; senior managers became, in a weird way, more focused on their shareholders than their customers. Quarterly earnings reports, once ignored by all but the most compulsive auditors and investors, suddenly became crucial to a company's public image. This was where [quarterly earning reports] a business could prove that its growth was on the proper, speedy trajectory. So, like everyone else, Enron began projecting, and then miraculously meeting, earnings targets four times a year, to glowing reviews from analysts and the business press. A company that missed its numbers got the same treatment in reverse. Wall Street analysts would hammer the company and the stock price plummeted. (Swartz with Watkins, p. 69)[17]

Kenneth Lay, fully supported by Jeff Skilling and Andy Fostow, determined that Enron should meet substantial growth targets—10 percent to 15 percent, or more—each year. They thought that this would be easy. Enron was now trading futures contracts in electric power as well as natural gas, and the total demand for electric power was huge, 20 times the size of the market for gas. The companies operating in that industry tended to be large and slow, accustomed to the regulatory approval process that was just ending. Enron, on the other hand, was large and fast, accustomed to the competitive price system that was just getting started within the natural gas and electrical generating industries. Enron had the mathematical models, computer capabilities, experienced traders, cultural attitudes, and funding methods needed for speed and growth. Skilling gave a talk in 1995 on his expectations for success under the new conditions in the combined energy (electricity and gas) industry, and tried not to gloat:

> I don't know who is going to win. They [the winners] will have to be very fast-moving; this market is moving at just unbelievable speed . . . They are going to have to be very creative; we don't know what the products and services are going to look like five to 10 years from now, so you will have people designing those. I think that competitive advantage won't be based on assets any longer. It won't be based on pipes and wires and generating plants; it will be based on intellectual capital. (Fox, 2003, pp. 75–76)[18]

[17] From Power Failure: The Inside Story of the Collapse of Enron by Mimi Swartz and Sherron Watkins, copyright © 2003 by Mimi Swartz. Used by permission of Doubleday, a division of Random House, Inc.

[18] From the book Anatomy of Greed: The Unshredded Truth from an Enron Inside by Brian Cruver. Copyright © 2002 by Brian Cruver. Appears by permission of the publisher, Carroll & Graf Publishers, A Division of Avalon Publishing Group, Inc.

What went wrong? Enron had expanded globally, and was now operating in Europe, Asia, and Africa. Many of the public utilities in these areas were state-owned, and refused to issue futures contracts for the sale of electric power. Enron had to build its own generating plants in order to push its way into the newly unregulated markets abroad. Teeside, in northern England, was an example of one of those new plants. It was built to be a showcase: a large-capacity, high-efficiency, gas-fired co-generation (produce both steam and electricity) project that relied upon Enron's ability to pull together many diverse players into one totally integrated effort. The gas, at the time still classified as a waste product of crude production, would come from the North Sea oil fields, and be processed by a major petroleum company in Scotland. The steam would be used by ICI Polymers, a division of one of the largest chemical firms in Europe, for industrial processing, and the electricity would be distributed through local utilities for retail sale to consumer and commercial customers alike. The plant design was very advanced: it took half the land of equivalent coal-fired plants, produced half the carbon dioxide emissions of those plants, and employed half the number of workers. The only problem was the lack of substantial competition for the use of the North Sea gas; Enron had signed long-term contracts based upon its anticipated price curves, but the competition never developed; consequently, Enron wound up paying above market rates for the gas despite the existence of numerous hedges, which relied upon non-existing contradictory trends. The Teeside plant was unprofitable, but it was not shut down. Kenneth Lay was disappointed, but not abashed:

> "For Enron [it was originally seen as] a triumph of the corporation's multitasking capabilities—a sort of hard asset version of the existing supply contracts in that Enron was able to pull together many facets of a complicated project. "We believe Enron is uniquely qualified to develop all aspects of a large integrated natural gas project such as the one at Teeside," said Lay . . . "Rather than resisting change, we're trying to lead it and prosper from it." (Fox, 2003, p. 47).

Dabhol, in southern India, was another example. The plant, once again of very modern design, had been built to generate electric power for sale to Maharasthra, India's poorest state, using liquefied natural gas transported by refrigerated ships from the oil-producing nations bordering the Red Sea. Enron owned 70 percent of this project; Bechtel, which had done the construction, owned 20 percent; and General Electric, which had supplied the equipment, owned 10 percent. Elections changed the ruling party in Maharasthra, and the new officials claimed that the contract price per megawatt hour that had been negotiated with the prior administrators was far too high. Allegations were openly made that this contested contract price had been approved only as a result of extensive bribery payments, and popularly believed, Enron had essentially hedged the purchase price by having a subsidiary contract with the Indian national government that required that entity to buy the electric power if the state of Maharashtra reneged, but the bribery allegations made this a "third rail: you're dead if you touch it" political issue. The Dabhol plant was closed down, and put up for sale at 20 percent above construction costs; there was no adjustment made for the presumably far lower price that would be received for an unused power plant in a politically hostile nation.

There were objections within the company to the refusal to recognize, and reevaluate, these failed power projects. All of them had been transferred to Enron Global Power, a publicly traded subsidiary in which Enron owned 52 percent of the stock and large pension funds and wealthy individual investors the balance. James Alexander had been appointed to be head of that subsidiary. He was responsible for renegotiating the contracts and then either starting or selling the plants. Asked to take over one more failed project, he complained to Kenneth Lay that the current market value should be substituted for the past construction cost for each plant, and that the losses should be recognized. This, he continued, was almost impossible given that the company's performance measures and incentive payments were based totally on projected profits, and would penalize severely any recorded losses. Almost everyone in the company would lose, he explained, if the accounting records were corrected, but it was necessary to do so for financial accuracy. His recommendations were ignored:

> Lay listened to Alexander's recounting of the conflicts of interest and suspicious accounting practices for about fifteen minutes. Then he grew distant. He wouldn't meet Alexander's eyes, and he stopped responding. Finally he said, "I'll take it up with Rich [Richard Causey, chief accounting officer at Enron]." The meeting was over. (Swartz with Watkins, 2003, p. 70)[19]

Other problems came in the use of mark-to-market accounting to establish the value of long-term contracts for trading non-energy commodities such as scrap metal, raw steel, waste paper, packaging materials, etc. Futures markets for natural gas and electric power were well established. and the resultant price and cost curves projected far into the future were thought to be reliable. Futures markets for the non-energy commodities were not as well established, particularly abroad, and consequently, the price and cost curves based upon market forces were not as reliable, and sometimes not even available. Personal estimates of the traders had to be used in the place of the market-based models. Each trader had a price curve for his or her commodity, constructed partially from market data points but primarily from personal projections, and he or she would fight fiercely for the validity of that price curve. Why? Because his or her semi-annual evaluations, salary increases, bonus payments, stock options, and even continued employment under the rank and yank system all depended upon the recorded profit that came from the price curve. Brian Cruver, the MBA from the University of Texas who went to work for Enron just eight months before the collapse, noted this problem in his first few weeks upon the job:

> Enron, more than any other energy company, dealt in commodities and derivative structures that were far too unusual to have an established [futures market] price. It was an issue of liquidity. If the deal required a price on something that was rarely bought and sold, then the price had to be made up . . . The trader's expertise on a commodity was difficult for someone from RAC [the Risk Assessment and Control Division at Enron] or Arthur Andersen to credibly question . . .
>
> This was mark-to-market accounting, and Enron linked individual bonuses to this mark-to-market value. As a result, the strategy was less about booking profitable deals or controlling the risk of deals, and more about booking as many of the biggest [and most computationally complex] deals possible. (Cruver, 2003, p. 80)[20]

[19] From Power Failure: The Inside Story of the Collapse of Enron by Mimi Swartz and Sherron Watkins, copyright © 2003 by Mimi Swartz. Used by permission of Doubleday, a division of Random House, Inc.

[20] From the book Anatomy of Greed: The Unshredded Truth from an Enron Inside by Brian Cruver. Copyright © 2002 by Brian Cruver. Appears by permission of the publisher, Carroll & Graf Publishers, A Division of Avalon Publishing Group, Inc.

Allegedly, it was possible, when trading derivatives, to separate risks from returns and to price both by open market exchanges in a complex series of hedges. But, errors could be made and losses then would occur. Serious errors were made and severe losses had occurred in the energy trading division of Enron in the third quarter of 1997. That division had been assigned a goal of a $100 million profit for that quarter, but instead they would have to report a loss of $90 million, for a combined shortfall of $190 million. That shortfall would affect the profit reported by the company at the conclusion of the quarter, and the steady growth in quarterly profits that was felt to be essential in maintaining the confidence of the investment community and the price-to-earnings ratio of the company. Enron had never missed its earning targets. Jeffrey Skilling, the CEO, told the traders to quickly find a way to recoup the loss and regenerate the profit. There were weekly and then daily meetings. None of their proposals seemed certain to work. Skilling felt they were not being innovative enough. "You're looking for your lost car key under the streetlight because the light's better there" (Swartz with Watkins, p. 92). Look elsewhere was his unstated command. They did so, and found a potential gold mine.

The energy trading division had been buying companies, and investing in plants, that could convert natural gas to electrical energy at times of high demand and—consequently—high prices. These were the "peaking" plants. It would be possible, one of the members of the energy trading division suggested, to look upon these plants as purchases for eventual resale rather than investments for immediate use. If they could be classified as purchases for resale, then their values could be increased through "mark to-market" accounting to cover this shortfall in profits and—given the large reservoir of value in those plants—future shortfalls as well through the use of optimistic price curves. Sherron Watkins, a co-author of one of the books about the success and failure of Enron that have been used as the basis for this case, had, years earlier, worked as an auditor for Arthur Andersen. That company, she felt, could not and would not approve. But, she had forgotten the pressures that were being placed on the auditing partners at Andersen:

> By the mid-1990s it was clear that Andersen needed Enron more than Enron needed Andersen, both for the prestige [of representing this large and well-known firm] and for the billings, which were closing in on $1 million per week. Consequently, as Enron pushed Andersen to approve ever more aggressive accounting techniques, Andersen had more trouble pushing back . . . Given that, it was not surprising that Andersen's Enron team signed off on the plan to use mark-to-market accounting to help cover the $190 million loss. (Swartz with Watkins, p. 96)[21]

Sherron Watkins expressed her concerns informally to Kenneth Lay, but received no encouragement to continue. The general attitude among the senior executives within Enron seemed to be that Arthur Andersen was acting properly, that they were being paid very substantial fees to be both innovative and aggressive in the interests of the firm, and that both of those qualities were needed to adopt Old Economy accounting rules to New Economy financial needs.

[21] From the book Anatomy of Greed: The Unshredded Truth from an Enron Inside by Brian Cruver. Copyright © 2002 by Brian Cruver. Appears by permission of the publisher, Carroll & Graf Publishers, A Division of Avalon Publishing Group, Inc.

Lastly, the special purpose entities developed by Andy Fastow had been intended to hide debts; it was soon discovered that they made an equally suitable means to hide losses. The state-of-the-art generating plants abroad that had not worked out quite as planned could be put into a package and then sold to a group of outside investors who needed to supply only a minimal (3 percent) amount of equity, with the balance in debt guaranteed by a pledge of unissued shares of Enron stock. The peaking-power plants within the United States that had been overvalued through mark-to-market accounting could also be put into a similar package and also sold to a group of outside investors under the same 3 percent equity and 97 percent debt guaranteed by unissued shares of the company's stock.

The early financial packages, particularly those that contained the gas exploration and supply contracts from the Gas Bank, had worked out very well for outside investors. Pension funds—such as CALPERS (California Public Employees Retirement System)—insurance companies, and investment banks had competed to invest because they received high cash flows and excellent capital returns. But, as the SPE vehicles were increasingly used to hide losses, the cash flows dwindled and the capital returns disappeared. It became more and more difficult to place these packages. Andy Fastow again came up with a solution. He, his family, and—to some extent—his friends would supply the needed 3 percent in equity, borrow the balance backed by unissued shares of Enron stock, and attempt to rescue the failed project or projects. This was illegal, because (1) it contravened the clear requirement that control of the entity had to be outside Enron, and (2) it ignored the conflict of interest that would occur between Andy Fastow as a senior executive at Enron and Andy Fastow as a private investor in the SPE. Benefits that went to Fastow and his family and friends clearly could not go to the stockholders of Enron. However, these transactions were again approved by Arthur Andersen, the auditing firm, with the provision that the conflict be at least partially revealed in the company's annual report. On page 48, in footnote 16, of the 2000 report, the following statement appeared:

> In 2000 and 1999, Enron entered into transactions with limited partnerships (the Related Party) whose general partner's managing member is a senior officer of Enron. The limited partners of the Related Party are unrelated to Enron. Management believes that the terms of the transaction with the Related Party were reasonable compared to those which could have been negotiated with unrelated third parties. (Cited in Cruver, p. 60)

Jeff McMahon, then treasurer of Enron, objected strongly to the conflicts of interest inherent in the special purpose entities financed by Andy Fastow, hierarchically his superior, and arranged to meet with Jeff Skilling, president and CEO of Enron. According to a handwritten note of that meeting, Jeff McMahon complained that, "I find myself negotiating with Andy on Enron matters, and am pressured to do deals that I do not believe are in the best interests of the shareholders" (Fox, p. 202). According to McMahon, Skilling ended the meeting by saying that he understood the concerns that had been expressed and that he would look into the matter. No further action was taken.

Early in 2001 the Enron stock price, which had been on a steep upward climb for nearly 10 years, began to falter. Apparently, the cause was a series of rumors about the decline in quality of the company's reported earnings and the absence of transparency in the company's accounting records. Then, in August 2001, Jeffrey Skilling resigned as chief executive officer, a post he had held for only six months. Kenneth Lay quickly replaced him and sent the following message to all employees, first saying that the departure was for "personal reasons," and then trying quell the natural concerns:

> I want to assure you that I have never felt better about the prospects for our company . . . Our performance has never been stronger; our business model has never been more robust; our growth has never been more certain; and most importantly, we have never had a better nor deeper pool of talent throughout the company. We have the finest organization in American business today. Together we will make Enron the world's leading company. (Cruver, 2003, p. 91)[22]

Sherron Watkins replied with what was to become, when presented months later to a Congressional Committee investigating Enron, her famous one-page memo. Originally sent anonymously, she acknowledged authorship the next day and requested a meeting with Kenneth Lay. She was worried, she said, that Skilling's abrupt departure would raise suspicions about Enron accounting practices, and she believed that those practices could not withstand outside scrutiny:

> Has Enron become a risky place to work? For those of us who didn't get rich over the last few years, can we afford to stay?
>
> Skilling's abrupt departure will raise suspicion of accounting improprieties and valuation issues. Enron has been very aggressive in its accounting—most notably [she named a series of the special purpose entities arranged by Jeff Fastow]. We do have valuation issues with our international assets and possibly some of our [energy trading] mark-to-market positions . . .
>
> The spotlight will be on us, the market just can't accept that Skilling is leaving his dream job. I think that the valuation issues can be fixed and reported with other goodwill write-downs to occur in 2002. How do we fix the [special purpose entities]? They unwind in 2002 and 2003, we will have to put up Enron stock and that won't go unnoticed.
>
> To the layman on the street, it will look like we recognized funds flow of $800 mm from merchant asset sales in 1999 by selling to a [special purpose entity] that we capitalized with a promise of Enron stock in later years. Is that really funds flow or is it cash from equity issuance?
>
> I am incredibly nervous that we will implode in a wave of accounting scandals. My eight years of Enron work history will be worth nothing on my résumé, the business world will consider the past successes as nothing but an elaborate accounting hoax. (Excerpts from Sherron Watkin's memo to Kenneth Lay, cited in Swartz with Watkins, pp. 361–362)[23]

Sherron Watkins followed up her original memo with a longer document providing greater detail about the accounting treatments of the special purpose entities and mark-to-market valuations that had concerned her. She then met with Kenneth Lay and

[22] From the book Anatomy of Greed: The Unshredded Truth from an Enron Inside by Brian Cruver. Copyright © 2002 by Brian Cruver. Appears by permission of the publisher, Carroll & Graf Publishers, A Division of Avalon Publishing Group, Inc.

[23] From Power Failure: The Inside Story of the Collapse of Enron by Mimi Swartz and Sherron Watkins, copyright © 2003 by Mimi Swartz. Used by permission of Doubleday, a division of Random House, Inc.

verbally expressed her concerns. Kenneth Lay asked Vinson and Elkins, the Houston law firm that represented Enron, to investigate the allegations. Their response essentially was that the accounting treatments, while aggressive, were not illegal; that those treatments had originally been approved by Arthur Andersen, the company's auditor; and that consequently no further action was needed.

Jeffrey Skilling's departure, while considered curious by outside observers, particularly those connected to the investment banks and brokerage houses on Wall Street, appeared not to trigger the suspicions and start the investigations that Sherron Watkins had anticipated. Enron's stock price stabilized at about $30 per share, down from more than $100 at the start of 2001. Kenneth Lay, and many of the other senior executives at Enron, spent much of their time attempting to reassure investors and employees, though, at the same time, they were selling large amounts of their own holdings of Enron stock:

> On September 26, Lay again told employees the company's stock seemed like a bargain and that the third quarter was "looking great"—only weeks before Enron would fall apart and its stock price plunge. "My personal belief is that Enron stock is an incredible bargain at current prices and we will look back a couple of years from now and see the great opportunity that we currently have."
>
> However, Lay made this series of comments touting Enron's stock not long after he and other senior executives had sold large amounts of their Enron shares. Between February 1999 and July 2001, Lay sold more that 1.8 million shares of Enron stock for total proceeds of $101.3 million . . . In all, Enron officers and a few directors unloaded a whopping $1.1 billion in Enron stock from January 1999 through July 2001. (Fox, pp. 252–253)[24]

The final ending, came with surprising quickness on October 16. Enron announced its earnings for the third quarter of 2001, which had ended September 30. Total recurring net income, it was said, had increased to $393 million, up from $292 million the year before:

> Our twenty-six percent increase in recurring earnings per diluted share shows the very strong results of our core wholesale and retail energy businesses and our natural gas pipelines. (Enron third quarter earnings report for 2001, cited in Cruver, p. 116)[25]

Apparently, the growth was continuing. Everything seemed to be well. But, then came the first shocker. Non-recurring charges of $1.01 billion were to be deducted from the stated earning figures, resulting in a loss for the quarter of $618 million. These non-recurring charges, Kenneth Lay explained, were to write off a few failed investments and to restructure a few poorly operating divisions. But, this was followed by a second shocker. There was to be a write-down of $1.2 billion in shareholders' equity, with the minimal explanation that this was associated with the "related party transactions" that had been briefly noted in a footnote to the 2000 annual report.

[24] Reprinted with permission from John Wiley & Sons, Inc.

[25] From the book Anatomy of Greed: The Unshredded Truth from an Enron Inside by Brian Cruver. Copyright © 2002 by Brian Cruver. Appears by permission of the publisher, Carroll & Graf Publishers, A Division of Avalon Publishing Group, Inc.

Enron had been forced to reveal the second "related party" adjustment because approximately $3 billion in notes issued by other special purpose entities was coming due, and clarification of the status of the related party claims was needed to permit sales of some of the pledged assets in order to be able to repay those notes. The company, apparently, had anticipated a subdued reaction to both the "non-recurring charges" and the "equity write-down" announcements. Enron executives believed, it would seem, that there was still a reservoir of trust and respect for their company among members of the financial community and that both adjustments would just be seen as long-needed but relatively minor corrections. Instead, there was a flurry of disappointment and anger. The *Wall Street Journal,* the next morning, in a front-page story, revealed that Andy Fastow, the chief financial officer of Enron, was the "related party" and was "eligible for profit participations that could produce millions of dollars [of profit for himself] in transactions with Enron." Brian Cruver, the MBA from the University of Texas who had started work at Enron only ten months earlier, described his reaction to this account:

> I sat at my desk and read through the article two more times. I stopped seeing the numbers and the partnerships and the Enron spin. I started to see a huge red stamp across the pages of the most respected business publication on earth. It read, "This company [Enron] cannot be trusted." (Cruver, p. 120)[26]

Other articles followed, in different newspapers and news magazines, with exactly the same message. Congressional hearings were scheduled, in an attempt to ascribe blame. Traders at other energy firms refused to deal with Enron, worried about their financial stability. Lenders at commercial and investment banks refused to negotiate with Enron, for exactly the same reason. The stock price plummeted. The company was bankrupt; it just took a few more weeks for everyone—investors, creditors, managers, and members of the general public—to formally acknowledge that undoubted fact.

Class Assignment

"Enron Corporation and the Road to Failure" is the last major case in this book. It will probably be assigned for the next to last class. This is the time to summarize in *your* mind what *you* have learned from this course. There are just three questions:

1. The first half of this case, up to the paragraph that starts "What went wrong?", focuses on the innovative culture, the demanding ethic, and the rewarding opportunities at Enron. Read that first half once again. Then, suppose you were one of the younger employees at Enron. Suppose also that you were one of the successful ones, that you always got "1's" and "2's" on your quarterly "rank and yank" evaluations, which made you eligible for large cash options and big stock bonuses. You enjoyed the challenges and were having a great time. But was there anything in that culture, that ethic, and those opportunities that made you suspicious that maybe this was all too good to be true? In short, during your first full-time job after graduation, what would tell you that it was time to get out? One of the major themes of this course is

[26] From the book Anatomy of Greed: The Unshredded Truth from an Enron Inside by Brian Cruver. Copyright © 2002 by Brian Cruver. Appears by permission of the publisher, Carroll & Graf Publishers, A Division of Avalon Publishing Group, Inc.

that *you* have to recognize serious moral problems, and then *you* have to decide what *you* should do about it. Leaving is always an option, but so is staying and trying to remedy the situation.

2. The second half of this case, after the paragraph that starts "What went wrong?", explains exactly that: what did go wrong. It starts with the use of past data points to forecast the future price levels of North Sea natural gas to fuel the company constructed and owned generating station at Teeside in northern England. What had happened in the past did not happen in the future, the hedges were worthless, and Teeside had to be operated with substantial losses. Another example was the negotiation of a contract to build and operate a liquefied natural gas-fired generating plant in Maharasthra, India's poorest state. The political parties controlling Maharasthra's government changed, and the newly installed officials refused to purchase the electric power generated by that plant at the contracted price, alleging bribery. Had the values of those two very unprofitable but very expensive generating plants been written down on Enron's balance sheet, that is "marked to market," do you believe that Enron could have been saved? Numerous managers at Enron asked that those values be written down, but were rebuffed. If you were to encounter a similar situation in your first full-time job after graduation, how would you make the argument for revaluation? Another of the major themes of this course is that if *you* decide that a given situation is wrong—based upon *your* balance of economic outcomes, legal requirements, and ethical duties—then *you* have to be able to logically convince others.
3. The last question is much shorter, but perhaps more difficult. Suppose that Kenneth Lay had asked Vinson and Elkins (the Houston law firm that had advised Enron for years) to evaluate the performance measures, the incentive payments, the prohibited procedures, and the leadership actions that were alleged to have led to the very large and very risky investment at Teeside and in Maharasthra, and suppose that you were part of a managerial consulting team employed by that law firm to make that evaluation. What—if any—changes would you have recommended? A third major theme of this course is that the moral aspects of management have to be combined with the practical aspects to be effective. Again, how would *you* have been convincing in presenting *your* recommendations?

Case 6-5

What Do You Want to Achieve in Life?

This is a very different case, and assignment. The following questions ask you to consider what you value in life, what goals you might set now so that—if you do achieve them—looking back later you could consider your life to have been successful. It would be inappropriate to discuss these very personal matters in a very public classroom. That is why there is a software program available that will enable you to record your responses anonymously. Those responses can then be totaled, and the totals converted to a chart or graph that can be displayed on a screen. I believe that the chart or graph, if your class is similar to the ones I taught when I was still active and not yet retired, will show major differences among the identified values and goals.

These differences will be among members of your class who probably are all of approximately the same age and status, preparing to start a career in management. Think how those differences would magnify if this survey had been conducted among the employees of a business firm or government agency, with different ages and different positions. Chapter 5, which you previously read, stressed the need for managers to be viewed as equitable and fair-to-all in their decisions and actions in order to build trust, commitment, and effort at the individual level and cooperation, innovation, and unification at the organizational level—all leading to competitive success in a changing global economy.

How do you do this in real life? In my view, you start by recognizing the differences in what people value and in what people want. Some people want money, position, and power. Other people want to contribute and to build something of which they can be proud. Still others want to improve the society of which they are a part. Most people are a mixture of all three of these groups. The objective of this case or—more properly—this survey is to start thinking about how these differences might be resolved and how people might be brought together in a cooperative, innovative, and unified organization. In short, this survey is about how to start thinking about what excellence in management really means.

Start by identifying your own goals and values. What do you want to achieve in life? What is important to you? Select your personal goals in money, lifestyle, position, performance, reputation, family, and church from the following listing. Add your social values on independence for yourself, interdependence with others, protection of the poor, equality among individuals, improvement of the environment, and peace among nations. I believe that this determination of what you want out of life, and your consequent definition of what you believe would constitute success in your life, is worth considering for at least one class session while you are in college or at graduate school.

Determine your goals and values by ranking each category from *6, which is the highest* in your priority, to *1, which is the lowest.* You may have as many 3's and 4's as you want, but limit yourself to one 6, which is then your highest goal or value, and to two 5's, which are your next most important goals or values. Pick at least one 1, which is your lowest goal or *value,* and two 2's, which are also far down on your list of priorities.

1. Increases in my wealth, and the power, possessions, and lifestyle that go with money, are important to me. 6 5 4 3 2 1
2. Promotions in my company, and the authority and privileges that go with advancement, are important to me. 6 5 4 3 2 1
3. Performance in my job, and the security and respect that go with achievement, are important to me. 6 5 4 3 2 1
4. Reputation within my community, and the political offices and social activities that go with prominence, are important to me. 6 5 4 3 2 1
5. Attention to my family, and the affection and companionship that go with family life, are important to me. 6 5 4 3 2 1
6. Devotion to my church, and the sense of community and sharing that are part of most religions, are important to me. 6 5 4 3 2 1
7. Independence in my personal life, and the ability to achieve my own goals and follow my own rules, are important to me. 6 5 4 3 2 1

8. Interdependence with my fellow human beings, and the opportunity to set social goals and adopt mutual rules, are important to me. 6 5 4 3 2 1
9. Protection of the poor, and the need to help others within our society who have been less fortunate than I, are important to me. 6 5 4 3 2 1
10. Equality among races, genders, and ethnic groups, and the need to offer courtesy, respect, and opportunity to all, are important to me. 6 5 4 3 2 1
11. Preservation of the environment, and the need to show greater restraint in the use of the earth's resources, are important to me. 6 5 4 3 2 1
12. Peace among nations, and the need to end oppression of any of the earth's peoples, are important to me. 6 5 4 3 2 1

Note: Please check your selections once again. Remember, 6 is your *highest* goal or value, and you should have only one of those, and then just two 5's for your *next highest* goals or values; 1 is your *lowest* goal or value, and again you should have only one of those, but then two 2's for your *next lowest* goals or values. The rest should all be 3's or 4's.

Case 6-6

The Shortest Case in any Undergraduate or MBA Program

Clarence Walton was the Dean of General Studies at Columbia University for a number of years, and then President of the Catholic College of America. He was also widely respected because he tended to express complex ideas in short but memorable terms. This characteristic is well illustrated from the following quotation taken from *The Moral Manager,* Ballenger Publishing Company, 1988, p. 4:

> Leadership, an ill-defined word, comes from understanding and respecting four crucial ideas: equality, justice, truth, and freedom.

Class Assignment

I will try to be equally brief with just two assignment questions. Do you agree with Professor Walton, or not, and why? If you don't agree, what four "crucial ideas" would you substitute?

Index

Q

R

S

T

U

V